DREAMING:

A

Cognitive-Psychological

Analysis

DREAMING:

A

Cognitive-Psychological

Analysis

David Foulkes
*Georgia Mental Health Institute
and
Emory University*

LEA LAWRENCE ERLBAUM ASSOCIATES, PUBLISHERS
1985   Hillsdale, New Jersey   London

The quotation, p. 12, is *from THE IDIOT by Fyodor Dostoyevsky, translated by Henry and Olga Carlisle. Copyright (c) 1969 by Henry Carlisle. Reprinted by arrangement with New American Library, New York, N.Y.*

The dream text, p. 152–3, is *from THE INTERPRETATION OF DREAMS, by Sigmund Freud, translated and edited by James Strachey. Published by Basic Books, Inc., by arrangement with George Allen & Unwin Ltd. and The Hogarth Press, Ltd. Reprinted by permission.*

Lawrence Erlbaum Associates, Inc., Publishers
365 Broadway
Hillsdale, New Jersey 07642

Library of Congress Cataloging in Publication Data

Foulkes, William David, 1935–
  Dreaming : a cognitive psychological analysis.

  Includes indexes.
  1. Dreams. 2. Cognition. I. Title.
BF1078.F618 1985   154.6′34   85-4426
ISBN 0-89859-553-3

Printed in the United States of America
10 9 8 7 6 5 4 3 2 1

Contents

259594

Preface

This book summarizes the findings of empirical dream psychology and interprets them from a cognitive-psychological perspective. As a review, it covers much the same territory as my earlier book, *The Psychology of Sleep* (1966), which discussed dream research within a largely psychophysiological framework. The shift here to a cognitive-psychological framework stems from the increasingly obvious inherent requirements of dream psychology and from the availability of a comprehensive psychology of waking cognition. Although this book is not a revision of the earlier one, it *is* addressed to a comparable audience: students and other nonspecialists who want a succinct summary of what is currently known about dreaming. The shift in interpretive focus, as well as the additional research in the years separating the two books, make this review much less "mindless" than the last. It now appears that dream psychology is beyond the stage of accumulating odd facts and at a point where those facts are beginning to coalesce in a comprehensive understanding of what dreaming is all about. That is an exciting development, and I hope that I've communicated some sense of that excitement in the text that follows.

I acknowledge specific debts I owe: to Sandra Cropsey and Lucia Edmonds, who typed successive versions of the manuscript; to Brenda Sullivan, who helped with the proofreading; to psychology students at Emory University, who watched the ideas behind this book grow, and who helped them along; and most of all to Nancy Kerr, who helped me to finally "get it right."

David Foulkes

Some writers on dreaming have marvelled greatly at this tendency of the sleeping mind to objectify portions of itself, and so to create imaginary personalities and evolve dramatic situations. It has seemed to them quite unaccountable except as the outcome of a special gift of imagination appertaining to sleep. Yet, remarkable as it is, this process is simply the inevitable outcome of the conditions under which psychic life exists during sleep. If we realize that a more or less pronounced degree of dissociation of the contents of the mind occurs during sleep, and if we also realize that, sleeping fully as much as waking, mind is a thing that instinctively reasons, and cannot refrain from building up hypotheses, then we may easily see how the personages and situations of dreams develop.

HAVELOCK ELLIS

Introduction

1. PURPOSE

This book brings some cognitive-psychological concepts to bear on a phenomenon—dreaming—previously thought to be the province of the psychoanalyst or the psychophysiologist. Its premise is unremarkable: Dreaming is a mental act with distinctive properties depending on a particular organization of mental processes. To understand dreaming, therefore, we need to identify those mental systems that are active while we dream and to characterize their modes of action and interaction.

It is my assumption that the sleeping mind is not functionally distinct from the waking mind; hence dreaming does not depend on mental processes or systems that are in any way unique to sleep. In recent years, cognitive psychology has made considerable progress in identifying some of the probable processing operations and representational systems of the waking mind. Thus, if dream psychology can specify the peculiarities of dreams and dreaming that require explanation, then cognitive psychology may provide the kinds of knowledge about mental processing and representations in terms of which such explanation must be sought.

My aim is to present a conceptual framework in which this kind of explanation of dreaming may be possible. I do not present a new "theory" of dreaming, so much as I suggest some new ways of thinking about dreaming that may stimulate significant empirical research from which more formalized cognitive theories of dreaming may someday emerge.

The building of bridges between two areas that psychology has contrived to separate is not without its risks, of course. First, no one can pretend to the kind of expertise in both areas possessed by specialists within either. Thus, my sampling and understanding of cognitive-psychological evidence may seem deficient to the specialist. Second, in rapidly developing fields such as cognitive psychology, institutional resistances accumulate against squandering the discipline's resources or compromising its credibility by wandering too far afield. For many cognitive psychologists, the study of dreaming probably is far afield. They may wonder whether there really are any interesting cognitive questions in dream psychology or whether a cognitive psychology of dreaming is even possible, since we do not know and cannot control the information processed during a dream. Third, inevitably there are also resistances on the part of those with a longstanding commitment to a particular subject matter when someone comes along with a new framework for studying it. The psychoanalyst, for instance, will want to know what's happened to "The Unconscious," and the psychophysiologist will want to know how one can explain dreaming without specifying its physiological basis.

These are risks I've chosen willingly (if not always happily) to incur, in the faith that there are (or will be) those who are interested in exercising their curiosity and imagination in thinking about the possibility of a scientific analysis of our mental life, in whatever form or state it occurs. Laypersons, for example, may be understandably reluctant to accept the dictum that there can be a science of waking cognition, but not one of dreaming. Students may wonder why their introductory texts only discuss dreaming in a chapter labeled "Personality and Psychopathology" and why their cognitive-psychological texts don't discuss it at all, when dreaming seems to be as mental or cognitive as any other kind of "thinking." From such sources, as well as from experimental psychologists themselves (at least while they are "off duty"), there is a reservoir of curiosity about dreams and dreaming to which cognitive psychology will one day have to attend. It is my hope that this book may help to hasten that day.

2. JUSTIFICATIONS

I've been emboldened to write this book, in part, by the substantial progress that cognitive psychology has made in clarifying the operations of the waking mind. For many years, academic psychology found all sorts of principled reasons for avoiding the mind and its peculiarly human manifestations. That, happily, is no longer the case, and it hasn't been so for at least two decades. The emergence and growth of mentalistic or cognitive psychology and of its affiliated disciplines (e.g., modern linguistics, psycholinguistics, and neuropsychology) have provided one of the great scientific success stories of our time. Morton Hunt has gone so far as to claim that "in a mere handful of years" these sciences have "discovered more about how we human beings think than we had previously learned in all of our time on earth."[1]* This is perhaps an extravagant judgment, but not an altogether implausible one.

Conditions in dream psychology also suggest the timeliness of realigning the study of dreaming with that of other mental acts (i.e., with cognitive psychology). The history of modern dream psychology consists, essentially, of two phases, associated with two distinct approaches, both of which apparently have about depleted their scientific productivity.

The modern psychology of dreaming begins with Sigmund Freud (1856–1939), who, almost alone among the psychotherapists of both his day and our own, thought of dreaming as a basic problem in scientific psychology. Freud's *The Interpretation of Dreams*[2] remains one of the great classics of psychology, not only because Freud wrote so well but also because he was the first psychologist to see the essential issues and problems in thinking about dreaming as a mental act. His solutions to those problems have not worn well, however, which can hardly be surprising because Freud's book was first (officially) published in 1900 and because it was necessarily written in the context of an entirely different understanding of the human mind and nervous system. After 1900, Freud had little more to say about dreaming, and most other psychotherapists were more interested in what dreams seemed to say about something else (conflicts, anxieties, etc.) than in dreaming as such. The clinical/psychotherapeutic approach (which persists to this day, but whose heyday was 1900–1950) essentially is more interested in using dreams than in understanding dreaming.

The landmark heralding the next phase of modern dream psychology was the discovery of Rapid Eye Movement (REM) sleep, and of its association with vivid dreaming.[3] Dreaming seemed to accompany, and only to accompany, a unique state of paradoxical arousal within sleep that included intermittent eye movements. To many excited researchers and observers it appeared that dreaming would at last find a genuine explanation—one framed in terms of the distinctive physiology of the state in which it occurred. But those hopes have now been largely dashed, both by the realization that finding a physiological basis for a mental act is not the same as explaining it, and by experimental data suggesting that dreaming is not in fact confined to REM sleep or to any other single body "state" (see Chapter 2). The psychobiological approach to dreaming (which also persists to this day, but whose period of greatest productivity was 1955–

---

*Raised numbers in the text indicate references and/or notes which appear at the end of each chapter.

1975) did uncover some important new facts about when, how often, and for how long people dream. These facts will be described in this book, and they constitute part of its foundation. However, the psychobiological approach did not prove to have as much to say about what dreams are, how they are put together, or what (if anything) they mean. That is, the psychological problems of dreaming identified by Freud remained (and will remain) largely unanswered by physiological observations and psychophysiological correlations.

However, as a method, if not as a source of potential explanation, physiological recording remains an invaluable part of modern dream research. Sleep recordings have some predictive value regarding whether a person will report a dream and what sort of dream a person will report when awakened. More importantly, we know that the strategy used in psychophysiological dream study—waking people up while they're dreaming (rather than, for example, simply asking them about their dreams in questionnaires)—is essential to understanding how our minds typically function when we're asleep. When this strategy is not employed, not only are many dreams totally forgotten in ways that bias our understanding of what dreaming typically is like, but those dreams that are remembered are remembered in ways that similarly bias our understanding.[4]

Moreover, using their "on-the-spot" strategy to collect dreams, psychophysiologists discovered some facts about dreaming that seem to suggest the feasibility of explaining the process cognitive-psychologically. They observed, for instance, that dreams typically are better organized and much less weird or bizarre than we might otherwise imagine.[5] That is, representative evidence of dream phenomenology itself does not sustain the idea that dreaming is radically different from much of our waking mental experience. Psychophysiologists also observed that, in early human development, dreaming changes in ways that reflect patterns of waking mental maturation.[6] Again, the implication is that an explanatory framework for dreaming might well use the same concepts as have evolved in (waking) cognitive psychology.

3. SOME COGNITIVE-PSYCHOLOGICAL CONCEPTS AND DISTINCTIONS

I've tried to write this book so that it will be comprehensible to those without detailed prior knowledge either of cognitive psychology or of dream psychology. Because the focus of the book is on dreaming, relevant concepts from dream psychology will be subject to leisurely discussion and considerable repetition in the body of the text. Moreover, the present state of scientific dream psychology is sufficiently simple that few of its ideas could be considered inherently difficult or generally unfamiliar. That is not the case, however, for the accessory discipline treated here— cognitive psychology. Therefore, to aid readers without much background (or those whose background may need a little refreshing), I want now to highlight a few of the major cognitive-psychological premises which underlie the chapters to follow. Actually, some statement of introductory premises also is required for those readers with considerable mastery of cognitive psychology, for (as these persons well know) cognitive psychology is less a unitary body of generally accepted theory than a sometimes disputatious family of diverse approaches. Thus, to say that one is taking a "cognitive-psychological" approach to something does not immediately indicate what that approach might be nor where its commitments might lie.

Cognitive psychologists generally begin with the assumption that the human mind is an *information-processing system.* Its activity, therefore, can best be described in terms of the processes by which information is manipulated and transformed. Often, these processes are set in motion by events in the external world. Something moves, and we watch it, trying to identify what this movement is and to understand what it may mean for us. Our mental processes can be described as *symbolic* to the degree that we can manipulate and transform information about objects or events even when they are not physically present, impinging on our sense organs, and when we are processing information regarding objects or events to which we have never had direct exposure. We can symbolize what is momentarily absent, and can imagine the distant or the impossible. The basis for symbolic behavior is *symbolic memory.* Symbolic memory refers to the fact that we have stored information that can be activated and manipulated on a purely mental basis (although we obviously also use this information while we are dealing directly with events in the world about us). This stored information consists of *mental representations—* information within the system that refers to the world outside the system.

Most research in cognitive psychology has tried to specify the processes by which we analyze and integrate *sensory* information so as to achieve durable mental representations, which can be applied in subsequent perceptual processing and behavioral regulation and used in later thinking.[7] In general, the approach has been a *constructivist* one. That is, it is assumed that the mind constructs representations which contain information about features of the world and about our options for relating ourselves to that world. The main effort has been to characterize the stages or subprocesses by which stimulus arrays in the world lead to representations in the mind.

Cognitive psychology has given considerably less attention to *spon-*

taneous mental processing—that is, to the use and transformation of representations in symbolic memory in cases where external events play no direct role in the engagement of symbolic activity and have little if any effect on the course of such activity. This obviously constitutes one major hurdle in any attempt at applying cognitive-psychological principles to the analysis of an act such as dreaming. My assumption, however, is that dreaming involves the same types of symbolic representations (memories) and the same kinds of processing systems as are implied by the study of our processing of information in the external world. Viewed this way, a cognitive-psychological account of dreaming must characterize the kinds of symbolic representations active in dream construction and the kinds of transformations these representations undergo during the formation of a dream. In drawing up such an account, however, some choices have to be made among the various models in cognitive psychology that describe the nature of symbolic memory and the processes by which information is encoded in it.

In line with the thinking of a number of recent analysts of cognitive-psychological research, I assume that there are what Jerry Fodor calls "modular systems" in which information is first analyzed.[8] For present purposes, the most significant of these systems are those by which *visual* information and *linguistic* information are processed. To describe these systems as "modular" implies the following points:

1.   They are domain-specific; that is, they deal only with information of a certain sort (e.g., visual or linguistic information).

2.   The output of these systems is relatively "shallow," that is, they do not produce representations specifying the meaning or significance of objects and events so much as information identifying objects and events.

3.   These systems are not so much "intellectual" as they are primitively "perceptual"—they are the mechanisms of perceptual identification and literal verbal comprehension rather than those of reflection and conceptual comprehension.

4.   Accordingly they are not, as such, the basis of individual differences in general intellectual or symbolic behavior.

5.   These systems are "hard-wired" into the human brain—while their operation may be subject to modification during development, the systems are not "learned," and their operation is (in appropriate circumstances) mandatory rather than a matter of conscious choice.

6.   To a considerable degree, the areas of the brain that mediate the operation of these systems, and even of their subcomponents, are discrete and specifiable (with damage to those areas leading to predictable forms of breakdown, for example, in visual perception or speech analysis).

7.   Because of the relatively limited "decisions" to be made by these

systems (e.g., "What did she say?" rather than "What did she mean?"), and in line with their automaticity, their operation is, as compared to that of deliberative thought, very fast.

8.   Finally, in agreement with previous characterizations, these systems are, in Fodor's terms, "informationally encapsulated"—the information at their access in interpreting inputs is limited to the sorts of specifically perceptual or linguistic information required to achieve their relatively limited goals.

In sum, Fodor's claim (which I accept) is that these modular systems only "present the world to thought"—they are input systems that prepare information in a form appropriate for conceptual comprehension, reflection, and eventual commitment to symbolic memory.[9] But they are themselves, once an input is specified for them, relatively uninfluenced by higher-order mental processes.

The designation of a specifically linguistic module—one that stands apart from the input systems dealing with nonlinguistic visual and auditory inputs—may be somewhat surprising. But it stands on a considerable (if not unequivocal) body of evidence. Moreover, this way of thinking about the role of language in mental functioning provides a convenient solution for an old problem: the relation of word knowledge to world knowledge. We possess and employ specifically linguistic knowledge—for example, knowledge about the sound patterns within and among words, and about the intralinguistic associations of words (e.g., "white"–"black"). This word knowledge has seemed sufficiently different from world knowledge that cognitive psychologists have sometimes used a different term to designate its hypothetical locus in memory: the "lexicon." But if word knowledge is represented similarly as world knowledge, why should the different objects of the two forms of knowledge make any difference? And if it isn't represented similarly, how is word knowledge represented and how does it interact with world knowledge?

In the judgment of many,[10] the wisest solution to these problems lies in thinking that specifically verbal knowledge is *procedural,* rather than a part of *declarative* or *propositional* knowledge (i.e., world knowledge). Specifically, lexical memory lies in a relatively encapsulated linguistic processing module which prepares sensory information for thought (or thought for verbal expression) rather than in the realm of thought itself. "Lexicon" refers, then, to stored information that is applied during the processing by which linguistic information is analyzed. It is procedural rather than substantive, in that it characterizes *how* verbal information is to be processed rather than *what* the world is like. In line with this procedural assignment of verbal knowledge, neuropsychological data have identified certain distinct regions of the dominant (typically the left) hemisphere of the brain that seem to be associated with the application of syntactic, phonetic, and other intraverbal knowledge in linguistic processing.

With this sketch in mind about how world-information is processed initially, we can now consider the question of how such information ultimately is represented in symbolic memory. Here, there are many different proposals, some of which describe the purported structure of substantive memory in elaborate detail. The failure of cognitive psychology to reach consensus is scarcely surprising, given the difficulty of the problem and the youth of the discipline. Some psychologists think that resolution of the problem may be inherently impossible. Others think that at least a few things can be said about what human knowledge representation must be like. My position is of the latter sort.

One issue regarding knowledge representation is whether it is (or how much it is) "analog." An analog representation is one whose significant features are "analogous" to those of the object or event represented. The clearest example of an analog representation in memory would be a kind of mental "film strip" that preserved most of the visual features of the events it symbolized. Some neuroscientists (but probably many fewer cognitive psychologists) think that our memories of events are somehow like mental pictures of those events. There's no doubt, of course, that we can image events or objects, but that doesn't necessarily mean that that's how they are coded in symbolic memory. We can also talk about events, but that doesn't necessarily mean that *that* is how they are coded in symbolic memory. As I've previously suggested, although knowledge may be expressible in words, words may play no direct role in symbolic memory. Verbalization may, rather, be a way in which information from memory can be *processed*. Likewise, I assume that imaging is a way by which information in memory can be processed, but not the form in which it is stored. In fact, dream imagery itself is probably the best argument against an analog storage theory. Some observers have made the point that the very detail of some of our imagery makes it unlikely that images are processed from nonanalog representations. Such detail, they say, could only result from details in analog storage.[11] But our *most* detailed and vivid imagery is dream imagery, and its content rarely corresponds to anything we would have stored as memories. The very novelty of our dream imagery argues for imaging as processing. And, as we'll see later, there are still further (developmental) data from dream psychology which contradict the idea of analog storage.

As to how information might be represented other than in picture (or sound, etc.) replicas, there also are many claims. I shall not specify, however, any *format* in which information is represented "abstractly" (i.e., in nonanalog form). That may never be knowable, and for the purposes of my discussion it doesn't really matter what the format might be. Two things seem reasonably clear, however, about what the *organization* of substantive memory must be like. What we know about anything includes knowledge about some of its features (e.g., we know that birds have wings and that they generally can fly) and knowledge about its relations with other things that we know (e.g., we know that birds are not mammals, that they seem to like to sit on tree branches and telephone wires, that they tend to fly away when someone approaches them, and so forth). Thus, our knowledge of the world must depend, in part, on a *conceptual feature analysis* of objects and events, and the sum total of our knowledge must conform in some way to a kind of *network organization* in which certain kinds of knowledge are more or less closely associated by features or context with other kinds of knowledge.

Another important proposal that has been made about knowledge representation in symbolic memory is that we should distinguish between *generic* knowledge (e.g., catsup is made from tomatoes) and *episodic* knowledge (e.g., I bought a jar of catsup at the market a week ago Thursday). That is, we can remember both relatively timeless facts and discrete events from our own life history. Endel Tulving, who has argued most forcefully for this distinction, thinks that the contrast between generic memory (which he calls "semantic memory") and episodic memory has to do with more than the kind of knowledge being represented.[12] He feels that generic and episodic memory are, in fact, two different systems.

In some respects, the differences described by Tulving have to do more with the way in which memories are processed than in how they are represented. For example, visual-perceptual and other sensory processing may be more common for life-history memories (I can "see" and "feel" what it was like when I was in the supermarket, whereas I may only "verbalize" my answer to the question about catsup's ingredients). Other differences described by Tulving may have to do with the accessibility rather than the representation of knowledge in memory (I have more difficulty "remembering" any particular trip to the grocery store—such trips tend to get mixed up with one another—than in thinking about timeless facts). Still other differences, however, seem sufficiently basic that Tulving's proposal of a qualitative difference in representation should be accepted (our life-history memories are all *self*-related and hence may depend developmentally on the emergence of a sense of a self to which events can be referred). Moreover, as Tulving indicates, neuropsychological data argue for the reality of his distinction. In certain forms of amnesia, for instance, people may forget significant portions of their life histories—or even their own identity—while retaining general information about the world.

Past the level of modular "input" systems, then, there are enduring symbolic representations of the world (and of the self). Some of these representations are generic, while others are part of an autobiographical memory system. But to leave our characterization of the human mind at this level is to lose sight of the kinds of processing which information must undergo once it passes through the input modules. It's easy to see several respects in which the sketch of the mind I've drawn up to this point must be lacking: It does not explain how information from the different modules is integrated (for example, blending sights and sounds into a unified impression of an event); it does not explain how the information from the input modules is analyzed for its conceptual significance; it does not describe how newly determined meanings are integrated with (and help to reorganize) what we already know; and it does not specify how, once we've interpreted an event, we plan and execute activity to reflect upon or deal with it. By and large, these sorts of processes of information transformation are nonmodular (or supramodular), in that they deal with information from different input systems, or with information that is sufficiently removed from its modular bases to be called "abstract." To the extent that the information processed *is* abstract, these transformations also seem to be nonmodular in the sense that they've proven more difficult to localize to particular brain centers. We are, in short, now in a realm of generalized information processing that fully deserves the label "thinking" or "intelligence."

As Fodor has suggested, it is precisely because of the generality (or informational *non*encapsulation) of these processes that they've been more difficult for cognitive psychologists to identify and describe.[13] Thus, the sketch of mind becomes less well focused at this point (unfortunately, just at the point of greatest interest). A few things may be said, however, about these higher-order mental processes. *First,* supramodal information integration seems to begin, in the brain, at a point where (unsurprisingly) the modality-specific input systems overlap. *Second,* the supramodal conceptual analysis of information seems to follow procedures reminiscent of those used in intramodal perceptual analysis. The difference is that the features analyzed here aren't just perceptual ones. Seeing portraits of Richard Nixon and Lyndon Johnson, for instance, can give rise to the conceptual-feature similarities: "Presidents of the United States", "left office under a cloud", etc. *Third,* information that has passed through this sort of conceptual analysis is committed to symbolic memory (thus, memory is not composed of visual film strips or other perceptual replicas, but of conceptually transformed and conceptually interrelated information). *Fourth,* although it is difficult to identify the principles by which conceptual understanding is accomplished, some clues about our conceptual repertoire can be gained by examining the development of conceptual reasoning in early childhood. Young children not only know less than we do, they also understand what they know in more primitive ways. It is possible, therefore, to describe the achievements children make as their comprehension improves, and thus to identify some of the processes of conceptual reasoning that we adults take for granted. This was the strategy followed by the Swiss psychologist, Jean Piaget (1896–1980), and it is one that is commonplace in cognitive developmental psychology. (As we'll see, this is a strategy which has also been applied profitably to dreaming itself.)

In considering how reasoning results in conscious awareness and overt behavior, several points also seem fairly clear. *First,* our overt behavior may be symbolically mediated without our being consciously aware of the reasoning processes involved. Because of this quite imperfect reflection of symbolic activity in conscious awareness, cognitive psychology cannot limit itself to the study of conscious experience. In fact, the rise of cognitive psychology is largely attributable to the development of investigative paradigms in which people don't have to be (and most often aren't) asked about their conscious experience. Rather, from their overt performances, the cognitive psychologist infers what people's mental strategies must have been and the most likely steps by which they implemented those strategies. *Second,* it appears that awareness of symbolic activity is a developmentally later-appearing achievement than is symbolic behavior itself. Being able to reconstruct, in "our own (conscious) minds," the nature of a reasoning process is always an uncertain and difficult business, but it seems especially problematic in early childhood.[14] *Third,* the generation of modality-specific experience and behavior seems to involve the same modular and nonmodular systems that are used in perceptual analysis. For example, there is considerable anatomical overlap between the modular brain areas serving speech perception and those serving speech production, and deficits in speech perception and in speech production generally accompany one another.[15] There is also good reason to think that the nonmodular mental "programs," that we use in production (for example, in making up a story), are the same ones we use in comprehension (in understanding stories told to us by others.) *Fourth,* it is more difficult to generate conscious modular experience (e.g., mental imagery) than it is to employ a modular system in perceptual processing. Young children whose perceptual performances seem quite adequate may, for example, have considerable difficulty in imaging objects or events purely in their "mind's eye."[16] *Fifth,* it likewise seems probable that, in the speech modality (where *overt* production is known to lag behind comprehension in early development), young children develop overt *speech* before they are able to *think consciously* in words and to use such inner speech representations to organize their behavior and experience. Thus, internally initiated conscious mental states—words or images "running through our (conscious) minds"—are by no means automatic accompaniments of symbolic activity and rarely (if ever) directly reveal the full nature of that activity.

In the preceding analysis, I've focused on the generation of conscious experience rather than on that of overt behavior for the obvious reason that dreams are conscious experiences. I've focused on visual imagery and on speech representations, because when we are conscious of some mental fact, that fact is often experienced in visual imagery or in the form of some kind of inner speech representation. These are the most frequent forms of concrete intramental awareness, and they are also the ones most prevalent in dreams. Dreams are, in fact, especially good examples of the principle that modular systems for the analysis of sensory data from the world outside also are potentially at the service of the world in our minds.

If the sources of our dreams lie in this world within—in what we know and remember—then in dreaming such information must be reorganized and transformed and then processed by modular systems so that we "see" and "feel" and "speak" in a conscious experience that we momentarily confuse with awareness of external reality. How all this could happen, in just the way it seems to, is a big puzzle—the puzzle of this book. Why, for example, do we experience our dreams as if they were life rather than thought? How can our awareness of *dream events* be so vivid, while we are so little aware of what our *minds* in fact are up to? How, Dostoyevsky wondered, can we be both so brilliant and so stupid in our dreams?

Sometimes one dreams strange dreams, impossible and unnatural, and upon waking you remember them clearly and are amazed by a very strange thing. You remember before anything else that your reason did not desert you throughout the whole dream; in fact you remember that you acted with extreme cunning and logic throughout; the long, long time you were surrounded by murderers trying to outwit you, disguising their intentions, behaving amicably while holding their weapons in readiness, and only awaiting some sort of signal; you remember how cleverly you fooled them at last, hiding from them; then you realize that they had seen through all your deceptions and were only pretending not to know where you were hidden; but you were clever and fooled them again. You remember all this clearly. But how in the same space of time can your reason be reconciled with the manifest absurdities and impossibilities with which your dream was filled? One of your murderers changed into a woman before your eyes, and from a woman into a clever, loathsome little dwarf—and you accepted all this instantly as absolute fact with hardly any surprise at all, and precisely at a time when otherwise your reason was it its highest pitch and showed extraordinary power, cunning, clarity, and logic.[17]

Yet dreaming is not an *altogether* different kind of symbolic act than one which is highly familiar (and reasonably comprehensible) to us—the conscious recollection and mental "reliving" of some event in our past experience. Freud once described dreaming as being simply "another kind of remembering."[18] What could he have meant by that? We rarely, if ever, *experience* our dreams as remembering, and, when we judge our dreams' contents, we generally have great difficulty in identifying anything that they could be remembrances *of.* What Freud may have meant is this: Despite the differences between conscious episodic recollection and dreaming, in each case we are able, "working purely from memory," to simulate the world of perceptual experience. Might not some of the same processes be involved? As we shall see (Chapter 3), young children's ability to experience dreams seems to be quite limited; young children's capacity for conscious recollection of particular events in their past seems to be similarly limited, and much less developed than their capacity for remembering procedures and facts.[19] Could there be a common explanation for these two deficiencies? If dreaming *does* employ some of the same processes as are involved in conscious episodic recollection, then the study of dreaming may be a good way of studying the development of that aspect of mind. (And, if Tulving is correct in asserting that conscious episodic memory is unique to the human species, then the study of dreaming may be a good way of finding out what's so special about our minds and selves.)[20]

However, the major task of a cognitive *dream* psychology is not so much to see in dreaming the *same* sorts of processes and systems that describe the waking mind, as to try to understand the *differences* in mental organization which are responsible for our experiencing dreams— rather than recollective imagery or verbal thoughts—when we're asleep. My premise (and the justification for this brief overview of the waking mind, as cognitive psychology sees it) is that the peculiarities of dreaming can be explained in terms of some kind of reorganization of many of those same mental processes and systems that we employ in waking perception and thought.

4. ON THE QUESTION OF DREAM INTERPRETATION

Freud's *The Interpretation of Dreams* can be viewed as an early attempt to explain the process of dreaming in just this way. But Freud also used his book to present a scheme for determining what the contents of individual dreams "mean." Ever since, it's been difficult for most people even to imagine that a book on dreams might be written in which meaning is not the central concern. This, however, is such a book.

Although my final chapter is devoted to an analysis of what people are looking for when they ask to have their dreams interpreted (and of how likely they are to be successful in their quests), my major interest lies in trying to understand what occurs *during* the act of dreaming. My position is that questions about the significance, function, and meaning of individual dreams can best be asked in terms of some realistic analysis of the kind of mental act that dreaming is.

Thus, my primary concern is with *how* we are thinking when we're dreaming, rather than with *what* we are thinking when we're dreaming. This is in the tradition of cognitive psychology more generally; it takes a *process-oriented,* rather than a *content-oriented* approach, to the human mind. Within the framework of dream psychology, this book can be placed in the tradition of Havelock Ellis' (1859–1939) *The World of Dreams.*[21] Without the tools of today's cognitive sciences, Ellis rather nicely portrayed dreaming as "the inevitable outcome of the conditions under which psychic life exists during sleep," and diligently set about trying to understand just what those conditions were.[22] Interestingly, for those who disbelieve any cumulative trend in dream psychology, his conclusions in many ways foreshadow those advanced here.

In thinking about what a process-oriented dream psychology might be like, a useful analogy can be made to the process-oriented psychology of language: psycholinguistics.[23] In recent years, psycholinguists have made considerable progress in describing how we produce and comprehend speech and how, developmentally, we come to be as skilled as we are in using linguistic symbols. This progress has been made even though psycholinguists have focused not on *what* people say so much as on *how* they say it.

Regarding human speech, it's clear that we generally cannot predict precisely what people will say, even when we have substantial knowledge or control of their environments. In this respect, there's an obvious parallel with dreaming. The unpredictability of our dreams has seemed to many observers to cast dreaming well beyond the boundaries of any possible empirical science. The problem does seem to be enormous, because the "environment" in which dreaming occurs is a wholly internal (intramental) one, and it seems to lie not only outside external control and knowledge but also outside our own control and knowledge. Other people cannot predict what we dream, nor can we ourselves.

Even if we cannot predict specifically what people will say, it often seems relatively easy, after the fact, to determine a relationship between what they've said and (a) what they meant to say and (b) the situation that gave rise to their intentions to say what they did. In the case of dreams, however, people typically profess not to know what their own dreams mean. They're not aware of having intended to dream the dreams that they did and can only wonder about what, if anything, they "meant" by them. Professional interpeters of dreams claim to be able to fill this breach, and, through their theories of human nature and their knowledge of dreamers' life circumstances, claim to be able to reconstruct the situations that give rise to dreams and the reactions to those situations that the dreams embody. To less credulous observers, however, it hasn't been clear how one can be sure that an interpeter is right, and the presence of so many different interpretive systems and of so many radically different readings of individual dreams is far from reassuring.

It seems reasonable, then, that cognitive dream psychology not begin with the assumption that dreams are meaningful in some specifiable, quasilinguistic way, but should start with the sorts of basic investigations of the process of dreaming that may ultimately help to identify ways in which dreams have meaning. Here is where the analogy to psycholinguistics may be helpful. Without being able to predict what people will say, and also in the absence of commitment to particular theories about how people decide what they "mean" to say, psycholinguists have been able to clarify the processes by which human speech is produced. In the same vein, it may be possible to describe the processes by which dreaming is accomplished—how we dream—without making an a priori commitment to what, if anything, a dream "means" to say. Just as there is a discipline of psycholinguistics for the study of the form of language processing, so too it may be possible to have a discipline of *psychoneirics,* devoted to the study of the forms of mental processing that occur during dreaming (*oneiric,* from ancient Greek, is an adjective designating dreams). This book takes the position that there can be just such a discipline, and tries to describe what it might look like, how it might proceed, and what its goals might be.

Two major goals can immediately be identified. The first, and logically prior, one is to describe dream phenomena. We need descriptions first of all of what dreams are like—of what seem to be their distinctive properties. But we also need descriptions of the cognitive processes that seem to be involved in the generation of dream experience and of how they seem to be operating during dream production. The second goal of cognitive dream psychology is explanatory. Through models specifying the mental systems active during dreaming, and their modes of action and interaction, we should be able to begin to explain why dream experience has the properties that it does.

A book committed to this strategy will not contain detailed interpretations of individual dreams. This admission may strike some readers as a disappointing one. If you are such a reader, I urge you to check your disappointment until you have had an opportunity to read the rest of the book and to begin to appreciate some of the power of its approach. Then you may decide whether your curiosity about your own dream life really is better served by a more traditional kind of dream book, in which you are fed a rich supply of dream material and are astonished (and sometimes puzzled) by the versatility with which the author seems to be able to interpret the content of these dreams. In making your judgment, you might also ask yourself whether the traditional content-interpretive approach has, in fact, led to any cumulative, reliable knowledge about dreams and dreaming (for this is what we expect from any empirical science). I think that it has not, and that this is why, after almost a century of "deep" dream interpetation, the time is ripe for a fresh approach, particularly for one that ties the study of dreaming to the very best efforts now being made to understand the waking mind. Those efforts are largely process-centered; so, therefore, is this book.

NOTES

[1] Morton Hunt, *The Universe Within,* New York: Simon and Schuster, 1982, p. 13.

[2] Sigmund Freud, *The Interpretation of Dreams,* New York: Basic Books, 1955 (originally published, 1900).

[3] Eugene Aserinsky and Nathaniel Kleitman, "Regularly Occurring Periods of Eye Motility, and Concomitant Phenomena, During Sleep," *Science,* 1953, *118,* 273–274.

[4] See, for example, David Foulkes, "Home and Laboratory Dreams: Four Empirical Studies and a Conceptual Reevaluation," *Sleep,* 1979, *2,* 233–251 and V. S. Bose, "Dream Content Transformations: An Empirical Study of Freud's Secondary Revision Hypothesis," Ph.D. Dissertation, Andhra University (Waltair, India), 1982. The results of these studies (conducted, respectively, with children and young adults) argue that typical home-recalled dreams are different from typical REM-awakening laboratory dreams, not because of the different setting in which dreams are collected, but because of the more representative sampling of dreams in the laboratory. In line with this conclusion, a study by Frank Heynick ("Theoretical & Empirical Investigation into Verbal Aspects of the Freudian Model of Dream Generation," M.D. Dissertation, State University, Groningen [The Netherlands], 1983) found that on-the-spot awakenings at home (random phone calls were made to subjects during the night) produced dream reports like laboratory REM reports and unlike spontaneous home reports.

[5] E.g., Frederick Snyder, "The Phenomenology of Dreaming," in Leo Madow and Laurence H. Snow, eds., *The Psychodynamic Implications of the Physiological Studies on Dreams,* Springfield, Ill.: Charles C Thomas, 1970, pp. 124–151.

[6] David Foulkes, *Children's Dreams: Longitudinal Studies,* New York: John Wiley and Sons, 1982.

[7] Ulric Neisser, *Cognitive Psychology,* New York: Appleton-Century-Crofts, 1967.

[8] Jerry A. Fodor, *The Modularity of Mind,* Cambridge, Mass.: Bradford Books, 1983.

[9] *Ibid.,* p. 101.

[10] E.g., Fodor, *op. cit.;* Endel Tulving, *Elements of Episodic Memory,* New York: Oxford University Press, 1983.

[11] Jerry A. Fodor, *The Language of Thought,* Cambridge, Mass.: Harvard University Press, 1975, p. 194; Roberta L. Klatzky, *Human Memory: Structures and Processes,* 2nd edition, San Francisco: W. H. Freeman, 1980, p. 210.

[12] Tulving, *op. cit.*

[13] Fodor, *The Modularity of Mind.*

[14] Jean Piaget, *The Grasp of Consciousness: Action and Concept in the Young Child,* Cambridge Mass.: Harvard University Press, 1976 (originally published, 1974).

[15] Catherine A. Mateer, "Motor and Perceptual Functions of the Left Hemisphere and their Interaction," in Sidney J. Segalowitz (ed.), *Language Functions and Brain Organization,* New York: Academic Press., 1983, pp. 145–170.

[16] Jean Piaget and Bärbel Inhelder, *Mental Imagery in the Child,* New York: Basic Books, 1971 (originally published, 1966).

[17] Fyodor Dostoyevsky, *The Idiot,* New York: New American Library, 1969 (originally published, 1869), p. 471. Quoted with permission of the publisher.

[18] Sigmund Freud, "From the History of an Infantile Neurosis," in *Three Case Studies.* New York: Collier Books, 1963 (originally published, 1918), p. 239.

[19] Tulving, *op. cit.;* Daniel L. Schacter and Endel Tulving, "Amnesia and Memory Research," in Laird S. Cermak (ed.), *Human Memory and Amnesia,* Hillsdale, N. J.: Lawrence Erlbaum Associates, 1982, pp. 1–32.

[20] Tulving, *op. cit.,* p. 1.

[21] Havelock Ellis, *The World of Dreams.* Boston: Houghton Mifflin, 1922.

[22] *Ibid.,* p. 185.

[23] There are many books on psycholinguistic research and theory. One that may be especially useful in the context of thinking about parallels with psychoneirics is: Donald J. Foss and David T. Hakes, *Psycholinguistics: An Introduction to the Psychology of Language,* Englewood Cliffs, N. J.: Prentice-Hall, 1978.

1 What Dreams Are

Despite widespread disagreement on how to interpret dreams, there has been general agreement, at least since the publication of Freud's *The Interpretation of Dreams,*[1] about what dreams are.

1. DREAMS ARE INVOLUNTARY SYMBOLIC ACTS

One of Freud's major theses about dreaming was that dreams are a form of thought or symbolic activity. The major question of his book was why we think in a different way when we are asleep than we do when we are awake. This is still the central concern of dream psychology. One dimension of difference between dreams and at least some of our waking symbolic behavior is that dreams are *involuntary*. That is, we are generally surprised on awakening from a dream because we didn't consciously will that we would dream it. If you think of our waking speech, we generally end up saying something that bears some relationship to what we *wanted* to say. But dreaming generally doesn't seem to express any coherent set of wishes or wants at all. At least, we're generally unable, after having dreamed, to figure out why we dreamed what we did, or what, if anything, we meant to express or establish by having dreamed it.

But involuntary ideation is by no means foreign to our waking experience. In fact, in implicitly taking problem solving or reasoning as our model of what waking thought typically is like, we probably greatly overestimate the voluntary control that we exert over the flow of conscious waking ideation. Often, when we are not occupied with the demands of reality—and sometimes even when we are—unbidden thoughts and images "pop into" consciousness. And, although we may be momentarily bemused or astonished by these thoughts and images, we don't seriously doubt that we somehow conjured them up. They are *our* thoughts and images, even if we may not be able to say "where they came from" or why they popped into consciousness just when they did.

With dreams, however, our willingness to accept involuntary ideation as our own is somewhat reduced. Thus, we can find many otherwise sensible people who seem to want to believe that their dreams are not their own thoughts, but are instead messages from the gods, or from other people or planets. There is a sense in which these people are right in denying their personal responsibility for their dreams, for the "persons" they know themselves to be did not willfully participate in creating these dreams. One of Freud's contributions, however, was to show that we are more than the people we consciously think ourselves to be, and that much of what we do with our minds does not depend on voluntary control or planning.

These points are now generally accepted by psychologists of many different persuasions, and their status in no way depends on accepting Freud's particular hypotheses about the constituents or operations of the hypothetical mental system he called the Unconscious. For example, the earliest experimental psychologists proposed to study waking thought by having subjects describe ("introspect") their conscious experience as they solved simple problems. As you can probably also verify from your own experience, research subjects were much better in solving the problems than in describing how they were able to, and they were often unaware even of having exerted volitional control over the process of coming up with their solutions.[2] Conscious, volitional control is not a necessary feature of the effective organization or utilization of what we call the mind.

But how do we know that dreaming really is a form of *symbolic* activity—that it's some kind of involuntary *thinking*? Before Freud, it had been common for researchers to think of dreaming as a kind of faulty perception. The idea was that dreaming only occurred when the sleeper became sensitive to some external or body stimulus, like the sound of a passing vehicle or a cramp in the stomach. The dream was viewed as the dreamer's attempt to interpret the stimulus. However, because sleep in some (generally unspecified) way was imagined to impair one's perceptual faculties, he or she arrived at a faulty interpretation of the stimulus. That interpretation was the dream.

There were immense difficulties in accepting this view of dreaming even in Freud's day, and with the collection of still further data since that time, the equation of dreaming with perception is now altogether unsupportable. (1) The idea that the kind of interpretation given stimuli during sleep is more like incomplete or faulty seeing or hearing (etc.) than it is like conceptually rich thinking overlooks the detailed, temporally elaborated, and dramatic quality of our dreams. Even if dreams were to be instigated by randomly appearing stimuli during sleep, the process initiated by these stimuli would have to be more like a soaring flight of inner ideas than any kind of passive perception. (2) As Freud noted, and as more recent research[3] has verified, stimuli applied during sleep (e.g., moving the sleeper's leg, or spraying his or her face with water) do not reliably instigate dreams (at least the only dreams we can know about, those which people remember). (3) As Freud also noted, the same stimulus, when it is "incorporated" in dream imagery, can be associated with vastly different kinds of dreams. On one occasion, the water-spray may be associated with a drinking theme, on the next with a flood theme. Thus, it is difficult to see how the external stimulus as such could "explain" the ensuing dream. (4) The picture one gets in the case of most such incorporations, moreover, is of an already ongoing narrative which, if it deigns to "use" the stimulus at all, does so by interpreting it in a way that is consistent with the preexisting dream story. That is, the dream determines the fate of the stimulus, rather than vice-versa. (5) Since the discovery of Rapid Eye Movement (REM) sleep, and of its association with vivid dreaming, it has become apparent that dreaming is too pervasive, temporally extended, and cyclically recurrent in the adult human to be explained by infrequent, brief, and randomly occurring stimuli during sleep.[4] Moreover, experimentally controlled external stimulation has not been found to trigger (REM) dream periods. (6) We now also know that there are, in the visual system, other impediments to perception during sleep than the fact that one's eyelids typically are closed. Subjects who slept with their eyelids taped open and with their pupils dilated were still demonstrated to be functionally "blind" during sleep. They couldn't see (or dream about) the stimuli before their eyes.[5] The visual system is by no means electrically silent during sleep, but it seems to be internally "tuned"; that is, it is organized in a different way in sleep than when it functions as a sensory system.

Perhaps the most convincing demonstration that dreaming is a kind of thinking rather than any kind of perception comes from the study of people whose waking perception is normal (or adequate to navigate the waking world) but whose waking abilities to *imagine* or *think* about the world are in some way impaired. One patient, for instance, experienced a severe head injury that did not interfere with his waking visual perception. It did, however, totally abolish his previously highly developed ability to visualize "mentally." A builder's manager, he could no longer mentally visualize a plan, and had, instead, constantly to refer back to the blueprints. He claimed that, "When I dream, I seem to know what is happening, but I don't seem then to see a picture. I can dream about a person without seeing him."[6] This account suggests that the patient could dream only as he could mentally imagine the world—without visual imagery—not as he could see it. But this case, and others like it, are less than totally convincing, because the patient was not awakened during REM sleep and asked, then and there, to describe his dreams. As we now know, many dreams, and many details of dreams, are quickly forgotten if they are not described immediately after their occurrence (see Chapter 2).

It is useful, then, that we have at least two case studies which describe the REM dream reports of subjects with defects in waking visual imagination.[7] In both cases, the individuals were unable to solve mental problems in which a test figure must be rotated mentally in order to have the same orientation as a standard figure, and in which judgment must be made as to whether the figures are identical. For example, the standard figure might be the letter "J," and the test figure either the letter "J" tilted at a 120° angle from the upright or the letter "J" so tilted *and* also rotated three dimensionally so that its "tail" now faces to its right rather than to its left. It is assumed that, to solve such a problem, one must first rotate the test figure through "mental space" until it faces upright, and then determine if the figures match one another in this position. That is, solving the problem depends on one's ability to *imagine* movement through visual space. One person with task-specific inability to solve such problems never reported visual imagery in her REM dreams. The other was asked if a movie would describe the manner in which he experienced his dreams, and he replied, "I think a radio drama or tape with an occasional picture might be a better means of expressing . . ." how he experienced them. Both subjects were bright, and college-educated; neither was *generally* inept at problem solving. They had a specific waking inability to visually imagine movement through space, and their dreams were similarly devoid of movie-like imagery. The first subject had normal waking perception. The second subject, because of damage to the right hemisphere of the cerebral cortex, could see only in his right visual field, but by changing his angle of observation, was capable of taking in sufficient visual information to pursue a career successfully and unaided. Thus, the subjects' dream "disabilities" seemed to be related more to specific thought defects (in visual imagination) than to any visual perceptual disabilities. These individuals dreamed more as they could *think* about the world than as they could *see* it.

Such observations not only reinforce the idea that dreaming is more like thinking than like seeing, they also raise some interesting questions about the evolutionary history of dreaming and about the developmental history of dreaming in the human. When we wonder what dogs or cats and human infants dream, we seem to think that, because these creatures can see the

world, they ought to be able to dream of it as well. But, if dreaming is
more like thinking than seeing, then we ought to be considering how well
dogs, cats, and infants can think about the world—whether they can
symbolically reconstruct and manipulate in their minds the things they
know perceptually—when we consider whether or how well they can
dream. In Chapter 3, I review what is known about the early development
of dreaming in the human, and show that dreaming in fact seems to follow
a course dictated by intellectual growth rather than by perceptual competence. That finding offers still further support for the characterization of
dreaming as a *symbolic process*—something we do with our thinking
minds.[8]

2. THE SOURCES OF OUR DREAMS LIE IN WHAT WE KNOW

It is generally assumed that the sources of our dreams lie in what we
know, that their particular images can be traced back to whole units or
bits and pieces of memory and knowledge that we have acquired through
experience. There are some obvious difficulties with this assumption,
because in our dreams we often run across people, places, objects, and
situations which have no obvious counterpart in our waking life histories.
Nevertheless, the assumption is not an implausible one, and it is difficult
to imagine any alternative to it.

Freud sought to demonstrate the derivation of dream imagery from
memories and knowledge by having dreamers "free associate" to their
dream images. First, the dreamer recollects some particular dream image,
and then lets her or his mind wander where it will. Freud's idea was that,
since volitional control doesn't seem to be operative in creating dreams,
an undirected association process beginning with the dream image might
be able to travel back through, and permit the reconstruction of, the
associative pathways used in creating the image. Ideally, it would lead
back to one or more demonstrable source for every feature of the dream's
imagery.

In Freud's hands, free associations were supposed to lead back not only
to the sources of the dream's imagery but also to the motives that dictated
their use. That is, Freud thought that free association would suggest not
only where the imagery of the dream came from but also why the dream
was dreamed. His ideas about the *ultimate* sources of the dream—that
they lay in repressed sexual wishes and fantasies—are well-known, controversial, almost certainly wrong, and unessential to the argument here.
These ultimate sources were not, in fact, identified in the dreamer's associations at all, but were reconstructed by Freud's imposition of a particu-

lar theory on those associations.[9] Even though one rejects this theory, however, "free" associations themselves still can be useful in identifying what Freud might have thought of as the *proximate* sources of the dream—those lying sufficiently close at hand to have served as the mnemonic (memory) basis for the particular imagery of the dream. In this sense, there is only one thing that's novel about Freud's method. He's saying that if you can't think where in your past experience a particular dream image might come from, then it might be helpful if *you'd* stop thinking so hard about it and just let your *mind* do the job in its own undirected way.

Using this method, Freud found just about what you and everyone else who's wondered about the sources of her or his dream imagery would expect. Some of the imagery of the dream seemed to draw in a relatively direct way on experiences of the day before (the *dream day*). These experiences, encoded as memories, Freud called *day residues.* Sometimes day residues referred to important and emotionally impressive experiences of the dream day; sometimes they referred to the sorts of trivial waking events the dreamer might otherwise have imagined to be totally forgettable, had they not recurred in the dream. On the face of it, there seemed to be little rhyme or reason as to *what* impressions of the dream day appeared in the dream, although Freud thought it significant that *some* impressions from that day could almost invariably be demonstrated to be present.

From the perspective of contemporary thinking about human memory and thought, in which computer analogies run rampant, it is natural to think of dreaming as a kind of updating of one's memory "files." In wakefulness, so the argument goes, information is being processed too continuously to permit complete cross-tabulation with relevant knowledge already on hand. Dreaming either is the process by which, or is a token of the process by which, such cross-filing goes on during sleep, when no new information is being taken aboard from the outside world. On this view, the day residue content of our dreams indicates that reprocessing *is* occurring for dream day experiences, and the day residue itself may be a means by which relevant older knowledge is being addressed, accessed, or reorganized. Presumably, from the logic of mnemonic organization, it might not matter how impressive or significant the experience was to which the day residue referred: Its importance would lie in its pattern of potential connections with knowledge already in storage.[10]

This is one of many ideas about dreams that have at least a superficial appeal, but about whose real value one must entertain some doubts. Insofar as it proposes a function for dreaming in human information processing, it faces the obvious problem that there seems to be so little rationale for what particular day residues will appear in one's nightly dreams (see the discussion in Chapter 5). Also, insofar as it proposes that it is dreaming, rather than merely REM sleep, that accomplishes some information processing function, it would be nice to see the idea worked out with dream observations, rather than, as has typically been the case, with REM sleep measurements. How, precisely, could *the dream,* as we know it, achieve (or reflect) the sort of mental reprogramming that this model proposes? Is there any reason to believe that the particular forms of cross-filing evident in dreams, for example the imaginal fusing of the physical properties of two different persons in one dream character, serve any useful mnemonic function?

Freud observed that some memory of the dream day is generally recoverable in that night's dreams. But is there *invariably* a day residue in each dream of the succeeding night? We don't know. No careful census has ever been made of the time reference of discrete memories in large samples of REM dreams. Once again, because these dreams are subject to so much spontaneous forgetting, it would be necessary to answer this question by awakening dreamers at the end of each and every such dream. Otherwise, it might turn out that we systematically remember (or forget) dreams on the basis of whether or not they contain unequivocal day residues.

If one is willing to overlook this bias, there are some relevant data for spontaneously-remembered morning dream reports. For 4 years, Ernest Hartmann[11] wrote down whatever dreams he could remember as soon as he awoke. He also noted whatever day residue elements appeared in these dreams. He reported that, for "approximately 800" dreams, 463 day residue items could definitely be identified. Most referred to "unimportant" waking events (although it's hard to evaluate this judgment, without knowledge of the distribution of "important" and "unimportant" events in his waking life). Interestingly, although Hartmann's definition of "day residue" was elastic enough to include events from several days before the dream day, very few dreams referred to such events (but, of course, as life goes on, it may also be harder to remember and identify dream sources that are less recent than the dream day). Despite its shortcomings as hard evidence, the Hartmann study is a nice illustration of the kind of research that needs to be done on the mnemonic sources of REM dream imagery. Until such research is done, it will be difficult to take seriously the idea that the dream serves some assignable role in mnemonic reprogramming. That hypothesis currently is tenuous, both because it doesn't specify how the dream accomplishes this result, and because it doesn't rest on any sort of serious study of the content or quality of recent memory that is present in the typical dream.

As Freud found, and as we know, the discrete memories to which the dream refers are by no means limited to recent waking experience. Sometimes our dreams bring back persons, places, or situations dating back to childhood—things we weren't aware of for years and years. This may not happen often (and, again, it would be nice to know just how often), but when it does, it is terribly impressive. It can, for example, be an altogether moving experience to wake up and realize that you've been conversing with a parent who's been dead for 30 years. Freud thought that dreams sometimes demonstrated *hypermnesia: better* recollection than typically is possible in wakefulness. He recounts an anecdote of the French scholar, Maury, who had a dream of playing in a village street in a town where his father long ago had superintended the building of a bridge. In the dream, a uniformed watchman introduced himself as C. After awakening, Maury asked a maid-servant who had attended him in childhood whether she knew of such a man (he was not aware that he did). Her reply was that C. was, in fact, the watchman at the bridge at the time it was being built.[12] Such anecdotes are not totally convincing, because the maid-servant might, for instance, never really have known of such a man but simply accepted Maury's implicit suggestion that he existed. However, to whatever degree such hypermnesia is possible in dreams, it suggests an obvious limitation in our attempts to find the sources of our dreams. Sometimes they may lie in things we know, but don't realize that we know.

There are other ways in which the mnemonic basis of dreams may be defended, despite the fact that free association and comparable techniques won't always lead us back to some definite source or sources for the particular dream images we've experienced. There's a natural sort of bias in our thinking about memory which seems to suggest that everything we know must be a kind of photographic replica of things we've seen or a phonographic reproduction of things we've heard. The implicit simile is that memory is like a film and tape library, in which events are stored more or less in the way they happened. Tracing the sources of our dreams, in this context, is finding out which films/tapes or splices thereof have been used in generating particular dream images.

There is no compelling evidence for the generality of this kind of model of memory, either in the findings of the neurosciences or in those of the cognitive sciences. You may have read that brain surgeons can stimulate recollections by delivering small amounts of current through microelectrodes to the surface of the cerebral cortex. These recollections are experienced as if the (epileptic) patient is reliving specific events of her or his past life. In fact, there's little reason to believe that this is the case. The content of the patient's experience may seem to be real, but so too is the content of our dreams while we dream them, yet few of us believe that our dreams simply "replay" moments of our waking life history. Furthermore, independent evidence has not verified the life history correspondence of the fantasies that patients experience (very rarely, as it turns out) under brain stimulation; indeed, in most cases, given the generality of the "recollections," it's hard to see how it could have done so.[13]

It's undeniable that we (without the aid of microelectrode stimulation) sometimes seem able to recreate past situations in some detail, but it is not clear how accurate or general conscious episodic recollection is. For most of us, even the details of episodes that were highly significant at the time seem to evade recollection with frustrating ease and to become confused with the details of other situations, real or imagined. And of course, there are many more events from our past which we can't recollect at all than there are those that can be consciously re-experienced with even dubious fidelity. Finally, as was discussed in the Introduction, imagery *experiences* do not necessarily imply imagery *representations* in symbolic memory: It's possible that episodic recollections are generated from a memory base that is not at all like an analog library of mental films and tapes. In fact, the characterization of human information processing that is emerging from both neuroscientific and cognitive-psychological evidence suggests that this must be the general case.[14]

These lines of evidence indicate that human perceptual systems are information abstractors. Their goal is *not* to preserve perceptual inputs in the form of inner replicas of outer events. Rather, it is to extract the meaning of events from their surface forms. Reading may serve as a familiar (and apt) example. In reading this book, you are not processing the text so that every line you read will later prove to be retrievable from memory precisely in the form in which it exists in the text. Granted, you could read it that way, but if that were the only way in which you read it, you wouldn't have learned anything from it (think of children who recite poems simply as strings of words and who demonstrate this by the kinds of meaningless errors they sometimes make). You are reading for sense. You are abstracting ideas from what you read, you are organizing these ideas, and you are inter-relating them with things you already know. Literal replicas in the head can't give meaning to experienced events: The uninterpreted event is as meaningless inside as it was outside. In this sense, the mind is an interpretive system, and its goal is to organize and interpret experience, rather than to preserve it photographically or phonographically.

If this example strikes you as too academic, think of what you "know" about some friend. You have, let us say, known this person for many years. In the process of your exchanges with (and regarding) this person, there have been innumerable particular moments that you no longer remember. But from those moments, you have abstracted a generalized portrait of this person (as, for example, being reliable, a bit obsessive in her or his pursuit of certain occupational goals, somewhat neglectful of the niceties of social convention, slow but sure-witted at chess, unlikely to answer letters promptly, and so forth). Grafted onto this general portrait, there will be a pastiche of discrete ("episodic") recollections (for instance, an encounter in New York in 1969 and again in 1975, an inn in Vermont in 1979, a day trip to the beach in 1981). But these discrete recollections are almost more in the nature of illustrations of features of the more generalized portrait; taken together, they themselves would no more summarize what you know of the person than would the occasional artwork in a novel serve to represent its storyline or meaning for you as a reader. Moreover, the discrete recollections themselves seem to be less reliable than the general portrait (you and your friend, for example, can't agree on whether it was in 1969 or in 1975 that you ate oysters in Grand Central Station).

Thus memory, particularly if it is efficient,[15] is a repository of generalized knowledge, abstracted out of specific experiences that, themselves, no longer may be represented, or represented reliably. What implications follow from *this* model of mnemonic organization for the problem of tracing back the sources of our dreams? There are two major ones. First, it is *consistent* with what we know about memory and its organization that units and features of dream imagery should not always be traceable back to particular episodes in your past life, and that when they are traceable in that way, dream imagery may not faithfully reproduce those episodes. Second, to the extent that one believes dreaming must be based in what we know, then the form of dream imagery might be read as indicating some of the nonphotographic, nonphonographic (etc.) ways in which we *do* represent knowledge. That is, the formal properties of dream imagery can be studied as a way of determining how we know what we know.

The case for the proposition that dreaming is a knowledge-based process will find still more support when we look, in Chapter 3, at the development of dreaming in early childhood. Children unwittingly serve as subjects in a natural experiment on the role of knowledge representation in dream formation. They know less than we do, and they organize their knowledge differently. Their waking peculiarities of knowledge representation should be reflected in peculiarities in their dreams. As we shall see, they apparently are.

3. THE DREAM DRAWS ON DISSOCIATED ELEMENTS
OF MEMORY AND KNOWLEDGE

By the standards of what we take to be the typical (waking) organization of memory and knowledge, mnemonic activity during dreaming seems to be more diffuse. Freud, and many other observers, have commented on the fluidity of association evident in dreams. In dreams, much more than seems characteristic of waking recollection, things that don't seem to belong together are in fact found together. Memories from different periods of life apparently can freely intermix. A person we know only in context X may be found in a dream in context Y, while people usually associated with context Y are altogether absent.

Freud's (and others') typical observations with the free-association method, moreover, suggest that it is rare when a dream image can be traced to one and only one mnemonic determinant. Thus, even isolated images in dreams rarely seem to correspond in a literal way to any discrete experience in our waking life history. Dreaming is memory-based, but it generally is not, in the conventional sense, mere "remembering." It is a form of conscious recollection in which bits and pieces from various memory "files" seem to have been caught up together, although they pose, in the dream, as fitting together naturally in some unified impression.

There is, it must be admitted, some possibility of bias in the results of these free-association analyses. The method typically underestimates the degree to which we have generalized, as well as particularized, memory. Neither analysts nor associators generally construe free association as the search for generalized mnemonic determinants of images. They're looking, instead, for particular life-history events that bear some relationship to the dream's imagery. Perhaps this strategy has led them along diffuse mnemonic paths precisely because they've been tracking elusive *discrete* sources of dream imagery, while missing more obvious and more generalized mnemonic sources.

However, even at the level of more generalized representations of knowledge, there remains good reason to believe that the mnemonic basis of dreaming is, again by the standards of waking recollection, diffuse. Consider, for example, the representation of people in dreams, particularly their facial features, or physiognomy. For people we have seen relatively often, we can call up waking images that are relatively context-free. I now, for instance, can see my son Tom in my mind's eye. It is not any particular Tom—not the one I saw at breakfast this morning, nor the one who was kicking a soccer ball yesterday afternoon. It is just a generalized Tom. Its portrayal of his hair is relatively skimpy—perhaps I've become accustomed to considerable variation in this dimension of Tom's appearance. But it is quite definite in its portrayal of features lying in a zone bounded by eyes and mouth. This image is clearly not the most unchanging representation of knowledge I'll ever have: Two plus two has equalled four in my mind since at least age 3 or 4, while it's hard for me now, unaided by photographs, to recapture what Tom looked like 5 years ago. Yet my current image *is* generalized in the sense that it seems not to be read off of a "slide" portrait of any particular moment in my recent experience.

An interesting property of dreams is that such generalized physiognomic portraits can be intermixed in a single image. For instance, you can see a person who is partly person X and partly person Y.[16] These two people are imaginally fused as one. Another interesting case involving physiognomy and fusion occurs when the image of the dream clearly portrays (as you recognize *after* awakening) person X, but you know (in the dream) that the person you are seeing should be taken as person Y. Here, one generalized visual depiction (X) is aligned with another generalized, but nonvisual, package of knowledge (the "Y package"). In cases such as either of the two described here, there can be little doubt but that an associative fluidity underlines dreaming, which permits components or packages of knowledge to intermingle in ways we'd probably find a little bizarre had they been noted in our conscious waking thought. Even for relatively generalized knowledge, then, fusions and wide-ranging intermixtures of mnemonic representations occur in dreams. Elements of memory units can become dissociated from their "home" context and attached to relatively foreign ones.

This reorganization can be understood as a relaxation of the barriers that relevancy and logical interconnectedness generally impose on conscious recollection. We generally don't think of person X in the same context as person Y, because we don't think of them as being similar and don't encounter them together. Those barriers to the linkage of X with Y apparently are not so strong as to prevent our making such an association while dreaming. But the diffusion in mnemonic organization that occurs during dreaming should not be viewed simply as mnemonic *disorganization*.

Some observers would have us believe that dreaming is not an organized process at all, and that trying to explain the dreaming mind is like trying to explain what happens to a machine when a bunch of monkey wrenches have been thrown at it in a random way. In both cases, the argument goes, the system no longer works as a system, and it's fruitless to try to understand it as if it did. As we'll see momentarily, there are simply too many signs of organization in dreaming for this to be a credible argument. Likewise, there's also reason to believe that knowledge organization (memory) during dreaming evidences a *lawful* kind of diffuse activity.

Physiognomic fusions in dream imagery are a case in point. There are no systematic data on the incidence or nature of such fusions in REM dreams. All we have are selected anecdotes. Nonetheless, a guess may be hazarded about their (lawful) nature: They will be derived from the kind of conceptual analysis we perform of persons and their faces. That is, the kind of fusions that appear in dream imagery won't be random ones, such as you might get from juxtaposing random slices of the photographs of two different people. Rather, imaginal fusions should build on the pre-existing memory organization we have evolved for classifying and distinguishing people and faces. In analyzing facial information, we abstract salient dimensions of appearance, e.g., "bushy eyebrows," "wide mouth," "thick lips." During dream formation, features of the dimensional analysis of different persons may be exchanged. We might give person X, whose eyebrows are unremarkable, person Y's bushy eyebrows. But this would be an exchange within a system in which dimensions of facial analysis themselves are preserved. Thus, we would not form a composite image by fusing the left side of person X's face with the right side of person Y's face, because left–right is not a dimension we use in the conceptual analysis of faces.

From independent waking evidence, cognitive psychologists have, in fact, formulated models of knowledge representation in which people, objects, and events are represented by, or along with, the features that we typically assign to them.[17] From these models (or this evidence), it may be possible to predict what sorts of imaginal fusions will, and will not, appear in REM dreams. Such predictiveness, in turn, would establish that the formation of imaginal fusions in dream imagery is a lawful process. Namely, image formation is constrained by the ways in which we classify people, objects, and events.

Given this argument, you will see that there is also a complementary possibility. We might be able to use the evidence of feature dissociations in dream imagery to judge the kinds of feature analyses people perform in interpreting the world in the first place. The major point, however, is that some of what we take to be the disorganized way in which dream images can be formed may not be so disorganized after all. Peculiarities in the manner in which dream images blend features of different people or other concepts may lawfully reflect the ways in which we segment our knowledge of those people or concepts.

The kind of dissociation that we've been considering here (e.g., person X doesn't have her nose, but has person Y's instead) may also be relevant to understanding what many observers have taken to be the peculiar illogic of dream thought. For example, imagine that you dream that it's Saturday, and you're frantic about getting to work. You awaken, and find the dream very curious, because you know (now) that if it is a Saturday you don't have to go to work. You draw the conclusion that dream thought is illogical. The alternative possibility is that the conceptual implications of Monday have been merged with the concept of Saturday, and that this kind of dissociation too may be a lawful kind of "illogic" occurring within an organized mnemonic system, which merely betrays a somewhat greater propensity for systematic cross-filing in dreams than it does in wakefulness. The cross-filing might be shown to be systematic in that, for instance, you wouldn't ever dream that because it's Saturday, you have to read the newspaper, since you have no beliefs about how newspaper reading should be keyed to days of the week.

Totally unfamiliar representations in dream imagery can also be used to argue for diffuse mnemonic activation during dreaming. Such imagery lacks *any* clear resemblance to a corresponding person, place, or thing known in waking life. How can we dream of people we've never known? It's not difficult to see how some people, in our time and place as well as in others, have come to believe that these dream persons really must exist. It's hard to imagine that the kind of vividness and clarity of detail we experience in apprehending these characters could be achieved simply through make-believe exercises of the mind. One possibility, of course, is that these characters are fusions of units of knowledge about so many different particular people that they do not immediately reveal their basis in particular knowledge, and hence appear truly novel. We know that the features of two particular individuals can be fused in dream imagery, and there's probably no good reason to think that fusion has to be limited to the case of just two people.

As we've seen, however, not all of our knowledge is particularized. This is as true of interpersonal knowledge as of any other. We have generalized knowledge of dimensions of personal appearance and of patterns of interpersonal behavior. We can draw pictures of prototypic boys and girls, even if they are unlike any children of our acquaintance. We have general ideas about how children behave, even if no one child of our acquaintance embodies them. Such generic representations clearly might also serve as a knowledge-base in our dream construction of "unfamiliar" characters; that is, characters who seem unfamiliar to us in their overall aspect and who seem to not remind us featurally of any particular persons of our acquaintance. Given the broad description of human information processing as knowledge abstraction, this would seem to be the more likely route by which novel dream characters generally are created.

A related argument can be made from the comprehensibility of novel dream imagery—that is, its comprehensibility *as we dream it.* We're generally not puzzled by what we see or hear in our dreams (although we may later be puzzled as to what it "means" or how we came to dream it). We know, for example, that the man in the dream is "just a man"—an "everyman" who is no one in particular. But, if we have this means of interpreting novel dream imagery, then we have also demonstrated the kind of conceptual foundation from which such imagery could have been generated in the first place.

The developmental history of human knowledge organization is as yet poorly understood. It is plausible to assume that particular knowledge predates, and is a prerequisite of, generalized knowledge. But it's not clear that this is in fact the case. The objectification of knowledge children describe in their dream reports may offer some invaluable clues as to their more general conceptual development. For the present, we *can* note that children's dreams do offer some pertinent testimony regarding the major argument of this section—that dreams derive from a mnemonic base which is diffusely active.

Even in earliest childhood, dreaming seems not to be a "play-back" of undifferentiated global units of the child's waking experience. Like us, children are not merely "remembering" when they dream; they are reordering their memories and knowledge. From the earliest point in human development at which dreams are reported on REM awakenings, these dreams seem to involve the detachment of features of events and their recombination in forms that rarely, if ever, correspond to any particular event which the child really has experienced. For all the ways that the dreams of preschool children differ from ours, we hold this one formal feature of dreaming in common, and it must therefore be a critical element in understanding what dreaming is all about.

4. DREAMS ARE ORGANIZED MENTAL ACTS

From the perspective of their particular contents, it may seem odd to talk about organization in dreams. The hallmark of dreaming seems, rather, to be its unpredictable and quirky use of the knowledge and memories at its disposal. Even at the level of a waking appreciation of what we've dreamed, however, our typical dreams probably are not nearly so bizarre as we imagine. The basis of our waking impressions of our dream life lies in the few dreams we spontaneously recall out of the many that we really have. It is only in a "sleep laboratory" environment, where an experimenter arranges to awaken us systematically during the night, that a representative sample of our dream life can be gathered and exposed to our waking attention. Otherwise, our impressions of our dream life come from those dreams we chance to remember. There's good reason, however, to believe that those dreams are a biased portion of all the dreams that we produce and experience. We may happen to remember them precisely because they are odd or unusual. Representatively sampled REM dreams of children and adults, on the other hand, have been found to be generally plausible simulations of the texture of waking life experience. In fact, the major finding of laboratory dream studies has been just how ordinary and mundane the typical REM dream is.[18]

But the major argument to be made about the organized quality of dreams rests not on what we dream about and its real-life plausibility, but on the form of the dream experience itself. It has just been noted that during dreaming our dreams are relatively comprehensible. Presumably this is because they are organized comprehensibly.

It is possible, of course, to suppose that dream experience is poorly organized and that we only impose organization on this experience as we recall and retell it. We do tend to reorganize memories of *waking* experiences in ways that render them more sensible to us, and, even as we attempt to recall and retell our dreams, we often have the feeling that we're somehow making a better story of the dream now than we did when we dreamed it. We can almost feel ourselves losing details that don't fit and adding those that do. What dreams themselves are really like is impossible to say in any ultimate sense, because by the time I remember mine or you tell me yours, they're gone, and it's impossible to match the recollection or report with the original dream. Philosophers love to descend into mental morasses such as this, and they generally return with the message that we can't be sure that there are any such things as mental experiences at all, or that we can't be sure about anything at all. There are contexts in which such speculations have their usefulness, but I am going to assume that this is not one of them. Along with common sense, I'm assuming that there are such things as dream experiences.

If we take the further step of assuming that our immediate impressions on awakening are our most likely source of information on what dreams are *really* like, then I think that these impressions suggest that dreams really are formally organized experiences, rather than a chaotic sequence of ink blots that we structure only after the fact. Granted, my waking recollection of some novel I've read is systematically altered over time, but that cannot shake my (in this case, accurate) impression that the novel was coherently organized and not just a random collection of letters, words, sentences, paragraphs, or even chapters. It is my intuition also that although my waking recollection of a dream is no doubt subject to systematic change over time, there was still a coherently organized dream for me to remember in the first place.[19]

By "coherently organized dream," I mean to call attention to the following two characteristics of dream experience. (1) At a momentary level, what we mentally "see" or otherwise experience while dreaming is comprehensible. (2) Sequentially, the images or other representations that constitute the dream hang together well: Specifically, they cohere in the form of a narrative or story and/or they cohere in the same form as does much of our waking experience.

At the momentary level, dream imagery typically is neither "underloaded" nor "overloaded" with propositions or knowledge. The visual imagery of the dream, for instance, is neither filled with such a mass of detail nor so bereft of information that we are unable to recognize and interpret it. It conforms, in short, to the kinds of visual perceptions to which we are accustomed in the waking state. We see, "Yes, there's Paul, and he's walking through the department store, right by the counter with the valises and briefcases." Given that, while we're dreaming, we're not literally perceiving any such thing, this kind of organization is a symbolic achievement. Given (if we believe the evidence of the preceding section) the diverse mnemonic elements that may have contributed to that dream imagery, their fusion into such formally coherent imagery is a considerable symbolic achievement.

Both in apprehending reality and in experiencing dreams, we can interpret—in a kind of nonimaginal "description"—what we take to be the salient features of what we are seeing or otherwise sensing. Were dreaming so vastly different from waking mental functioning (and were dreams faithful to their presumably diverse mnemonic sources), it could have been otherwise. Dream imagery could contain so many superimpositions of representations of different events and objects as to be incoherent. But it's not like that. And the fact that it is not indicates that image formation during dreaming is subject to the same constraints of coherency as is the organization of our conscious thought and waking experience. That, in turn, suggests not only that dreaming is organized, but that it is formally organized by some of the same processes and structures that we use to order our waking experience.

Because dream psychologists have for so long studied the supposed meanings of dreams, or their physiological correlates, there are relatively few systematic descriptions of what dreams themselves actually are like. One direction for future research clearly would be to provide more information on the imagery of typical REM dreams. The preceding argument has, perforce, been based more on impressions than on systematic data.

The second respect in which dreams are well-organized formally is that, over time, dreams have a strong narrative quality. This is, in effect, a defining characteristic of what we call dreams. Unfortunately, precisely because narrative quality is inherent in "dreaming," we tend to take it for granted in thinking about explaining dreams. Maybe it's natural that our minds must somehow be or remain active during sleep—given, for instance, the kinds of brain activity associated with sleep. But it's by no means self-evident why we have to "think stories." Why shouldn't our thoughts jump around randomly over time? That question becomes an even more pertinent one when you consider the data suggesting associative flux in the memories used in dream production.

What has caught our attention about our dreams is that the narrative organization of dreaming—perhaps in response to this flux—occasionally breaks down in relatively spectacular ways. At one moment, you're visiting your grandmother; then, suddenly, you're taking notes in your calculus class. The only continuity in this dream—a fragment of a student's REM dream report—is in the continuing sense of self-participation. Otherwise, both the setting and characters are discontinuous from the first to the second scene. The question is, just how frequent is such dramatic discontinuity? Is it the norm or the exception in typical REM reports?

Here, there *are* some relevant empirical data. In a laboratory study, subjects were awakened after 5 minutes of REM sleep on several occasions. Each time they were asked to describe whatever dreaming they could remember, they were then asked to go over their dream reports, and to arrange them in chronological sequence—that is, in the order in which they thought that the dream events actually had occurred. Using this chronology, judges then divided the subjects' reports into broadly defined temporal units. A new temporal unit was scored whenever a new activity took place. Nonself characters and settings were noted for each activity unit. It was found that, on the average, only one out of eight temporal transitions in typical REM reports was accompanied by *both* setting and character discontinuity. In other words, the succession of REM dream imagery generally preserved either the nonself characters or the setting. If a dream is to evidence narrative development—the unfolding of a plot—it clearly would be unreasonable to expect *both* characters and setting to remain constant throughout a dream. But the finding of this study indicates that, when there is moment-to-moment change in the dream, it typically preserves either the characters or the setting, if not both.[20]

Thus, another actual REM dream report from the same study better catches the flavor of what typically happens as a dream unfolds (see Table 1.1). However odd its specific contents may strike you (who is "Computer?"), there can be no doubt that this dream contains a well-crafted narrative progression. It has character and setting continuity, but within this general continuity there is also plot development—dramatic tension is created at step 4, and is dissipated by step 9. The dream was thematically comprehensible to the dreamer as she dreamed it, and her report has made it thematically comprehensible to us. Neither she nor we may understand *why* she dreamed it, but what she dreamed was thematically organized—just as a waking story or any coherent slice of waking life is organized.

Thus, there is reason to believe that the thematic coherency of dreams can be achieved by some of the same processes and structures that we use to organize our waking experience. Precisely which ones, and how they're organized during dreaming, we don't yet know. Another direction for future research is to describe the kinds of skeletal formal outlines to

TABLE 1.1

Temporal Unit	Activity	Characters	Setting
1	Coming out of a church-school, walking past children on the playground.	Self, children	Playground
2	Getting to the gate.	Self, children	Playground
3	Turning around to operate the gate latch.	Self, children	Playground
4	Two girls separate themselves from the group of children, one asking the dreamer if "Computer" had said that the girl could have a drink.	Self, children, two girls	Playground
5	Responding "No."	Self, children, two girls	Playground
6	Girl saying, "Well, I want one."	Self, children, two girls	Playground
7	Responding, "Well, why don't you go ask him?"	Self, children, two girls	Playground
8	The girl running from the dreamer, as if to do this.	Self, children, two girls	Playground
9	Opening the gate.	Self, children	Playground

which well-remembered dream narratives conform. Are they literally like stories? If so, are cross-cultural variations in norms for weaving "good" stories reflected in cross-cultural differences in dream organization? Or does dream organization reflect some more basic organizing capacities which are more or less common to all humans, whatever their sociocultural experience? Are those capacities the same as those we use to organize waking conscious experience? Is this part of the reason why our dreams seem so "real" to us—like life rather than like thinking about life?

Developmental evidence (to be reviewed in Chapter 3) suggests that the kind of narrative organization we take for granted in our dreams is not present in children's earliest dreams. Rather, such organization seems to emerge only at that point in mental development where children's waking thinking begins to show internally regulated coherency (ages 5 to 7). This observation supports the idea that dreaming is, in fact, organized by the most generalized mental structures available: those we use to regulate waking thought and the flow of waking consciousness. In this context, it can't be surprising that dreams aren't *always* good, thematically coherent stories. For neither is the course of our waking experience.

Let me pursue this point just a bit further. In waking life, once we implement a plan, it dictates a certain coherency in our ideation and our activity. But we are never protected from events that will force modifications in that plan. Some of these events may be quite extrinsic: I decide I'm going to read a book, but the phone rings. Others may follow from my dogged pursuit of my plan itself—as I'm reading a book, I suddenly get some ideas, and I'm motivated to stop reading the book to jot down these ideas. In many cases, these ideas will bear only a tangential relationship to what I'd been reading, or to my original plan. Or, while reading a novelistic account of a meal, I may suddenly become aware of how hungry I am and get up to do something about it. It seems plausible to me to allow that, just as we can't regulate the flow of our waking experience with perfect order, so too, the unfolding of a dream narrative will be subject to some possibility of derailment, either as a function of unanticipated extrinsic events (such as memories newly activated since the narrative began), or as a function of circumstances inherent in the narrative itself. But, however narrative derailment is to be construed, the major point of this section is how truly rare it is. From the perspective of good form, the dream is not merely organized, it is generally a first-class organizational achievement.

5. DREAMS ARE CREDIBLE WORLD ANALOGS

Although created mentally, the dream is experienced as life rather than as thought. Why don't we recognize—as we dream—that we're only imagining or making up the contents in our consciousness? Why—until we wake up—do we take these contents as if they were part of life itself? There are two directions in which we might turn in trying to answer these questions: the believability of the dream, and the gullibility of the dreamer.

It is often stressed how "visual" dreams are, and that, since the visual imagery of our dreams is so vivid and "life-like," we interpret it as perception rather than imagination. But this account doesn't do justice to the multidimensional way in which dreams create world analogs.[21] In dreams, we can also hear sounds, smell odors, and so forth. More significantly, we experience our spatial localization in an imaginary environment. We feel our bodies move about in this environment. We initiate speech to other characters who also seem to exist within this environment, and they answer back. The simulation of what life is like is so nearly perfect, the real question may be, why *shouldn't* we believe that this is real?

The fact that the reality of our dreams does not depend on their *visual* imagery can easily be demonstrated. The data are the REM dreams of the congenitally blind. If these people are totally blind, they cannot mentally recreate visual experience at all. If they have minimal vision (e.g., if they can only see light versus dark, or can only detect the presence of large forms in their environment), they cannot create anything like the versatile visual imagery on which the vivid quality of sighted persons' dreams is supposed to depend. But the dreams of the congenitally blind are as rich as sighted peoples', and, contrary to stereotype, this does not seem to be the result of some compensatory use of other sense modalities, such as hearing or kinesthesis. Without the added props of sound and touch, these dreamers can as easily imagine themselves in some environment with geographical boundaries and with intervening objects and people as can sighted people. And, their dream "stage" and the drama that takes place upon it are taken to be no less real than are those of sighted dreamers.[22]

The apparent parallel here between current waking perception of the world and simulation of that perception in dreams may seem to be leading back toward the view that dreaming is a kind of perception. In this regard, a useful corrective is to consider the dreams of those whose blindness occurs after the age of seven. These people retain the capacity for generating visual mental imagery long after they cease to perceive the world visually. That visual imagination has become a system which functions independently of visual perception is demonstrated by the fact that these individuals dream coherent visual representations of people and places they've never known visually—that is, of people and places they've experienced only since their loss of vision. That the ages from 5 to 7 may constitute a watershed with respect to whether visual imagery is retained after blindness may indicate that it is at these ages that purely symbolic control of modular visual processing becomes systematized. At any rate, the dreams of the late-blinded recreate not the world they now perceive, but life as they can imagine it most fully. World analogs are created in dreams within the limits of *conceptual* representations and symbolic abilities, not merely within those of current *perceptual* processing.

Despite the lifelike quality of our multimodal analog dream worlds, there is also reason to suspect that our belief in them must depend on an impairment in our judgment. The belief, while dreaming, that dreams are real-life experiences, rather than imaginings, is known technically as "hallucination." The hallucinatory quality of REM dreams may depend in part on how life-like they are: For instance, in non-REM sleep, when the ability to simulate life experience seems to be relatively impaired, (e.g., dreams are much briefer[23]), people are also more likely to report that the contents of their sleeping minds were "thoughts," rather than dreams.[24] But this can't be the whole story, by any means, for many of the sketchiest and most momentary images reported from sleep are hallucinatory. That is, the dreamer believes in their reality, just as he or she believes in the reality of much better-constructed and temporally-extended world analogs. Even ill-constructed simulation is accorded belief. One subject, while falling asleep, reported making pudding in a pan; superimposed on this image was the word "COMMUNIST." The unbelievable image was believed.[25]

Why, then, are we so gullible during dreaming? Why do we take implausible story lines to be believable ones? Why do we take isolated images—of a piece of cake, for instance—as indicating the presence of real objects, rather than as stray mental images? Answers to these questions characteristically are rather vague. Freud thought that the capacity to discriminate perceptions from imaginings depended on the ability to perform motor acts.[26] Awake, you can open or shut your eyes and see whether the object disappears. You can move around it and see if its visible aspects change. You can reach toward it, and see if your hand makes contact with it. Asleep, these acts are impossible, and so "reality testing" is also impossible. The explanatory power of a motor testing hypothesis is questionable, at least unless it is made considerably more subtle. People have waking images with their eyes closed which are sometimes hallucinatory and sometimes not;[27] seemingly, there is no more effort at motor verification for the one class than for the other. Likewise, as we have just seen, sleep imagery is often hallucinatory, but sometimes it is not. The possibility of motor verification does not seem to discriminate these cases.

A more fruitful approach to the phenomenon (and one more in accord with the orienting assumptions of this book) is that our dreaming gullibility depends on some particular reorganization of waking information-processing systems. How, for instance, could we think about the gullibility problem in terms of the sketch of mental organization presented in the Introduction? Our first inclination might be to focus on the symbolic activation of modular systems during dreaming. If dreaming employs the same systems of perceptual and linguistic analysis that we use to analyze world information, then isn't it "natural" that we should confuse the results of symbolically-instigated activity in these systems with the results of their receptor-instigated activity? That is, to the degree that dreaming employs systems whose major function is the apprehension of what the world is like, then any activity in those systems is likely to be treated as if it reflected world events.

Two questions can be raised about this line of reasoning. The first is whether (and how) symbolic activity could instigate processing in systems designed for analyzing sensory information. There does seem to be some evidence suggesting common processing mechanisms in, for example, the analysis of optical information from the world and the ideational generation of "mental imagery." Thus, visual experience and mental imagery seem to interfere with one another in ways that suggest they compete for modular processing "space."[28] Presumably, when direct electrical stimulation of the cerebral cortex *does* result in lifelike imaginal experience in epileptic patients undergoing brain surgery, it is mediated by the activation of modular systems analogous to that occurring "naturally" during dream formation.[29]

The second question is whether symbolic modular activation, as such, could be sufficient to explain hallucination. Clearly not, because both episodic recollection—the conscious remembrance of some past event—and visual imagination can take place without a belief in the *reality* of the imaged events. There is, however, a more subtle, and perhaps a more revealing, objection to identifying modular processing with hallucination. Recent research on waking visual information-processing suggests that not even *conscious perception* itself can be construed as automatically following from or as a simple awareness of modular processing. Rather, conscious awareness seems to depend on further processing, which segments and organizes the outputs of modular systems, and which has some access to supramodular world knowledge.[30] That is, even conscious perception is a kind of *interpretation* of modular activity. Because dreaming is a form of consciousness, it must also depend on interpretive systems past the level of basic modular activity. Presumably it is the quality of interpretation given the modular activity, rather than the activity itself, which determines whether conscious contents are taken as being "real."[31]

Another proposal for explaining the reality-status we accord our dreams focuses on the absence of sensory inputs during dreaming; this is responsible both for the vividness of dream imagery and for its hallucinatory quality. Although, as we've already seen, dream imagery does not have to be vivid to be hallucinatory, the general rule is that our dream imagery is our most vivid imagery—the imagery that comes closest to simulating multimodal perceptual experience. What is it, in the waking state, that keeps us from comparable levels of vividness and reality-simulation in our symbolic imagery? The answer here would be that, in wakefulness, symbolic use of modular systems must compete with their use in sensory processing. It's difficult to get caught up in a dream world when the real world is still bearing down on you. In fact, when you consider those situations in which normal waking hallucination is most likely, they are precisely those in which sensory stimulation or variety is reduced (e.g., you're lying down in bed in a darkened soundproof room with your eyes closed.) But even in these circumstances, hallucination is more the exception than the rule, and when belief in the reality of imaginative experiences does occur, it is more intermittent and less continuous than it seems to be in dreams.[32]

Thus, it seems that we have to go beyond the level of modular activity, past even potentially unimpeded symbolically-driven modular activity, to understand dream hallucination. In particular, we need to consider the kind of interpretive processing that modular activity undergoes in dream formation. Allan Rechtschaffen, in an influential analysis, has described an attentional deficit during dreaming which he calls "single-mindedness."[33] During dreaming, our consciousness consists of a single "channel." Unlike most wakefulness, there are no accompanying "side channels," which reflect on the main channel (or which carry on other, unrelated activities); hence, when dreaming, we are typically unaware of where we are (in bed) or of what we are in fact doing (sleeping, dreaming). It may be this larger awareness of context that enables us to discriminate waking imagination imagery from perceptual experience. While we dream, we are no longer contextually aware.

Rechtschaffen further relates this absence of contextual awareness to two salient properties of dreams: their narrative organization and their forgettability. He suggests that the very reason dreams typically stay on a narrative track for as long as they do is that there is very little competing reflection to deflect them from their course. He further suggests that the absence of simultaneous channels to monitor the dream is related to our strong tendency to forget it. Typically, when we wish to remember something, we engage in what cognitive psychologists call "constructive processing"; that is, we interpret and organize what is going on as it is happening so as to facilitate the commitment of events to memory and their later retrieval from memory. While we dream, such processing is largely absent: we take the dream in passively. We don't reflect on it. We do interpret, at least at one level—we figure out what's happening. But we don't integrate that analysis very well with the rest of our knowledge. If we did, we might realize that what is happening is *not* plausible, and is therefore probably imagination rather than reality. In terms of the sketch of mind heretofore presented, our comprehension of dream imagery is more at the level of conscious interpretation of modular processing—we determine literally "what's happening"—than at that of conceptual reasoning—we don't relate "what's happening" very well with our more general body of self and world knowledge.

However, if consciousness itself is a kind of interpretation that makes some use of symbolic memory, then our dream comprehension can't be considered entirely insulated from our general world knowledge. And there is good evidence that dream experience is subject to supramodular ("conceptual") monitoring. That evidence is the thematic coherence of the dream, which implies bearing in mind what has already been dreamed so that what is to be dreamed next will be coherent with the ongoing narrative. The narrative integration of dreaming is conducted on more than a moment-to-moment basis. The dream is not just a chain of events loosely associated from one point to the next; rather, it conforms to an overarching narrative plan. In fact, it is by no means infrequent for a dream, having made a midcourse detour from its original concern, to return to it later. Consider, as a minor example of this process, how the woman, whose attention had been earlier deflected by the children, opened the gate to leave the schoolyard at the end of her dream, as she earlier had intended.

What's striking about this monitoring of the dream, and what may distinguish it from our generally more halting attempts at story generation when we're awake, is that it's not conscious. Rather, it's automatic. Or, to put it another way, it's not self-regulated. In this context, Rechtschaffen's "single-mindedness" denotes an absence of conscious *self*-monitoring in typical dream experience.

As will be described in Chapter 2, it seems to be a necessary part of the experience we call "sleep" that we lose a directive and reflective self. You can't fall asleep, or be asleep, if your waking self is still regulating and reflecting upon your conscious mental state. This loss of a sense of self may be the most profound difference between typical waking and sleeping states of conscious awareness and symbolic activity. From its consequences, we must assume that the intentional direction of symbolic behavior, reflection on conscious mental states, and the discrimination of life events from mind events are major, and largely undetachable, components of a mental system of self-regulation. Significantly, *waking* hallucination also seems to be associated with degradation in the functioning of this system (Chapter 2).

But the loss of self-regulation, on the evidence of dreaming (and of waking hallucination), does *not* entail a loss of the ability to create organized conscious states. Dreaming is our richest source of information on this other, unselfconscious form of organization, which we can impose on consciousness. Studies of children's dreams should provide the best (perhaps the only) kind of evidence on the development of this form of organization in the early years of human life. Both on conceptual grounds and on the basis of the best available current evidence (see Chapter 3), this organization is *symbolic*. That is, it is a form of higher mental process unlikely to be shared routinely with other organisms, but it is not regulated by a conscious self and it is not open to direct conscious awareness. It can only be known, as is true of so many other symbolic processes, by what it does.

Viewed this way, such regulation does not involve the comparison of conscious experience with the breadth of our world knowledge. In a dream, we may recognize "father," and evidence some familiarity with the sort of behavior we expect from him, but we don't remember that he's been dead for 30 years. This is another aspect of the brilliant/stupid nature of dream reasoning noted by Dostoyevsky. In involuntarily creating the dream, we produce imaginative, detailed, yet well-formed scenarios with a speed which probably greatly outstrips that of any analogous but consciously regulated mental performance; yet our ongoing interpretation of the dream is curiously limited and unreflective. In terms of the characterization of modular processes presented in the Introduction, however, these may be two sides of the same coin: the speed and automaticity of non-self-regulated conscious states may be related to the limited character of the interpretations produced therein and to the limited amount of knowledge employed in arriving at these interpretations.

The interpretations which we give dream experience as we're dreaming have a "shallow" character. They seem to draw on semantic (or world) information to the extent necessary for perceptual categorization and on specifically verbal knowledge to the degree that verbal labeling of, and common verbal associations to, categorical information are accessible while we are aware of dream events. But, also associated with the absence of self-regulation of conscious states during dreaming is an absence of the wider-ranging search, comparison, and coordination processes associated with *conceptual* understanding.

There may be an interesting waking parallel to this sort of deficit in conceptual comprehension. Howard Gardner and his associates have described a pattern of conceptual deficits in patients with extensive damage to the right hemisphere of the brain.[35] These patients fail to grasp the "point" of complex verbal communications. They don't integrate verbal information or draw appropriate inferences or morals from it. They are particularly handicapped in understanding verbal materials "in which contextual information is wholly or largely determinant—understanding the underlying intention of a question or comment, judging the plausibility of a particular fact within an adventure story or fairy tale, evaluating which of two jokes is funnier."[36] They are not defective (as are patients with left hemisphere damage) in the modular (phonetic, syntactic, intraverbal associative) aspects of linguistic processing, but they have considerable difficulty in processing verbal materials for conceptual understanding. In Gardner et al.'s image, the "narrowly programmed linguistic computer" of these patients is relatively intact, but their context-dependent conceptual comprehension is awry.[37] Thus, these patients have good *literal* comprehension of verbal texts, but they often have little comprehension *beyond* literal comprehension, and their sense of what is plausible and what is not is correspondingly impaired.

This pattern of deficits is especially interesting because it highlights another peculiar feature of dreaming. Although when we remember our dreams, we are sometimes struck by the marvelous metaphors or witty plays on words they seem to contain, during dreaming itself we seem to be ploddingly literal in our analysis of events, and also remarkably humorless. The patients' similar deficits remind us that our dreaming lack of appreciation of the figurative and playful uses of language and imagery are part and parcel of a more generally defective conceptual comprehension of dream events. In related ways, the performances of right-hemisphere-damaged patients and our own dreams may illustrate the partial separation of modular and supramodular (conceptual) processing systems and could contain suggestive evidence of what it would be like were we limited only to a modular level of conscious understanding.

There is, of course, a significant difference between our dreaming comprehension and the patients' comprehension of complex verbal materials. The verbal materials were created by the experimenters who tested the patients. The patients themselves seemed relatively unable to construct coherent narrative sequences.[38] The grand paradox of dreaming is that it is the *same* mind which constructs elaborate, creative, coherent narratives (with their metaphoric imagery and playful uses of words) and which then proceeds to interpret these narratives so literally (and stupidly). But this paradox, too, may be self-resolving. To the very degree that non-modular conceptual processes are involved in rapidly and efficiently organizing the dream, they may be unavailable for interpreting it. It is not necessary, then, to imagine that conceptual comprehension processes (which might lead us to more plausible interpretations of our dream imagery) are functionally obliterated during REM sleep; they may merely be otherwise occupied—in conceptual production. A key assumption here (one supported by the observations from Gardner et al.'s patients) is that structures or systems employed in narrative comprehension overlap with those employed in narrative generation.

This discussion has focused on those deficits of comprehension that lead us to assume that dream experience is life rather than imagination. It is admittedly speculative. Its purpose has been to indicate that there are some systematic ways of thinking about the hallucinatory quality of the multimodal world analogs we call dreams that go beyond the level of verbal redescription or everyday self-observation. These ways of thinking about the problem are systematic, in that they rely on cognitive-psychological concepts which have been demonstrated to be useful in explanations in other (waking) contexts.

To readers familiar with the recent interest in "lucid dreaming," it may seem that the whole focus of this section is wrongheaded. In lucid dreaming, you are aware that you are dreaming while you are dreaming, and you may even be able to make the dream go where you want it to.[39] I will make three brief points about the phenomenon.

First, lucid dreaming is quite rare—it is the exception that proves the rule of our generally unreflective and involuntary dreaming.[40] *Second,* because lucid dreaming is, on the face of it, a different mental organization from ordinary dreaming, it's not likely to be similar to ordinary dreaming in all other respects besides lucidity. Thus, the idea that self-conscious lucid dreamers can be trained to signal to us during sleep about what dreaming is really like has an inherent limitation. Since the system is no longer the same system, the observations may not be pertinent to ordinary nonreflective dreaming. *Third,* by the same token, however, the study of lucid dreaming can, more indirectly, help in the understanding of typical (unreflective, involuntary) dreaming. Lucid dreaming is a natural (or contrived) experiment in which certain features of ordinary dreaming are altered. By determining the consequences of that alteration on the whole nature of dream experience, we may be able to determine the role of absent self-awareness in ordinary dreaming. The key here is not that lucid dreamers can communicate to us during their dreams, but that the whole character of their dream reports may tell us at what cost to ordinary dream competence lucidity is achieved. For instance, at their more lucid moments, are lucid dreamers experiencing more bizarrely sequenced imagery?

6. DREAMS ARE SELF-REVELATIONS

Freud thought that dreams are "completely egoistic,"[41] and many other observers have been inclined to the same opinion. The whole institution of dream interpretation is built around the assumption that your dreams reveal you, the dreamer, rather than the ostensible referents of your dream imagery. Calvin Hall, who collected thousands of spontaneously remembered dreams and analyzed their contents, was impressed with how little these dreams seemed to reflect the scholastic, professional, economic, and political world of the dreamer. They were, instead, narrowly self-centered.[42] Indeed, the most frequently occurring character in REM dreams is the "self," who appears in roughly 95% of REM dreams.[43]

The case for egoism or self-reference in dreams is generally imagined to rest on more than just our own frequent appearance in our dreams. The dream protagonist, even if he or she is not literally me, may "stand in" for me, and may represent my situation or express my feelings. The situation of sleep (the world is tuned out; no one can observe what we "do") is thought to be conducive to a turning away from interests urged upon us by others and to a turning toward those of our own interests about whose cultivation the world is uninterested (or is disapproving). Think of how much of your waking ideation is under the direct or indirect control of others, and of how guilty you may feel when you are caught "lost in a daydream" by someone else. Nightly, our dreams afford us the culturally sanctioned luxury to think in however self-centered a way we please, and it is widely believed that this is just what we do.

All of these ideas have an intuitive kind of plausibility. The questions to be raised here are: (1) whether they seem generally to be correct and (2) to whatever extent they are correct, how they can be reformulated in terms of a realistic model of how dreams are created. A first step in answering these questions is to distinguish several senses in which egoism has been attributed to dreams and dreaming.

Dreams *are* completely egoistic in the sense that their sources lie in our minds, rather than in the world. (As we have seen, even when external stimuli present during sleep can be shown to influence the dream, they typically do so on the mind's own terms.) Dreaming is knowledge-based, and the generalized knowledge and discrete memories that serve as its base are those in the dreamer's own mind.

This does not necessarily mean that the knowledge being processed during dreaming is *self-knowledge* or *self-referential* knowledge. Self-knowledge consists of the generalized ideas we have formed of our own unique mind–body constellations: that we're short and generous, for example (even if, by other persons' evaluations, we're neither). Self-referential knowledge is autobiographical: my "earliest memory," for instance, is of sitting on a step in a backyard in Newark, New Jersey, watching my mother hang out some laundry. (Here, too, the match with other observers' realities may be far from perfect. That particular backyard scene, plausible as it is, may never have happened to me. My autobiographical knowledge is not a sure guide to what happened in my life; it only indicates my current ideas about what happened.) The question about self-knowledge and self-referential knowledge is whether it's invariably activated and processed during the formation of our dreams.

That there most often (but not invariably) is a self-character in our dreams, and that this character is typically experienced as being continuous with the self that we know from our waking experience, indicates that self-knowledge must generally be activated and processed during dreaming. Otherwise, there'd be no self, or an unfamiliar "self" in our dreams. But it still remains to be demonstrated whether self-knowledge plays a *significant* role in the creation of dreams. We are not always, even when present, central characters in our dreams. Even when we are, the intermixing of knowledge during dream construction means that we will sometimes assume roles that are borrowed from our knowledge of others. This is the other side of the coin, which asserts that others can represent portions of our self-knowledge. Thus, not everything which "we" do in our dreams should be taken as *self*-revelation.

Does the dream invariably draw upon self-referential knowledge? In particular, does it (as most interpretive systems assume) "work through" current or historical "concerns" arising out of unsatisfactory or unsatisfying episodes in our life history? These questions should probably be answered in the negative. That is, we should not *assume* self-reference in these senses before collecting relatively unbiased data about what kinds of memories and knowledge are used in dream formation. The free-association method, as we've seen, is generally biased toward the collection of autobiographical material. Our own minds, even if we are not avowed Freudians, may be primed to think about the sources of dreams in this same way. Since the dream *is* a life simulation, and since we're (generally) *in* this real-world analog, then it *must* be connected up with events from our other (waking) life. Given these biases, however, it must surely be instructive how often both professional dream interpreters and relatively untutored dreamers fail to come up with convincing parallels between what happened in the dream and events in the dreamer's waking life. Most professional interpreters probably would agree with the amateur's assessment that not all dreams are equally (self-) revealing, or even (self-) revealing at all.

Moreover, as we've also seen, the references the dream does make to discrete events in the dreamer's life are by no means limited to *significant* waking experiences. Sometimes the memories of daytime events used in dream construction seem highly inconsequential. It was in recognition of this situation that Freud saw that he'd have to *interpret* (impose a theory upon) the memories elicited in free-association in order to document their personal significance to the dreamer.

Thus, there's no plain and simple evidence on which to base the belief that dreams are egoistic in the sense that they invariably deal with our immediate personal goals, interests, or situations. Sometimes they clearly do so; but often they do not. From the former instances, one can draw a general rule that self-interest must always be present, and then proceed to interpret all dreams following that rule. That seems to be what many interpreters of dreams do. But even they often have to admit failure. (Or, what amounts to the same thing, they focus on only part of a dream or on only one dream in a larger group of dreams which seems to meet their needs. Or, what also amounts to the same thing, they come up with clumsy and tortuous interpretations which seem testimony more to their inventiveness than to that of the dreamer who dreams the dream.) All these failures occur in the context of a dream sample that's probably already biased in the interpreter's direction. Ordinarily (outside a sleep laboratory, where dreams can be sampled representatively), we may better remember those dreams that *do* hook up in an obvious way with our waking life experience. When laboratory experimenters say that adequately sampled REM dreams are relatively "mundane," "dull," or "uninteresting," they're suggesting that the run-of-the-mill dream is *not* highly self-revelatory.[44]

At the level of the evidence reviewed thus far, then, we're left with only two clear facts about the dream's power to reveal the mind of the dreamer. First, because the dream is knowledge-based, it's bound to reflect some of the ways in which the dreamer mentally represents her or his world. However, because of the way dreams intermix different units of memory and knowledge, the dream's reflection of them may be fragmented (and, therefore, of more interest to the cognitive psychologist interested in knowledge representation than to the interpreter who's looking for unified and personally significant "concerns"). Second, because there generally is a self-character in dreams who's continuous with the waking self, the ways in which that character is portrayed *may* reflect waking self-knowledge (but one should consider seriously the possibility that any novel "revelations" about the self emerging from such analyses are really reflections of knowledge of others that happens to be mixed with the dream's self-attributes).

These rather modest conclusions about the revelatory power of dreams come from a consideration of the *content* of dreams, and of how that content may be used to gauge the *content* (knowledge representations) of the dreamer's mind. There's another interpretive possibility, however, which may be far richer. The focus of content interpretation must be on *what* you know (or believe or feel), and on how dream portrayals reflect these things you know. Among what you know, as we've seen, is yourself: there's a you in your mental representation of the world, with generalized attributes and a particularized history. There's another self, however, besides the self that's known. This is the self that knows.[45] This self, the Active-I, is the system which generally oversees the conscious processing of knowledge. It is the self we refer to as "I" when we say things like "I think of myself. . ." This self is also distinctive: no one else, we imagine, ever thought just the way we think. We can imagine this even if we're not thinking of ourself. We're talking about *how* we experience, rather than about *what* there is to be experienced.

As we've seen in the last section, major components of our waking Active-I seem to be lost as we enter sleep. We lose our sense of volitional control over the contents of our conscious awareness. We lose awareness of where we are and what we're doing. We lose the self-reflectiveness that permits us to perform independent calculations of the plausibility of the contents of our consciousness.

Still, there's something intensely *personal* about most of our dream experience. Experiencing a dream is not at all like the experience of practiced Zen meditators, for example, who may report "empty awareness" with no sense of self.[46] To be aware of "events", as we are in dreams, seemingly implies a distinction between the knower and the known, hence the persistence of a self which knows.

Thus, it seems that we must qualify the dichotomy drawn in the previous section between the voluntary self-regulation of conscious states and the involuntary, automatic regulation that is present in dreaming. The latter can't be entirely unselfconscious. Consciousness is a form of information processing—a kind of interpretive activity—in which *some* level of self-regulation is necessarily implied. The difference between the voluntary regulation of conscious states and the kind of regulation seen in dreaming must be more of degree than of kind.

This conclusion implies that consciousness itself, as we most typically know it (either awake or asleep), depends on a certain kind of self-development. Hence, it may be viewed as a cognitive achievement, one which is probably only slowly attained in early development. The study of dreaming helps to raise the question as to how voluntary and "involuntary" self-regulation are interrelated developmentally, and it may also someday help to answer that question.

But we already know some ways in which self-regulation (in the new sense just introduced) does characterize dreaming. The very coherence of dreaming, both momentarily and over time, suggests that involuntary self-regulation is constrained by rules similar to those followed in voluntary self-regulation. Moreover, as we'll see in the next chapter, we are able to remember a whole dream when we're awakened from REM sleep—not just its last fleeting image. This extended accessibility of dreaming to conscious autobiographical recollection also presupposes some persistence of self-consciousness during dreaming.

If the analysis of dream formation given to this point is reasonably accurate, then dreaming must be viewed as a relative triumph of this sort of self-regulation over the particular knowledge representations to which it is applied. That is, the dream produces order out of mnemonic flux. The token of this order is the formal coherence of the dream: the residual tokens of flux are the sometimes bizarre contents (e.g., "Computer") on which order is imposed. Interpretively, then, it may make more sense to focus not on the interpretation of dream contents for what they say about the "me" side of the self but on the interpretation of the formal organization of the dream for what it says about the "I" side of the self.[47] Whether our dreams are *about* us, they are organized and experienced as *our* dreams. In this sense, they must have a great deal to tell us about who we are. Also in this sense, the self they can reveal may be a less than familiar one to our conscious self-reflection, and may justify (on somewhat different grounds) the dream interpreter's faith in the unique self-revelatory nature of dreams. We'll consider this argument again in the final chapter of this book, in the context of a discussion of whether and how dreams have "meaning."

NOTES

[1] Sigmund Freud, *The Interpretation of Dreams*, New York: Basic Books, 1955 (originally published, 1900). This book is the classic introduction to modern dream psychology. It demonstrates a masterful grasp of the scientific issues posed by dreaming, but its own

positions are not necessarily always carefully reasoned. A précis of Freud's arguments and an indication of some powerful objections to them can be found in David Foulkes, *A Grammar of Dreams*, New York: Basic Books, 1978, ch. 4.

[2] An excellent account of this research can be found in George Humphrey, *Thinking: An Introduction to its Experimental Psychology*, New York: John Wiley & Sons, 1951.

[3] See, for instance, the account in David Foulkes, *The Psychology of Sleep*, New York: Charles Scribner's Sons, 1966, ch. 7.

[4] Until the discovery of REM sleep, in which the cerebral cortex of the brain is highly activated (as it also is during wakefulness), sleep was thought of as a state of passive disengagement from the world. In this context, it may have made some sense to think of the mind "shutting down" during sleep, and of whatever mental activity that occurred as necessarily being driven by external stimulation. But the existence and nature of REM sleep indicate spontaneous (internally regulated) activation of the brain during sleep, and presumably are compatible with the hypothesis of spontaneous (inner-regulated) activation of the mind during sleep.

[5] Allan Rechtschaffen and David Foulkes, "Effect of Visual Stimuli on Dream Content," *Perceptual and Motor Skills*, 1965, *20*, 1149–1160. This experiment, incidentally, is not one you want to try on your own, at least without referring to the details of the original. Provision must be made, for instance, for keeping the cornea moist during periods in which the eyelids are artificially elevated.

[6] W. Russell Brain, "The Cerebral Basis of Consciousness," *Brain*, 1950, *73*, 465–479. This quote is from p. 470.

[7] Nancy H. Kerr, David Foulkes, and Gregory J. Jurkovic, "Reported Absence of Visual Dream Imagery in a Normally Sighted Subject with Turner's Syndrome," *Journal of Mental Imagery*, 1978, *2*, 247–263; Nancy H. Kerr and David Foulkes, "Right Hemispheric Mediation of Dream Visualization: A Case Study," *Cortex*, 1981, *17*, 603–610 (the quote is from p. 606).

[8] It obviously is more difficult to imagine evidence that would resolve the question of subhuman dreaming. For a consideration of some of the issues involved, see David Foulkes, "Cognitive Processes during Sleep: Evolutionary Aspects," in Andrew Mayes (ed.), *Sleep Mechanisms and Functions in Humans and Animals: An Evolutionary Perspective*, Wokingham, England: Van Nostrand Reinhold, 1983, pp. 313–337.

[9] See the discussion in Foulkes, *A Grammar of Dreams, loc. cit.*

[10] For one influential version of this sort of reasoning, see Edmond M. Dewan, "The Programing (P) Hypothesis for REM Sleep," in Ernest Hartmann (ed.), *Sleep and Dreaming*, Boston: Little, Brown and Company, 1970, pp. 295–307.

[11] Ernest Hartmann, "The Day Residue: Time Distribution of Waking Events," paper presented to the Association for the Psychophysiological Study of Sleep, Denver, 1968.

[12] Freud, *op. cit.*, p. 16.

[13] See the discussion by Ulric Neisser, *Cognitive Psychology*, New York: Appleton-Century-Crofts, 1967, pp. 167–170 and by Elizabeth Loftus, *Memory*, Reading, Mass.: Addison-Wesley, 1980, pp. 50–54.

[14] For a relevant neuroscientific account, see A. R. Luria, *The Working Brain: An Introduction to Neuropsychology*, New York: Basic Books, 1973. Since cognitive psychology has, by and large, defined itself as the study of human memory, almost any text in the area can be consulted. Particularly good sources include Roberta L. Klatzky, *Human Memory: Structures and Processes*, 2nd edition, San Francisco: W. H. Freeman, 1980 and John R. Anderson, *Cognitive Psychology and Its Implications*, San Francisco: W. H. Freeman, 1980.

[15] For how disabling it would be if one *did* have something approaching total literal recall, see A. R. Luria, *The Mind of A Mnemonist*, New York: Basic Books, 1968. Luria's patient, "S," had excellent memory for the particulars of his experience; his ability to organize and

abstract from these particulars was correspondingly poor. He ultimately became a professional mnemonist, performing feats of (literal) memory for audiences, the occupation for which his talents were best-suited.

[16] Freud, *op. cit.*, p. 137ff., gives an example.

[17] See, for example, Donald J. Foss and David T. Hakes, *Psycholinguistics: An Introduction to the Psychology of Language*, Englewood Cliffs, N.J.: Prentice-Hall, 1978, ch. 5.

[18] On adults' laboratory dreams, see Frederick Snyder, "The Phenomenology of Dreaming," in Leo Madow and Laurence H. Snow (eds.), *The Psychodynamic Implications of the Physiological Studies on Dreams*, Springfield, Ill.: Charles C Thomas, 1970, pp. 124–151. On children's laboratory dreams, see David Foulkes, *Children's Dreams: Longitudinal Studies*, New York: John Wiley & Sons, 1982. If you think there's something specious about estimating "typical" dream life from dream reports collected in an "artificial" laboratory situation, you are not alone. Many researchers have been concerned that features of the laboratory environment may change dreaming (or dream reporting), so that laboratory collected reports are not at all like typical dream experiences. For evidence that this concern is relatively groundless, see David Foulkes, "Home and Laboratory Dreams: Four Empirical Studies and a Conceptual Reevaluation," *Sleep,* 1979, *2,* 233–251.

[19] One form of the concern about how well dream reports reflect dream experiences stresses the modality translation needed to get dream imagery into the words of a dream report. The imagery of the dream may be poorly organized, it is argued, but we inevitably make it appear more organized than it is when we translate it into the logical structures of language. Thus, because of the modality translation problem, we think that our dreams are more organized than they really are. But there is no modality-translation problem in reporting speech from dreams (Frank Heynick, "Theoretical & Empirical Investigation into Verbal Aspects of the Freudian Model of Dream Generation," M.D. Dissertation, State University, Groningen [The Netherlands], 1983). Heynick points out that, "of all the stuff dreams are made of, dream speech is unique in its being amenable to direct reporting in the modality in which it was experienced . . . (p. 11)." He emphasizes the considerable degree to which the logical structures of speech seem to be present in dreams themselves, a fact conveniently overlooked by those who imagine dreams to consist only of illogical sequences of vague visual images. His findings are, that although few dream speech episodes are simple "replays" of speeches recently made or heard by the dreamer, most are syntactically correct and pragmatically appropriate. That is, they are grammatically well-formed, and they are appropriate to the imagined dream context in which dream speakers find themselves.

One strategy dream psychologists have adopted for studying how recollection changes dream reports is to compare reports on mid-night awakenings with those given of the "same dream" the following morning. This can't answer the question of differences between the original experience and the *first* report in any definitive way, but differences between first and subsequent reports might suggest mnemonic factors that also influenced the original report. Typically, some systematic differences are noted between first and later reports of the same dream. For example, there may be the addition of feelings appropriate to dream activity but not originally reported to have accompanied it, and a tendency for originally unfamiliar characters to be identified as familiar ones. Significantly, however, there does not seem to be a general tendency for dream events to become more logical or less bizarre on the morning retelling. See V. S. Bose, "Dream Content Transformations: An Empirical Study of Freud's Secondary Revision Hypothesis," Ph.D. Dissertation, Andhra University, Waltair (India), 1982, and Foulkes, *loc. cit.*

[20] David Foulkes and Marcella Schmidt, "Temporal Sequence and Unit Composition in Dream Reports from Different Stages of Sleep," *Sleep,* 1983, *6,* 265–280.

[21] I'm using the term "analog" here in roughly the same sense as does Julian Jaynes in *The Origin of Consciousness in the Breakdown of the Bicameral Mind,* Boston: Houghton Mif-

flin, 1976, ch. 2. It should be emphasized that the term as used here refers to the form of imaginal processing and takes no stand as to the mnemonic base ("analog" versus "abstract") of such processing (cf. the Introduction).

[22] The findings on the dreams of the blind in this paragraph and the next are taken from Nancy H. Kerr, David Foulkes, and Marcella Schmidt, "The Structure of Laboratory Dream Reports in Blind and Sighted Subjects," *Journal of Nervous and Mental Disease*, 1982, *170*, 286–294.

[23] Foulkes and Schmidt, *loc. cit.*

[24] David Foulkes, "Dream Reports from Different Stages of Sleep," *Journal of Abnormal and Social Psychology*, 1962, *65*, 14–25; Allan Rechtschaffen, Paul Verdone, and Joy Wheaton, "Reports of Mental Activity during Sleep," *Canadian Psychiatric Association Journal*, 1963, *8*, 409–414.

[25] Gerald Vogel, David Foulkes, and Harry Trosman, "Ego Functions and Dreaming During Sleep Onset," *Archives of General Psychiatry*, 1966, *14*, 238–248.

[26] Sigmund Freud, "Metapsychological Supplement to the Theory of Dreams," in *General Psychological Theory*, New York: Collier Books, 1963 (originally published, 1916), 151–163.

[27] David Foulkes and Stephan Fleischer, "Mental Activity in Relaxed Wakefulness," *Journal of Abnormal Psychology*, 1975, *84*, 66–75.

[28] Lee R. Brooks, "Spatial and Verbal Components of the Act of Recall," *Canadian Journal of Psychology*, 1968, *22*, 349–368; see also Ronald A. Finke, "Levels of Equivalence in Imagery and Perception," *Psychological Review*, 1980, *87*, 113–132.

[29] It's interesting to note that the cortical areas whose stimulation results in the most "dreamlike" experience are not, on other evidence, thought of as centers of specifically *visual* information processing. In a telling phrase, Wilder Penfield (*The Excitable Cortex in Conscious Man*, Springfield, Ill., Charles C Thomas, 1958) called these areas the "interpretive cortex."

[30] Anthony J. Marcel, "Conscious and Unconscious Perception: An Approach to the Relations between Phenomenal Experience and Perceptual Processes," *Cognitive Psychology*, 1983, *15*, 238–300.

[31] The developmental implications of such a view of consciousness will be considered further in Chapter 3. Obviously, the view is consistent with some of the evidence alluded to in the Introduction regarding young children's difficulties in reconstructing symbolically and reflecting on what they are doing behaviorally.

[32] Foulkes and Fleisher, *loc. cit.*

[33] Allan Rechtschaffen, "The Single-Mindedness and Isolation of Dreams," *Sleep*, 1978, *1*, 97–109.

[34] Klatzky, *op. cit.*

[35] Howard Gardner, Hiram H. Brownell, Wendy Wapner, and Diane Michelow, "Missing the Point: The Role of the Right Hemisphere in the Processing of Complex Linguistic Materials," in Ellen Perecman (ed.), *Cognitive Processing in the Right Hemisphere*, New York: Academic Press, 1983, pp. 169–191; Nancy S. Foldi, Michael Cicone, and Howard Gardner, "Pragmatic Aspects of Communication in Brain-Damaged Patients," in Sidney J. Segalowitz (ed.), *Language Functions and Brain Organization*, New York: Academic Press, 1983, pp. 51–86.

[36] Garnder et al., *loc. cit.,* p. 188.

[37] *Ibid.*

[38] Dean C. Delis, "Hemispheric Processing of Discourse," Ph.D. Dissertation, University of Wyoming, 1980.

[39] On lucid dreaming, see Patricia Garfield, *Creative Dreaming*, New York: Simon and Schuster, 1974, and Stephen P. LaBerge, "Lucid Dreaming: Directing the Action as it Happens," *Psychology Today*, January, 1981, 48–57.

[40] Rechtschaffen, *loc. cit.* For two subjects selected "because they were bright, verbally articulate, awakened quickly, and reported dream content in great detail," only 2.4% of 168 REM reports were characterized by any dream lucidity at all, and that was episodic rather than continuous. On difficulties in controlling dreams, see Mary Lloyd Griffin and David Foulkes, "Deliberate Presleep Control of Dream Content: An Experimental Study," *Perceptual and Motor Skills,* 1977, *45,* 660–662.

[41] Freud, *The Interpretation of Dreams,* p. 267.

[42] Calvin S. Hall, *The Meaning of Dreams* (rev. ed.), New York: McGraw-Hill, 1966, p. 11.

[43] Snyder, *loc. cit.,* p. 134.

[44] Bill Domhoff, "Home Dreams versus Laboratory Dreams: Home Dreams are Better," in Milton Kramer (ed.), *Dream Psychology and the New Biology of Dreaming,* Springfield, Ill.: Charles C Thomas, 1969, pp. 199–217.

[45] William James, *The Principles of Psychology,* vol. I, New York: Dover Books, 1950 (originally published, 1890), ch. X.

[46] Philip Kapleau, "Editor's Introduction," in *The Three Pillars of Zen,* Boston: Beacon Press, 1967, pp. 3–24.

[47] For a related argument, see Phillip McCaffrey's convincing "formal" reinterpretations of the dreams of one of Freud's patients in *Freud and Dora: The Artful Dream,* New Brunswick, N.J.: Rutgers University Press, 1984.

2 When Dreams Occur

The major question of this chapter is whether dreaming is confined to some one body-state (with REM sleep the prime candidate), or whether it can occur throughout sleep and even in the waking state. A second question is raised by evidence of the pervasiveness of dreaming. How, if we dream so much, do we remember so little of what we dream, and are we so little aware of how much dreaming we do? These questions are approached as they apply to adults. The occurrence and development of dreaming and dream recall in children are discussed in the following chapter.

1. DREAMING AND REM SLEEP

It's now general knowledge that there is a peculiar kind of sleep in which our brain and central nervous system are highly active rather than dormant. It's also widely known that one index of this central activity is the periodic occurrence of REMs, and that REM sleep is associated with the occurrence of vivid dreaming. The discovery of REM sleep and of its association with dream reporting was made by Eugene Aserinsky and Nathaniel Kleitman and published as a brief note in *Science* in 1953.[1] Since then, there have been many popularizations of this finding and of the psychophysiological approach to dreaming it promoted. The message of such popularizations often seems to be that the new observations and methods have made it possible for dream psychology to pass from a prescientific phase into a genuinely scientific one, in which questions

54

about dreaming will be answered by the "hard" facts of neurobiological observation.

If this is the message you've received about what REM dream research has done or can do, you've been badly misled. No neurobiological description of the state of the brain during dreaming will ever prove sufficient to answer the questions of dream psychology. The questions we raise about our dreams—What are their sources? How are they put together? What do they mean? What function do they serve?—are questions posed at a psychological level. Their ultimate answers will have to be psychological as well. Mental questions cannot be answered by neurobiological observations. No microscope or brain scan, however powerful or complex, will ever reveal what a dream is or the mental acts by which it is constructed. Psychology deals with questions which arise in an alternative frame of reference (a "functional" one) from that of the neurobiologist. The language of psychological explanation can't be reduced to, and in general may not even be similar to, that of neurobiological analysis of brain function. Indeed, if one takes as one's goal the relationship of these two frames of reference ("mind–body" research), there's good reason to believe that psychological investigation has priority. First, one must establish the functional patterns of mental organization; then and only then will you be able to examine their (probably various) correlates in neural activity and organization. A neurobiology of learning presupposes that you know what learning is; a neurobiology of dreaming must also presuppose that you know—psychologically or functionally—what dreaming is.[2]

Thus, insofar as a science of *dreaming* is concerned, the relevant question about any approach is how much it has contributed to our understanding of dreaming as a *mental act*. By this criterion, scientific dream psychology began well before Aserinsky and Kleitman's discovery of REM sleep. Also by this criterion, dream psychophysiologists have made contributions mainly at the level of helping us identify when dreaming occurs, rather than identifying what it is, what it does, what it means, or how it is accomplished. And, as we shall see in the remainder of this chapter, the very contributions dream psychophysiologists have been able to make have had the unwitting effect of unraveling earlier hopes that the mysteries of dreaming could be approached through any "hard" facts about the physiological organization of REM sleep.

The early findings of the dream psychophysiologists that have withstood the test of time are these: In the adult, REM sleep seems to be accompanied by relatively fluent (imaginal, story-like) dreaming. On immediate awakening during or at the end of a REM period, laboratory subjects give relatively lengthy accounts of dreams which they believe happened just before they awoke. REM periods occur cyclically throughout the night, with the first one occurring after 90 or 100 minutes of non-REM sleep and lasting an average of about 10 minutes. As the non-REM/REM cycle recurs throughout the night, REM sleep takes up a progressively larger portion of it, so that, by morning, REM periods of 30 or 40 minutes in length are not unusual. Over the course of a typical night, roughly 25% of sleep is REM, 75% non-REM. Allowing for memory lapses, and for the fact that a given REM period can be associated with multiple dream "episodes," the longer the REM period, the more dreaming a subject generally reports. Dream time seems to approximate real time—or at least waking thought or imagination time. Thus, dreams do not happen in a "flash." On all of this evidence, we regularly spend at least 1½ hours during each night's sleep producing reasonably vivid, imaginal, story-like dreams, the great majority of which we regularly seem to forget. These naturally "forgettable" dreams can be remembered only if, as in a sleep laboratory, we're awakened while having them. The content of these dreams generally portrays situations and sequences of events which are not wholly out of line with those we might expect to experience in our waking lives.[3]

One major hope of the early dream psychophysiologists has not been realized. "REM sleep" is a relatively gross and long-term characterization of patterns of physiological activity, which can be strikingly different from one moment to the next. Most significantly, there are moments of REM sleep in which eye movements actually occur; they often are preceded by distinctive ("sawtooth") wave forms in electroencephalogram tracings of the spontaneous electrical activity of the cerebral cortex (as recorded by small metal-disc electrodes placed on the intact surface of the scalp). But there are also stretches—sometimes long ones (lasting a minute or more)—of REM sleep when there are, in fact, no eye movements occurring. Because the phasic or episodic activation reflected in eye movements also tends to coincide with other forms of such activation—increased variability in breathing, for instance—REMs can be interpreted as signs of a more generalized activation that periodically intrudes upon the background conditions of REM sleep. An early goal of dream psychophysiologists was to be able to show that physiological changes occurring *within* REM sleep were predictably related to particular kinds of changes in the accompanying dream experience. Perhaps, for example, dreaming was visual only when there were eye movements, or perhaps there were changes in one's visual regard in the dream only when there were eye movements. With such signs, they even contemplated that one could read changes in the form of a subject's dream experience as they were occurring simply by looking at recordings of physiological variables during an ongoing period of REM sleep.

By and large, this strategy hasn't worked out. Dreaming seems to go

on, even vivid visual dreaming, whether or not there is actual eye movement activity during the accompanying REM period. Qualitative changes
in recordable physiology during REM sleep don't seem consistently to
reflect changes in the quality of subjects' dream experiences.[4] Indeed,
Rechtschaffen's discussion of the "single-mindedness" of dreams was
paired with his identification of the "isolation" of dreams, and one of his
prime examples of how the dream is isolated is how *poorly* it seems to
reflect the dreamer's organismic condition. In the adult male for instance,
most REM periods are accompanied by penile erections, yet it is only
rarely that these REM periods are accompanied by sexually arousing or
even sexually related dreams. The isolation of dreaming from the body of
the dreamer can't, of course, be total. There's some reason to believe, for
instance, that, in a very nonspecific way, discontinuities in dream narratives may be associated with moments of phasic REM activity.[6] That is,
when a relatively dramatic change in cortical (and, one must suppose,
mnemonic) activation occurs, there's *some* sort of change in the accompanying dream.

For the most part, however, the dream seems to continue relatively
oblivious to events and changes occurring in physiological systems other
than those which must play a central role in the dream's production.
Unfortunately, it's precisely the symbolic-memory and conceptual organization systems of the human mind—those most critical to the initiation of
dreaming—about whose physiological bases we currently remain most
ignorant. The organismic "isolation" of dreams, then, may simply reflect
the facts that: (1) dreaming is a complex symbolic activity; (2) the sorts of
physiological variables that at present can be well measured for interrela-
tion with dream content are not highly related to complex symbolic activity. In any event, once dreaming is set in motion during REM sleep, it
seems to have a life of its own, a life only very imperfectly reflected in the
psychophysiological measurements for which we currently have tech-
nological capability. It's a life, in short, which we'll have to describe and
understand psychologically, if at all.

The larger disappointment of REM dream research, however, lies not in
its inability to track down details of dream elaboration within REM sleep
by concurrent physiological recording, but in its discovery that dreaming
can and does occur outside REM sleep. REM sleep generally may signify
dreaming; however, dreaming does not require REM sleep. It can occur in
a variety of states, including wakefulness. In their enthusiasm to nail
down an exclusive relationship between dreaming and REM sleep, the
early REM researchers seem consistently to have understated the prevalence of dreaming in non-REM sleep and at sleep onset, a prevalence
noted both before their time[7] and since. Typically, about 90% of laboratory awakenings from REM sleep are associated with the reporting of

preawakening ideation. At least the same percentage is observed at sleep onset, despite the fact that REM sleep does *not* occur at that time. In addition, roughly 60% of non-REM awakenings result in the report of some preawakening mental activity.[8]

Proponents of an exclusive relationship between dreaming and REM sleep have raised two types of questions about these reports of mental activity outside of REM sleep. (1) Were they *credible* reports? That is, were subjects describing mental activity which actually occurred during non-REM sleep (or at sleep onset), or were they confusing their pre-awakening mental state with something else (e.g., an earlier REM dream, mental activity as they woke up)? (2) Was the mental activity subjects reported really *dreaming,* or was it something else (e.g., a thought, an unrelated sequence of mental images)?

Based on several different criteria, it is now generally agreed that reports of ongoing mental activity during non-REM sleep and at sleep onset are credible.[9] The mind often really is doing something at sleep onset and during non-REM sleep. Coherent answers to the second question, *what* it is doing—dreaming, or something else—have been somewhat harder to come by. This has been the case because, until psychophysiological dream research helped to acquaint us with the variety of mental experiences we can have during sleep, dreaming often was defined as *any* mental experience occurring during sleep. We now see that such an all-inclusive definition is not very helpful in either describing or explaining the mind's activities during sleep. However, it's been difficult to come up with an acceptable system for classifying these activities.

2. DREAMING AND NON-REM SLEEP

Consider, for example, the variety of experiences people can report on non-REM awakenings. Significantly more often than on REM awakenings (in one study, on fully 20% of all non-REM awakenings[10]), subjects report "thinking" about something. They're not simulating life, they're just thinking about some aspect of it. Fairly often, the object of their thought is some aspect of their workaday world: an I.R.S. employee contemplates the amount of support you need to claim someone as a dependent, or a student "thinks" about an upcoming examination. Sometimes, the object of their thought is described topically rather than in any way that lends itself to propositional analysis: "I was thinking of Italy." (Of what *about* Italy? The subject seems not to know.) What these "thinking" reports often seem to have in common is that, paradoxically, they don't give evidence of much thinking. That is, subjects describe the object of their mental concern, but they typically don't describe having done much real thinking about it. They haven't actively thought *through* anything; their thinking has not been to any particular point or in the service of any particular goal. Occasionally, the lack of active, constructive thinking is so striking that the subject describes the experience as simply remembering, rather than thinking about, some real-life situation ("I was rehearsing my parents' conversation with me on the phone last night"). "Remembering" reports also are given significantly more frequently on non-REM than on REM awakenings.[11]

There are some *imagery* reports from non-REM awakenings that have an odd quality, because they also don't seem to lead anywhere. An object is pictured, but it is not part of any larger narrative context. A teenage girl imagines a pineapple, for instance: not a pineapple sitting any place—much less a pineapple anyone is thinking about eating—just a pineapple. More often, however, non-REM reports with imagery portray a dream fragment or even a small-scale scenario, and as many as half of non-REM awakenings can produce a report with this kind of dreamlike quality.[12] For example, a man "dreams" of asking a friend for a hammer so that he can fix something in his apartment. A woman dreams she's in a car, and then it starts up and she can see the passing landscape through the window. On rare occasions, the non-REM dream gains momentum equal to that of any REM dream. For example, in a study in which the typical subject's REM dream (reported after 5 minutes of REM sleep) had 5.5 "discrete temporal units" (nonsynchronous activity descriptions) one dreamer had a non-REM report with 22 such units.[13] Full-scale dreaming clearly is not as prevalent during non-REM sleep as during REM sleep. But it can and does occur there. This fact has an immediate and significant implication: The peculiar physiological organization of REM sleep cannot be the only means by which the brain organizes itself for dream production.

The bewildering diversity of non-REM reports has seemed, to those who want to believe in one-to-one mind–body parallels, proof of these reports' incredibility. How could the same organismic state be associated with so many different kinds of conscious mental contents? (Despite considerable organismic variation *within* non-REM sleep, it has not been possible to relate this variation in any coherent way to the kind of report a subject will give when awakened.) Descriptively, too, it's been hard to think of a term (or set of terms) that could embrace all the different sorts of reports that people give on non-REM awakenings. A commonly proposed dichotomy is that non-REM reports are more "thought-like" and REM reports are more "dream-like." But in fact, more non-REM reports than not have the quality at least of a dream fragment if not of a dream scenario. And, as we've just seen, the prototypic non-REM "thinking" report doesn't seem to reflect very much genuine thinking (an active process which transforms objects of thought, progresses over time, and even reaches conclusions).

It has probably already occurred to you that, given the discussion of well-formed (REM) dreams in the previous chapter, there's a way out of this conceptual and terminological mess. Non-REM sleep may often reveal different degrees or kinds of breakdown in the same processes that serve fluent dreaming in REM sleep. If this is true, then the processes of dream formation are the same in non-REM and REM sleep, but their engagement is more limited or segmented in non-REM sleep than is typically the case in REM sleep. If this argument is correct, then the "failures" of effective dream construction in non-REM sleep may be much more revealing of how dreams typically are put together than a whole slew of well-formed REM dreams.

For example, one major basis for figuring out the units and stages of mental operations during *speech* production has been the analysis of slips-of-the-tongue.[14] Thus, when a speaker says "Stop beating your *brick* against a head wall," with the stress on "brick" just as if it had been (the intended) "head," we see that stress is assigned to a syntactic "frame" for utterance before particular words are selected to fill that frame. We also see that, more generally, syntactic organization and word selection are discriminable aspects of speech production.[15] By analogy, however dull or ill-formed non-REM mental experiences may be, they can also be defective forms which illuminate the more general process. Through non-REM reports, we may be able to observe the separate and separable components which are fused in typical REM dreaming, and which give it its fluent, formal coherence.

This is a kind of argument (and perhaps the only one) that *does* make sense out of the diverse reports people give on non-REM awakenings. Memories are activated during non-REM sleep, but not in a diffuse way. Isolated units of recent episodic memory may find favor in a manner that is not true in REM sleep. What's activated, apparently, is moderately likely to be something that's of more than passing interest to you and that's been on your mind recently (i.e., during the dream day). That's not always the case, however: Sometimes isolated bits of generalized knowledge are activated (and one "dreams" of pineapples, etc.). But, because mnemonic activation is discrete and episodic, there's no occasion for the dream production system to be revved up so as to blend and make thematic sense of what is activated. What's activated already makes an elementary, episodic kind of sense.

In the more typical non-REM case (i.e., you "dream" instead of "think"), however, mnemonic activation is more than discrete, but less than diffuse. The full dream production system is engaged to make sense of this activation. Since this activation is neither highly diffuse nor continuous, the ensuing dreams are typically brief—neither involved nor involving. On rare occasions, however, the mnemonic activation of non-REM sleep approaches a level of diffusion and continuity that's more generally characteristic of REM sleep, with the same results: well-formed, temporally extensive, dream narratives. Those occasions probably are not totally unpredictable, being more likely to occur in the later hours of sleep, when, by physiological criteria, non-REM sleep shows greater cerebral-cortical activation. Otherwise, the hypothesized lack of diffuse mnemonic activation during non-REM sleep also agrees with this state's relative lack of diffuse cerebral-cortical activation.

This account is no doubt greatly oversimplified. For example, in treating mnemonic activation as stimulus, and organizing structures as response, this description ignores the possibility that organizing structures may themselves contribute to mnemonic activation. It's a familiar story, for example, that once our minds get revved up to carry out some operation, they take on a power of their own, and it's hard to turn them off. Ask any insomniac. But among the considerable virtues of this account is that it helps to tie together the diverse kinds of mental experiences people have during non-REM sleep in terms of a common mechanism—the degree of diffusion and continuous diffusion in mnemonic activity. As applied to differences between REM and non-REM dreaming and to differences within non-REM dreaming, moreover, its hypotheses about states of mnemonic diffusion do conform to observable states of gross physiological activation in the cerebral cortex.[16] Finally, it is the crowning virtue of this account that it proposes that we have one dream production system, rather than two (or many). That is, it explains non-REM dreaming as involving (in typical cases) some measure of degradation in the operations of the same dreaming system that is generally working at full steam during REM sleep. This is a virtue, because scientists are always looking for explanations that require relatively fewer, rather than relatively more, structures or processes.

In summary, the proposal is that: (1) mnemonic activation generally is less diffuse and continuous in non-REM than in REM sleep, but (2) the dreaming processes available for organizing whatever activation does exist are the same throughout sleep. There are additional observations that are consistent with each part of the proposal.

In one study, for instance, fairly typical findings were made regarding quantitative differences between REM and non-REM reports: 93% of REM but only 67% of non-REM awakenings yielded reports of mental content; 80% of the reports from REM sleep but only 40% of those from non-REM sleep had a dreamlike thematic sequence (two or more discrete temporal units); the typical REM report (after only 5 minutes of REM sleep) was 5.5 units long, the typical non-REM report was 1.3 units long. All of these differences suggest the kind of lesser engagement of dream production mechanisms in non-REM sleep previously discussed. An additional finding, however, suggests that the reason for this lesser engagement may be lesser mnemonic activation. Per unit of dream or dream fragment ("thought-like" reports were excluded from the analysis), there were fewer non-REM than REM dream characters. (The result comes from a comparison in which a subject's REM and non-REM reports were matched for their overall length.) Presumably, less elaborated dream imagery would reflect less mnemonic instigation.[17]

A possibly related observation has been made regarding the particular kinds of contents subjects report on non-REM awakenings. These contents have been called "superficial," for example, or they have been compared to the kind of nondirected ideation that seems to lurk on the fringes of our waking consciousness.[18] One interpretation of these characterizations is that they're saying that there isn't much *derivational complexity* behind non-REM ideation. That is, such ideation doesn't stem from diffuse or profound mnemonic sources, and what contents it has haven't been subjected to much transformation between memory and dream. For example, when a 9-year-old boy reports non-REM dreams in which he's watching a bullfight or flying a helicopter or eating giant cookies, we don't find it difficult to imagine that these dreams are drawing in a pretty obvious way on what might have been some of his waking daydreams or idle fancies. Such fantasies would not, we suppose, portray central concerns in his life so much as certain whims that his waking imagination might sometime idly have entertained.[19] Likewise, in the study in which dreams were divided into temporal units, a relatively prominent characteristic of non-REM reports was coherent imagery that portrayed neither characters nor settings. For instance, there were dreams of a pen writing on a drum, shelves with jars of purple liquid on them, and a big piece of yellow cake with whipped cream and a cherry on top. This imagery was not indistinct—there didn't seem to be anything wrong with the processes for creating imagery. It was just that there didn't seem to be much impetus for image-making processes to "say" very much, or to say anything very interesting or significant to the dreamer.[20]

Finally, the temporal unit study also produced evidence suggesting that the processes which give dreaming its temporal or narrative coherence over time are, on those occasions when they are engaged in non-REM sleep, operating in the same manner when (much more frequently) they are engaged in REM sleep. Specifically, regardless of whether they were matched for length, REM and non-REM dreamlike reports did not differ in the quality of their thematic or narrative elaboration. The rule in both conditions was for dreaming *not* to show wholesale moment-to-moment discontinuity (with both characters and settings changing), and characters were equally likely to persist from one moment of the dream to the next in each condition.[21]

It can't be argued that non-REM dream (or ideation) reports are the same as those from REM sleep. Demonstrably, they're not. Reports of an absence of dreaming, of just thinking or remembering something, and of single-unit dream fragments occur significantly more often on non-REM awakenings than on REM awakenings. Full-fledged dream narratives occur significantly more often on REM than on non-REM awakenings. In one study, it was demonstrated that judges could guess from which stage paired REM and non-REM awakening reports came with almost 90% (versus 50% chance) accuracy.[22] The questions raised here have to do with the interpretation of these differences. (1) Do they indicate that dreaming can occur only in REM sleep, and not in non-REM sleep? (2) Do they indicate qualitatively different mechanisms of dream formation in REM and in non-REM sleep? My answer to each of these questions is no. Fully formed, coherent dream narratives can and do occur in non-REM sleep, and the means by which such narratives are constructed are the same whether dream formation occurs in non-REM or in REM sleep. There is only one dream-production system, and its full engagement is not limited to any one kind of sleep.

I've attributed those undoubted differences found between *typical* non-REM and REM awakening reports to the relative absence of diffuse, continuous mnemonic activation, and to the consequent lack of impetus for the dream-production system to get a full workout during non-REM sleep. Thus: (1) there are fewer reports of any sort of conscious ideation on non-REM awakenings; (2) there are more non-REM reports that consist of either untransformed thought or isolated images; and (3) even the typical non-REM *dream* is brief and sketchy.

You may have wondered, throughout this section, whether typically observed REM and non-REM dream-report differences could simply be due to faulty memory, rather than to true differences in the amount or kind of ideation being experienced. Maybe dreaming is the same in non-REM and in REM sleep; it's just better remembered on REM awakenings. It certainly makes sense to think that people sometimes forget their dreams. That is the interpretation typically given to the fact that on about 10% of *REM* awakenings, a person may not remember a dream. But the question here is whether there's systematically *more* forgetting of non-REM dreams than of REM dreams. Obviously, we can't tell for sure because, as noted in Chapter 1, we have no way of knowing people's experiences of dreams except through their reports of them. It is sometimes suggested, however, that the relative lack of cerebral-cortical activation during non-REM sleep indicates a mind that's relatively incapable of processing material for longterm mnemonic storage. However, it can be argued equally well that this lack of activation indicates a mind that is relatively incapable of creating conscious mental experiences to be remembered in the first place.

One line of evidence that supports the idea that REM versus non-REM differences in dream reports reflect real differences in dream experience comes from some of the peculiar contents people report on non-REM awakenings. As we've already seen, these include relatively unreconstructed fragments of recent or general memory. They also include a relatively large number of reports of coherent imagery having neither characters nor settings (for example, the piece of yellow cake). It's hard to think of these reports as representing "partial" recall of dreams that are similar to REM dreams. Would you remember the mnemonic source of the dream, and forget the dream itself? Would you remember incidental details and forget the characters, settings, and activities? Memory cannot be the only, or the major, determinant of sleep-stage differences in dream reports.

3. DREAMING AND SLEEP ONSET

Perhaps you've had the experience, while reading or watching television or sitting in a lecture hall, of starting to fall asleep and of then "catching" and waking yourself. If you're like most people, you may have noticed that you'd started a dream before you woke yourself. Research has confirmed everyday impressions that dreaming often accompanies sleep onset: In one study, for example, the typical subject reported dreaming on 75% of awakenings during the electroencephalogram stage viewed as transitional between wakefulness and non-REM sleep.[23] Two aspects of this finding should be emphasized: (1) The transitional stage is *not* REM sleep, and, in particular, is not accompanied by the phasic or episodic cerebral-cortical activation that helps to define REM sleep. (2) The 75% figure refers not just to reports of some kind of ideation ("thinking," "mental imagery")—*that* figure is close to 100%—but to reports of dramatic, hallucinatory imagery: you see some situation portrayed that you take to be real. In short, you're *dreaming,* and you're doing it outside the state of REM sleep.

Dreaming at sleep onset is not an important observation because it represents a lot of the dreaming that we do. Quantitatively, non-REM sleep, even if we have full-fledged dreams only occasionally during it, is the more significant exception to the idea that dreaming occurs only in REM sleep. This is because you typically spend 5 or 6 hours each night in non-REM sleep, while the distinctive waking-sleeping transitional period of interest here may last from only 30 to 60 seconds—if you fall off to sleep easily and without interruption. The importance of sleep-onset dreaming lies elsewhere than in its pervasiveness. Specifically: (1) sleep-onset ideation is more likely to be dreamlike than non-REM ideation; (2) there are discriminable stages of ideational organization as we pass from wakefulness to sleep that reveal separate components of the fully functioning dream-production system; and (3) there are individual differences in ideational organization in the transition between wakefulness and sleep, which may also help to identify critical features of that same system. These points now will be discussed in order.

(1) When sleep-onset reports are rated for the possession of so-called "dreamlike" qualities (sensory imagery, hallucination, bizarre content), they tend to be relatively more like REM reports than are typical non-REM reports.[24] It also has been reported that sleep-onset and REM reports are not highly discriminable. That is, judges found it difficult to guess which report was REM and which was not when the other report class was sleep-onset (and perhaps more difficult than when the other report class was non-REM). The judges could identify the awakening stage in REM versus sleep-onset comparisons only 63% of the time. This seems to indicate considerable overlap between REM and sleep-onset reports.[25] It was also found that, when analysis was limited to dreamlike reports judges could discriminate better on the basis of global guesses than when using a rating scale that employed the criteria of imagery, hallucination, and bizarreness. In their free guesses, the judges evidently used some information other than that used on the rating scale.

That additional information may well have been the length of the report. In the temporal-unit study referred to in the discussion of non-REM reports, it was found that dreamlike (dramatized) reports with some thematic sequence (more than one temporal unit) occurred on 80% of REM awakenings but on only 47% of sleep-onset awakenings. Furthermore, while REM reports (collected after 5 minutes of REM sleep) contained an average of 5.5 discrete temporal units, the figure for sleep-onset reports was 1.6 temporal units. Both of these differences were significant, and in both respects sleep-onset reports were more like non-REM reports than like REM reports.[26]

Drawing these bits of evidence together, it appears that dreamlike processing of the REM variety is more likely to occur at a typical moment in the transition to sleep than in non-REM sleep proper, but that the kind of mnemonic activation required to sustain full-fledged dreaming has a predictably briefer time course at sleep onset than during REM sleep. Given the brevity of the transition period, this is hardly surprising.

(2) When observations are extended from the transition period itself (a stage-1 electroencephalogram) *back* to the relaxed wakefulness from

which it issues and *forward* to the non-REM sleep into which it soon changes, one can see a reasonably reliable progression in conscious mental experience. During a relaxed waking state ("alpha-rhythm" electroencephalogram), conscious thought becomes highly likely to be conducted in or with visual or other kinds of mental imagery. Some people sometimes lose track, during this "objective" waking state, of the fact that their imagery is in the mind rather than of the world. However, most often this pre-sleep imagery is not hallucinatory: it's recognized as images passing through your conscious mind. As drowsiness proceeds, voluntary control tends to be lost. That is, there is a succession of imagery that you didn't will to be there. The contents of your consciousness happen to you, rather than "you" causing them to be there. In the transition to sleep itself ("stage 1"), voluntary control is absent altogether, and now you're quite likely to be hallucinating, just as you do in your REM dreams. You take what you see and hear to be "really happening," rather than as some involuntary thoughts that happen to be flashing through your mind. Correspondingly, your imagery has a dramatized quality: you are generally seeing a situation, complete with characters acting within a setting.

In terms of one analysis, your imagery also is "regressive." This term is owed to psychoanalysis, and it implies a particular model of the organization of the mind—one no longer considered very useful by most cognitive psychologists. What is meant by this term at a descriptive level is the following:

(A) There may be defects in coherent image formation (e.g., you see part of a scene, but not all of it—a setting for instance, hasn't "jelled" yet; or, you see superimpositions—such as strawberries superimposed on a train station).

(B) There may be defects in linking imagery to reflective thought (you're imaging one thing while thinking about something else).

(C) There may be defects in narrative formation; that is, sequences of images are not interrelated by any overriding theme or storyline.

(D) The content of well-formed imagery is weird—you see, for instance, people living inside a human chest cavity, or you dream that as you wave your hand over a town, its lights grow dimmer.

The interesting thing about changes like these is that they are momentary. Typically, as you pass into sleep proper (a stage-2 electroencephalogram), regressivity declines. You are still dreaming, but your dreams (or, more accurately, dream fragments) generally are coherently formed. Their contents are reasonably plausible, rather than weird. As with most non-REM dream fragments collected elsewhere in the night, those that occur when you first reach sleep itself are relatively good simulations of the form and substance of waking experience. Thus, whatever "regressivity" occurs in the transitional period is a brief flurry of disorganization or craziness that soon gives way to the typical kind of mental organization generally evident in non-REM sleep. Moreover, even during the transition period itself, only about half of subjects' reports are "regressive."[27]

On the model developed thus far about the mental processes involved in dream production and the mental conditions that call these dream processes into play, it's clearly possible to reinterpret the regressivity findings nonpsychoanalytically. To fall asleep is to lose the "Active-I," which directs conscious thought and monitors the activities and sensations of mind and body. Indeed, to the extent that the Active-I returns "in sleep," as for instance, in lucid dreaming, there's evidence to suggest that the electroencephalogram patterns of wakefulness tend to return as well.[28] If you were consciously directing your thoughts, were aware that they were thoughts, and were aware that you were lying in your bed, and that your roommate or spouse had just entered the room, could you still be "asleep"? Although a dream self-character is not to be identified with the Active-I of wakefulness, there may be enough potential linkage between the two that you even tend to avoid portrayal of the self at sleep onset. In the temporal-unit study which found non-REM reports to contain fewer overall characters than REM reports, it was observed that sleep-onset reports were less likely than REM reports to contain one specific character—the *self*.[29] The familiar maxim that you should count sheep to fall asleep may not be so far off base. You have, at least, to let your mind lose *you* and find some other focus for its waning attention.

Thus, relinquishing voluntary control over the flow of one's conscious thought seems to be a necessary condition of sleep induction. A subsequent condition is the loss of orientation: you're no longer aware that you are lying in some particular bed in some particular place. The suppression of an Active-I can only be complete, however, when you finally lose track of the difference between thought and reality—when "your mind" no longer exists.[30] At this point, whatever is "on" your mind is taken as being really "in" the world: you're hallucinating.

The fact that rates of reporting ideation at all points in the transition between wakefulness and (stage-2) sleep are so high suggests that the relinquishment of the Active-I is not, at first, accompanied by a massive *general* loss of mental activation. You can't turn your mind down as readily as you can lose the Active-I responsible for organizing many of its waking encounters with the world. Indeed, as we've seen, the mind's activities persist, at a diminished level, throughout much if not all of non-REM sleep. But as you enter sleep, you have the particular problem that the state you've just been in is no other kind of sleep, but wakefulness. Both physiologically and psychologically, waking levels of activation can only be slowly dampened. For example, even when REM sleep occurs at sleep onset—as it does in narcoleptics, patients subject to inappropriate daytime "sleep attacks"—there's evidence that properties of waking consciousness such as volitional control, orientation to place, and discrimination of imagery from reality are more often present than they are in more typically placed (post-non-REM) REM periods.[31] For narcoleptics, lingering activation of wakefulness apparently can be augmented by and intermingled with the newly arising activation of REM sleep. The more general point, however, is that because overall levels of cortical and mental activation are only gradually diminished at sleep onset, there's reason to think that relatively high levels of *mnemonic* activation or facilitation persist into this period. They do so, moreover, in a peculiar kind of mental "field," one in which the standard mechanism of conscious waking mental organization and regulation—the Active-I—is absent.

Thus, the "regressivity" observations suggest what might otherwise have been expected. Freed from its standard waking regulation, mnemonic activation at sleep onset is widespread or diffuse. This is indicated by formal characteristics of image formation (superimposition, fusion), by formal characteristics of thematic sequencing (unrelated successions of imagery), and by the weirdness of dream contents (putting people, for instance, inside a chest cavity). In short, at sleep onset, the ideal conditions exist (if what has been said earlier is correct) for the engagement of the human dream-production system.

But why isn't the dream-production system turned on sooner or more completely? Why, in the transitional period, don't we have more coherent imagery and image sequences and more generally plausible dream content? Why, instead, do we sometimes see only the fragmented workings of the dream-production system, half-baked image formation, and little or no narrative coherence? Here, one can only speculate in ways that don't readily lend themselves to verification. If dreaming began too early, would it threaten to subvert the transition to sleep? Would it carry along with it the possibility of emotional accompaniment which would disrupt one's passage into sleep? (Emotion generally seems lacking in what little dreaming does naturally occur in the transition period.[32]) Is voluntary self-regulation still so liable to being "reawakened" that attempts to replace it with some other organization must be delayed? On a kind of least-effort principle, has our mind learned to adapt to diffuse mnemonic activation in the transitional period with a set of stopgap measures in the knowledge that that activation won't last very long? Does it correctly anticipate that such mnemonic activation will soon be sufficiently manageable to be handled in much the same way as that in non-REM sleep—without full-fledged dream production?

Sometimes, there *is* dream production on the REM model at sleep onset. My impression, however, is that its incidence probably is overestimated by laboratory studies. In research on sleep-onset dreaming, subjects have often been awakened again and again as they fall off to sleep: start to fall asleep→ awakening and report→ start to fall asleep→ awakening and report, etc. Understandably, this makes them somewhat self-conscious about falling off to sleep and about what's going on in their minds as they do so. Often, they seem to "catch" themselves just after their electroencephalogram has indicated the transition period or sleep itself, and they return to an earlier phase. The result may be a prolongation of the sleep-onset process, and a consequently greater than usual opportunity to dream a REM-like dream. The same thing may happen at home when we know we have to sleep and try so hard to do so that we can't ever quite seem to get all the way there. The more typical case for most of us, however, must be a relatively quick transition period and relatively little dreaming of a temporally extended sort.

We do know, however, that when for whatever reason, dreaming really *does* get going at sleep onset, it seems not to be different from that which occurs in REM sleep. The main dimension of difference, as already noted, is the relative absence of a self character. The absence is only relative, in that the self character is present more often than not at sleep onset. It's just not so omnipresent as during REM dreams of the same thematic length. But, when matched for length with REM reports, sleep-onset dreams seem to have roughly the same kind of formal properties and thematic coherence as do REM dreams. If the typical sleep-onset dream has seemed a little peculiar ("regressive"), that peculiarity perhaps should be understood as reflecting the fact that the typical sleep-onset dream is a short one, a single dream fragment really. REM dream fragments of the same sort also are a little peculiar, and in the very same ways. For instance, failure to articulate images by providing a setting or background for characters or objects is about equally as frequent in single-unit REM reports as it is in single-unit sleep-onset reports.[33]

Thus, however the typically less-than-total engagement of the human dream-production system at sleep onset is to be explained, it offers similar opportunities as during non-REM sleep for observing components of that system. In REM sleep, the system typically is too well-integrated to make such observation feasible. At sleep onset, however, there are especially rich opportunities to observe the production of images which are attempts at integrating diverse mnemonic elements. Precisely because there's relatively little narrative sequencing going on, image formation can better be viewed in terms of its momentary mnemonic determinants. It isn't necessary that an image be sensibly coherent with its predecessor, only that it deal with its current sources. The truth to the claim that sleep-onset ideation is more dreamlike than non-REM ideation seems to lie more at the level of image formation than at that of narrative sequencing. At a momentary level, at least, the processing of memories and knowledge is richer than in non-REM sleep. Because of residual waking activation, there probably are more memories to process. Because the sleep-onset dreamer can readily be alerted and induced to comment upon them, it should be particularly useful to study the way in which memories are transformed into dream imagery at sleep onset.[34]

(3) There's evidence suggesting greater person-to-person variation in how dreamlike conscious experience becomes at sleep onset than during REM sleep. By and large, it is the fate of *all* of us to experience imaginal, storylike dreams during REM sleep. It seems that, in some sense, we have more choice about how we shall think in the transition to sleep. Not surprisingly, differences in thinking at sleep onset have been related to waking differences in self-regulation. Self-acceptance and a willingness to indulge in fantasy go along with relatively fanciful or dreamlike sleep-onset ideation; they do not, however, predict the quality of REM ideation.[35] Given the gradual relinquishing of voluntary control implied by sleep induction, these findings make sense. They indicate that some people "let themselves go" more easily than others, and that some people "hold on" longer than others. Although reasonable, these findings require much elaboration. What particular features of dreamlike reports are subject to inter-individual variation? What do these features suggest about the dream constructional processes involved? What are the significant dimensions of waking conscious self-regulation to which the dream differences might be attributed?

Another potential source of stable individual differences in sleep-onset dreaming might lie, as suggested earlier, in differences in how easily people typically fall asleep. Moreover, even for people who fall asleep readily (say, reach stage-2 equally quickly), there are stable electroencephalographic differences in how they do so. For some subjects, very high amplitude bursts of relatively low frequency ("theta") activity suddenly appear, against a characteristically low amplitude waking and stage-1 background. For other subjects, the slide into sleep tracings is more gradual and subtle. Such differences might reflect differences in the psychological organization of sleep onset.[36]

However, the standard electroencephalogram stages themselves (alpha, stage 1, stage 2) seem not to be highly reliable accompaniments of the changes in mental organization at sleep onset. In previous discussion, I've mentioned two sequences: the electroencephalographic, and the mental—the change from voluntary thought to involuntary nonhallucinatory thought to "regressive" hallucination to "nonregressive" hallucination. I've also indicated their most common association with one another, namely: waking/nonhallucination, stage-1/regressive hallucination, stage-2/nonregressive hallucination. But, even when *not* indexed by these physiological stages, the psychological sequence is still observed. The psychological order is the same, although it is indexed by other than the standard physiological changes. Regression and hallucination might have started in "waking," for instance, with nonregressive hallucination associated with the stage-1 transitional period. This is a significant observation, because it indicates that the mental changes are not just reflections of the physiological changes. They evidently have a logic of their own. For instance, a consistent correlate (precondition) of regressive content was the loss of effective self-regulation (loss of voluntary control over ideation, loss of orientation, loss of ability to discriminate images from percepts). Fully 94% of the regressive reports were accompanied by one or more of these signs of loss of self-regulation.[37] This intra-mental correlate of regression was far superior to any potential physiological correlate. The lesson of this observation is a general one: The occurrence and nature of dreaming can better be explained in terms of the organization of mental systems (and, at sleep onset, in terms of individual styles of mental organization) than as simple offshoots of currently available physiological measurements.

4. DREAMING AND WAKING

In trying to track down the mental experiences subjects had during brief moments of phasic activation within REM sleep (see: "Dreaming and REM Sleep"), experimenters had to ask subjects not to report all the dreaming they could remember but just to describe what was happening at the moment before they were awakened. This was necessary since subjects were being awakened after physiological recordings had indicated a period of phasic activation lasting for only several seconds. One difficulty in establishing the subjective significance of this physiological activation, obviously, might lie in the difficulty of this introspective task. How easy is it, in any state, to isolate the contents of consciousness in a very brief period occurring just before you suddenly were alerted (and perhaps startled)?

Some experimenters, therefore, decided it might be useful if subjects serving in this sort of sleep study had the chance, while awake, to "practice" reporting the mental experiences they had had just before being given a signal. Consequently, sessions were arranged in which subjects were wired up for recording electroencephalograms and eye movement activity during the daytime. Each subject then would lie down on a bed, in a moderately illuminated room, under the instructions to "relax, but stay awake." The physiological recordings allowed the experimenters to ensure that wakefulness was, in fact, maintained. At random intervals (which the subject erroneously was led to believe were related to the particular state of her or his physiological tracings), the subject was alerted (by calling her or his name) and asked to describe "the very last thing going through your mind just before I called you." The conditions, in short, were just like those of a sleep or sleep-onset dream study, only the subject wasn't asleep when signalled.

As you might expect, some subjects were made rather self-conscious by these arrangements. When signalled, they might, for instance, report that they were thinking about "what to think about!" However, most subjects were able to relax and to relinquish some degree of voluntary control over the contents of their consciousness. The consequence of subjects' willingness to "let themselves go" was that they sometimes described, on being signalled, having just had mental experiences which could only be described as dreamlike. That is, they experienced multimodal sensory imagination which was dramatic in form and which, for the moment at least, was experienced as reality rather than as imagination. They had been, however, briefly, *hallucinating*—this despite the fact that their physiological recordings said that they had been "awake." The average incidence of hallucinatory ideation on such occasions was 24% in the first study of this sort,[38] and figures close to 20% were found in two subsequent studies.[39] Typically, subjects would report that, while hallucinating, their subjective state had been the same as their "objective" one: they thought they had been "awake and relaxed."[40] Sometimes, however, subjects would look back at what their minds had been doing, and decide that they couldn't have been awake. As one young woman described it: "Evidently I was in a different world."[41]

In what sort of world *do* people immerse themselves during such waking reveries? One young woman believed, on successive signals that: she had been back in her old home town, standing in front of the drug store; her boyfriend had been sitting in her dormitory room drinking beer, as she thought about how upset she was with him; she had been in her dormitory room again, this time smoking a cigarette; a man had been leaning out a window, taking pictures of the clouds (she had been concerned that he might be leaning out too far and might fall). Another young woman believed before the signal that she had been pressing down on a pulsating vein or artery, trying to stop its bleeding. Still another young woman believed, before the signal, that she'd been watching a sentencing in an "oldtime" court of law: a judge with a powdered wig sat high above a horseshoe-shaped set of tables as he pronounced sentence on a young man with short black hair. All of these experiences were thought, at the time, to be really happening, although, in each case, the subjects lay undisturbed on their beds in a closed, slightly darkened room and although, in each case, they were physiologically "awake."

There apparently are, then, such things as *waking dreams*—or, at least, waking-dream fragments, for none of the situations cited above seems to have had much narrative development. This lack of thematic development probably isn't just related to the fact that subjects most often were invited to describe only the very last moments of their mental experience before the signal. When the interview question was more general,[42] comparable results were observed, and hallucinatory belief seemed to attach itself only to briefly visualized moments of the larger stream of the subject's consciousness. As one subject described it, "When I could picture it best and hear it best . . . I felt more like it was really going on, like it was something that was just happening to me, except that that would have only been just an instant there."[43] Momentarily, then, it is possible to lose one's bearings, and to confuse one's own mental imagery with events taking place in the world—despite the fact that one is awake.

Aren't such experiences indications, however, that the subjects were *really* falling asleep? The most obvious evidence suggests that they were not: neither by physiological criteria nor by their own judgments did sleep or sleepiness seem to be present. Moreover, by physiological criteria, the subjects often went through an entire waking-recording session (which, apart from the interviews themselves, may have consisted of 25–30 minutes) without *ever* showing signs of physiological sleep, even though their randomly sampled reports suggested a relatively high incidence of hallucination. Of course, one can answer the question in a definitional way: If they're hallucinating, they *have* to be falling asleep. But the implication of this approach is pretty much the same: If our relaxed wakefulness is intermittently infiltrated by sleep, then it still remains true that what we typically take to be the waking state is capable of supporting the formation of fragmentary dreams.

Furthermore, there is some evidence to suggest that the formation of waking-dreamlike ideation is not just like that of sleep-onset dreaming. In the study of regressivity (illformedness of imagery or imagery sequences and/or weirdness of content) at sleep onset, for instance, over half of the regressive reports were hallucinatory.[44] That is, subjects typically believed in the reality of what they were experiencing. When waking ideation was evaluated in the same way, however, regression and hallucination seemed to occur more independently of one another. Thus 77% of the regressive reports were *not* hallucinatory and 70% of the hallucinatory reports were *not* regressive.[45] It seems, then, that in "loosening" your control of waking ideation, you may experience either crazy mental contents (but not believe in them) *or* hallucinatory belief (but of relatively plausible contents)—one or the other, but rarely both together.[46] Unlike sleep onset, the experience of regressive ideation in relaxed wakefulness typically is not associated with hallucinatory belief. Nor is there evidence that the momentary experience of "plausible" hallucinations needs to be preceded—as at sleep onset—by a phase of regressive ideation. It looks, rather, as if what are *successive stages* of conscious mental organization at sleep onset are *alternate possibilities* in relaxed wakefulness. The hallucinatory alternative might be viewed as one in which the waking sense of self has been traded off for a whole-hearted engagement of the organizing schemata that guide the transformation of diverse mnemonic sources into coherent dream imagery. The regressive strategy, on the other hand, seems to retain some waking sense of self at the expense of less than full engagement of these same schemata. At any rate, these strategies seem to be differently (i.e., more independently) deployed than at sleep onset.

If one is willing, then, to grant that the kinds of ideation we have been discussing are *waking* (rather than sleep onset), the other major question is to what extent they are *dreaming*. To the degree that hallucination is lacking, a major defining property of dreaming is also missing. Even when hallucination is present, moreover, plot development and narrative progression typically are not. The same is true, of course, of many sleep-onset and non-REM reports. As is also true for sleep-onset and non-REM reports, however, this defect does not necessarily imply that waking hallucinations are undreamlike, or that they are constructed by some altogether different means than are REM dreams. In fact, the waking dream fragment (i.e., a nonregressive hallucination) and the waking proto-dream (i.e., a regressive nonhallucination) may be but two more specialized instances of the partial engagement of processes or conditions involved in true (i.e., REM) dreaming. In particular, the former may indicate the prevalence of the involuntary, consciousness-organizing schemata of such dreaming, while the latter may bear especially rich testimony to the mnemonic diffusion underlying such dreaming.

The most generally observed dreamlike feature of thought samples from relaxed wakefulness was the absence of voluntary control over the contents or direction of one's conscious awareness. Indeed, on about half of the experimental signals, such control had been lost.[47] This loss of voluntary control would seem to be a precondition for hallucinating: 91% of self-reported waking hallucinations were accompanied by self-reported loss of control. Loss of voluntary control probably also facilitates regressivity, particularly the experience of "bizarre" contents in one's ideation (e.g., hairy men in a human chest cavity): only 25% of reports judged to be regressive in this way were associated with reported maintenance of voluntary control.[48] Thus, as in sleep, it seems that some relinquishing of regulation by the Active-I is conducive to the production of other features of dream thinking. Yet the data also suggest that it's difficult to be awake and to relinquish self-regulation entirely or for any sustained period of time. Thus, the contents of your relaxed waking consciousness typically are both sensible and known to be just thoughts passing through your mind. And, as we have seen, you generally do not simultaneously relax your regulation of the sensibleness of these contents and your evaluation of them as being internally produced.

Nonetheless, your Active-I is in relative abeyance. Yet you remain awake, your cerebral cortex stays relatively activated, and your mind accordingly is subjected to continuing mnemonic impetus. The impetus is mnemonic rather than external if, like the subjects in the studies described above, you're in an unchanging and relatively boring environment. It's continuous, in that, in these same studies, subjects almost always could report *something* passing through their minds before they heard the signal to report their ideation. In part, then, we have the conditions for dream generation.

There is, for example, mnemonic activation that is at least partly released from the focal organizing control of the Active-I, and therefore at least partly diffused. One-third of the waking reports judged regressive in one waking study, for instance, were so judged because of combinations of ideational elements in ill-formed image composites or sequences (like the strawberry superimposed on the train station). Another third were imaginally well-formed, but the resulting imagery juxtaposed contents in a way judged "weird" by standards of waking plausibility (like the hairy men in the human chest cavity).[49] These are indications of the simultaneous processing of discrete mnemonic units. Likewise, however internally plausible was the situation subjects hallucinated while awake, that situation generally was not a remembrance of some one particular event from their recent life history. Rather, as in night dreaming, the imagined situation drew in a more inventive way on different bits of discrete memory and generalized knowledge.

There is good reason to believe that the sort of stable individual differences in conscious mental processing observed at sleep onset have even greater scope in relaxed wakefulness. For those who desperately want to hold onto their voluntary self-control and to forestall any drift to dreamlike ideation, for instance, the resources to ensure these outcomes surely are much more available in wakefulness than at sleep onset. One imagines that people who habitually report, during thought-sampling experiments, that they are thinking something about the experiment did not invent this dream evasion technique then and there. Rather, they've probably adapted to the experimental situation techniques that they use more generally for maintaining hyper-vigilant self-control. Likewise, other individuals probably can let their thoughts drift somewhat without ever reaching the point of hallucination.[50] It's also tempting to believe that persons who do momentarily experience bizarre and/or hallucinatory ideation while awake do so as part of a more general strategy of self-regulation. At present, however, we know little about such matters, and they are obvious candidates for future study.

Some readers may relish the idea that there are such things as waking dreams and see them as a natural part of the larger fabric of human imagination. For those readers, the necessary cautionary note is that, at least as observed in the laboratory (where the "waking" part best can be verified), normal volunteers generally seem to experience only very brief moments of actual hallucination. Mental contents that are weird in content, form, or formal sequence probably are somewhat more generally experienced, and can persist over a longer time course, but they most often are not truly dreamlike. They're experienced as thoughts, rather than (as in dreams) reality. Furthermore, when hallucination does occur, it seems that mental contents are not markedly more weird or imaginative than when it does not.

Other readers may find the idea that any sort of dreamlike experience could occur when one is awake a rather implausible one. The idea that we can think weird thoughts while awake is not, perhaps, altogether foreign to our own experience. However, the idea that sane individuals hallucinate while awake may be more difficult to accept. The findings of the laboratory studies described here are not, however, new ones. Waking hallucination in normals has been reported ever since serious observation has been made of human mental states. It was documented by that great 19th century scientific dilettante, Sir Francis Galton, and his observations have been replicated many times.[51] As one pair of investigators noted, "one wonders how many times a finding must be made before it ceases to be surprising."[52] The acceptance of normal waking hallucination seems to depend on transcending rigid dichotomies about waking versus sleeping, and normal versus abnormal, thinking. These dichotomies have found much support in the rationalist tradition in Western culture. But they don't seem to be accurate, and they're a definite obstacle to describing how our conscious minds really work.

The evidence reviewed in this chapter suggests that dreaming is not bound to any particular state—neither to REM sleep nor to sleep more generally. The interpretation advanced here is, rather, that dreaming is a phenomenon which occurs in the presence of certain *mental* conditions: the relative absence of sensory stimulation and of the processing of such stimulation, the relinquishment of an Active-I, and persistent and relatively diffuse mnemonic activation. The mind has an involuntary organizing system to consciously interpret this residual, intramental activation in such a way that it makes sense, both momentarily and sequentially. The sense this system makes of its sources is related to the kind of sense that we impart to conscious experiences more generally. However, because its sources are different than those of waking perceptual experience and of much waking ideational experience, the synthesis achieved by the dream may seem strange by ordinary waking standards. But what the dream-production system is trying to accomplish is not strange at all. It's aiming at the same goals as those of conscious mental functioning more generally: the organization and interpretation of "what's happening."

On this view, dreams (or mental experiences that are somehow dreamlike) will occur whenever requisite conditions for the activation of the dream-production system are met, *providing that* such a system is available to respond to them. The availability of such a system seems to be limited in early childhood in ways that depend on the more general development of mental organizing structures and processes (see Chapter 3). It must also be limited, even in adults, by other concurrently active structures and processes of mental organization—those whose activity, for instance, keeps us "awake" when we still are.

The impetus to fully engage the dream-production system, when it is present and potentially available, depends on how well and how continuously requisite eliciting conditions are met. These conditions seem most generally to be present during REM sleep, but they also can occur during non-REM sleep and at sleep onset, and (at least momentarily) even when we are both physiologically and experientially awake. That full-fledged dreaming can and does occur outside REM sleep indicates that the mental act of dreaming is not bound to the physiology of one state. That *less* than full-fledged dreaming is the more frequent observation outside REM sleep provides us with marvelous opportunities to learn how the system works when it works well. It's in just those instances when everything is *not* in place and not smoothly integrated that we can best observe the separate components of the human dream-production system, and best understand how they must work together as well as they typically do in REM sleep.

5. FORGETTING DREAMS

Much of this book is about the role of memory *in* dreaming. That is, my primary concern is to review and evaluate evidence regarding how a dream-production system operates on memories and knowledge (as inputs) so as to achieve life-simulating dream narratives (as outputs). But there is, of course, another important context in which to consider memory and dreaming: memory *for* dreams. Freud suggested that the problems of how dreams are put together and why they are forgotten most likely are interrelated. He thought that a mental function of "censorship," whose role in dream construction could be seen in the way certain memories were treated and valued, also was responsible for the widespread forgetting of dreams.[53] His particular ("repression") hypothesis has proven to be inadequate both conceptually and empirically.[54] But his more general idea may still be valid: Something about the way in which dreams are created may be related to why they so often are forgotten.

There actually are two major questions about the forgetting of dreams. (1) Why, in general, are dreams so easily forgotten? (2) Why can some people remember relatively many of their dreams, and others relatively few? My interest here is to discuss the first problem in a fairly comprehensive way. The second problem is treated only by implication, namely, only insofar as it is related to individual differences during dreaming itself. Clearly, there is much room for individual variation *after* the dream is dreamed (in how likely you are to wake up from it, in how attentive you are to your first waking impression of it, in how likely you are mentally to rehearse—and elaborate—this first recollection, and so forth). But these differences shade into factors that are not unique to the remembering of dreams. It's important that interpersonal differences in remembering dreams can be attributed to some of the same factors that mediate memory for other (waking) experiences, but insofar as these factors introduce no new principles as applied to remembering dreams, they are not discussed here.[55]

Donald Goodenough has identified "the key question" about memory for dreams as "why dreams are so much more difficult to recall than waking experiences".[56] This, in fact, seems to be the big problem. Granted that most dreams are relatively plausible simulations of waking life situations, in almost every dream there's at least something peculiar going on that you would view as highly memorable if it had happened in life. In the dream, however, it (and its context) seem to be highly forgettable. Had the subject with the "Computer" dream (Chapter 1) not been deliberately awakened while it was happening, she almost surely would have slept through it and later would have been unable to remember any of it. But it's not just reasonably mundane dreams that subjects forget. Although we can't be sure in particular cases, it seems likely that many of the more impressive REM dreams laboratory subjects sometimes report—ones with vivid sensory imagery, strenuous self-participation, and intense emotional accompaniment—also would have been lost to later recollection had they not been deliberately interrupted by an experimental awakening. Had the dreams been real-life experiences, rather than imaginary simulations of such experiences, it seems almost impossible to believe that, even a few minutes after they happened, they'd be totally forgotten. Yet, when awakening is delayed only several minutes after the conclusion of an undisturbed REM period, subjects typically no longer can recall the associated REM dream.[57]

Although one major finding of psychophysiological dream research is how relatively plausible the typical REM dream is, the contents of REM dreams don't seem inherently forgettable. One should bear in mind, too, that REM dreams aren't fleeting impressions, but temporally extended sequences which can continue for 30 or 40 minutes. *Content-centered* explanations of dream forgetting won't work: It's not the forgettability of *what* we dream that generally leads to our forgetting it. How, then, are we to understand the other major finding of psychophysiological dream research: that we forget most of the (considerable) dreaming we do?

We think we know that all this dreaming is going on because of the results of laboratory research. We know, for instance, that people have multiple REM periods each night. We also know that, if systematically awakened during or at the end of these REM periods, people generally will describe a relatively lengthy dream which they believe they've just experienced. Finally, we know that, if these first impressions and recollections of the dream are of sufficient interest to a sufficiently alert person to lead that person to rehearse and reflect upon the dream just after it occurred, the dream generally will be recollected (in some form or other) the following morning—and perhaps later as well.

That the immediate transition from dreaming to waking seems to be critical to remembering dreams has suggested two variants of a *state-centered* explanation of our typical amnesia for our dreams. State-centered theories of dream amnesia seem to be most popular among physiologically oriented students of dreaming. Accordingly, the psychology of such theories typically is not well worked out.

One sort of state-centered theory points its finger at non-REM sleep, which typically follows our sleep-onset and REM dreaming and almost all of our non-REM dreaming as well. There must be something about non-REM sleep, according to the argument, that prevents us from transferring what's in our immediate (or "short-term," or "working") memory back into our long-term memory.[58] We can't "consolidate" our short-term impressions into stored memories because the physiology of non-REM sleep is somehow incompatible with the maintenance of the mental processing systems that normally perform (perhaps "unconsciously") such consolidation.

Supporting the idea that sleep interferes with the transfer of immediate impressions into retrievable memories is the observation that we don't simply forget *dreams* during sleep. Perhaps you've had the experience of waking someone during the night and briefly conversing with them only to have them deny the next morning that the awakening or conversation ever took place. Perhaps someone has cast you in the role of unwitting victim in such an encounter. Either way, the exchange was sufficiently detailed and appropriate to lead the awakener to believe that the awakened person was mentally processing it at the time. Later, however, only the person who remained awake could recollect it. Experimenters have verified that mid-night encounters with their subjects sometimes are totally forgotten the next morning, and Goodenough has concluded that "the acquisition of information is *very generally* impaired during sleep."[59] You don't just forget dreams during, or closely adjacent to, sleep, but anything that happens to you.

The other variant of a state-centered explanation of our amnesia for dreams is a state-dependent one. The concept of state dependency rests on the observation, for example, that subjects who learn material while intoxicated may be better able to recollect it later if they are intoxicated than if they are sober. The idea is that reintoxication reinstates the situation of the original learning, and may, therefore, provide more effective "retrieval cues" than does a state of sobriety.[60] On the state-dependency hypothesis, the dream of one REM period would best be recalled in a subsequent REM period. It sometimes seems, in a dream we can remember, as though we took material from earlier dreams, which we can't remember apart from the recurring material. A dream setting may, for instance, seem familiar, even though it's not recognizable from our waking life. We have the experience in the dream of "remembering" that we've been here before.

Apart from whatever intuitive appeal such examples have, it is difficult to verify the state-dependency hypothesis of dream amnesia. Thus, I generally will not know the content of my first REM-period dream of the night unless I awaken from it. At that point, the dream is no longer unique to one state: I experienced it in REM sleep and recalled it while awake. Only if I know the content of that first dream independently of my second REM-period dream of the night can I be sure that I have, in fact, recollected something in a state-dependent way. The state-dependency concept is not without its problems as applied to states other than sleep. Goodenough's conclusion regarding dream amnesia is that, although the state-dependency hypothesis is not without its attraction, "the evidence for an explanation of this sort is not very compelling at this time."[61]

State-centered explanations that implicate non-REM sleep in dream amnesia also face a major problem. Just as laboratory dream subjects are often surprised to discover how much night dreaming they do, so too subjects in "thought sampling" studies have been moved to comment on how unaware they'd been of their aptitude for experiencing dreamlike ideation while awake. The suggestion is that we also do a lot of waking dreaming that we generally forget. Non-REM sleep cannot be the culprit here. Presumably, one could retain a state-dependency hypothesis, and talk about a variety of "sub-states" within wakefulness that are relatively isolated from one another mnemonically. But then states would no longer be defined independently of their mental correlates, because there's no strong evidence at present that waking dreaming has unique physiological indicators.[62]

The most general problems with either state-centered explanation of dream forgetting, however, lie elsewhere. *First,* the concept of state, insofar as it's defined physiologically, is not an explanatory construct in psychology. What explains dream amnesia (or any other possibly state-related psychological phenomenon) can't be the physical state; rather, it has to be the organization of mental functions prevalent in that state. *Second,* state-centered explanations of dream amnesia typically focus on what happens after the dream occurs—on the subsequent appearance of some other state than that in which the dream occurred. But the key to why we forget our dreams may lie in the organization of mental processes during dreaming itself: The very act of dreaming may sow the seeds of the apparent mnemonic loss of its processed contents. Thus, it may be more fruitful to approach the problem of dream amnesia from a *process-centered* perspective, and to ask what it may be about the act of dreaming itself which makes its contents less memorable than those of our mental activities as we process world events.

This strategy has several advantages. To the extent that there is some degree of overlap between physiologically defined states and psychologically defined forms of mental organization, the processing-centered approach can retain—on conceptually more appropriate grounds—some of the attractiveness and plausibility of the state-centered approach. However, by focusing on properties of dream processing, the approach can more easily be reconciled with the observation that such processing is not inalterably tied to any one body-state. As we have seen, we can dream in any one of four such "states": REM sleep, non-REM sleep, the transition from wakefulness to sleep, and wakefulness itself. There is little reason to believe that amnesia for dreaming is any different simply as a function of the state in which dreaming occurs. Such amnesia *may* be related to the degree to which the dream-processing system is engaged—and that may (statistically) be state-related—but the operative variable would still be the process rather than the state.

The major advantage of thinking about dream amnesia from a processing perspective is that it allows us to make substantial use of the considerable scientific literature on waking remembering and forgetting.[63] As I demonstrate, this literature can supply a useful context for considering the remembering and forgetting of dreams. I also show that considering the remembering and forgetting of dreams in this context demonstrates some limitations in waking memory research for which dream observations may provide a necessary corrective.

Memory research suggests that the possibility and the quality of one's conscious recollection of events is a joint (interactive) function of two variables: how an event is originally encoded, and the number and nature of the retrieval cues available at the time recollection is attempted.[64] Let's first consider the role of *retrieval cues* in memory for dreams.

One suggestion about why we forget our dreams starts from an observation noted earlier: Although dreams are, in a general way, relatively plausible life-simulations, they are not exactly like any situations we have encountered or are likely to encounter in our waking experience. Dreams are, in short, just a little odd when compared with the typical texture of our waking lives. What this means, in the context of retrieval cues, is that we're unlikely to ever come across a waking situation just like that in our dream—the sort of situation that causes us to say,"*Now*, I remember! I once had a dream just like that."

This sort of explanation for our waking amnesia for dreams does have two useful properties: It explains why the forgetting of dreams is so widespread (dreams are, in general, odd), and it explains why we generally forget our dreams—regardless of the state in which they occur (since, for example, waking dreams may be no less odd than REM dreams). Nonetheless, there are strong grounds on which to doubt its adequacy.

First, although our dream experience, as a totality, may be unlike anything we encounter in waking life, our dreams contain representations of persons, places, objects, and events which, considered singly, we do frequently encounter in waking life. That's what is meant by saying REM dreams are "generally plausible" simulations of our waking life experience. Moreover, the more frequent form in which we experience delayed, cue-stimulated dream recollection is of precisely this sort: we see Ms. X and suddenly recall an odd dream we had about her last night. The problem here is that, because our REM dreams are generally plausible—i.e., they make reference to familiar features of our waking life experience— we should be able to recall most of them on the basis of this kind of cuing. But we don't.

This may not be as major a problem as it first seems, however. As Tulving has pointed out, most often we are not stimulated to reminiscence of prior *waking* experiences by the appearance of cues that helped comprise those experiences. Every time I order a Heineken beer, I am not immediately flooded with recollections of past times when I have done so. Tulving observes that we don't know what it is that causes some cues to stimulate episodic reminiscence—to put us into what he calls the "retrieval mode".[65] Novelty may have something to do with it. The second time I stay at a particular hotel I may be stimulated to think back to the first, but by the tenth time I may simply have general knowledge of the hotel rather than much vivid recollection of any one past set of experiences there.[66] Thus, precisely to the degree that the people (places, objects, etc.) in my dreams *are* familiar, they may not be terribly effective cues to stimulate recollection of my most recent (dream) encounter with them.

There is another objection to a simple retrieval-cue explanation of dream amnesia that is not so easily turned aside. The general point of such an explanation is that retrieval cues may be insufficient for waking dream recall because dreams are, by waking standards, odd. On this argument, the more odd the dream (i.e., the less it refers to cues we're likely to encounter later in our waking life), the less well we should be able to remember it. But comparisons of dreams that people first remember on REM awakenings with those they remember the following morning seem to indicate that, the odder the dream, the *better* it is recalled.[67]

It may be objected that, on the original experimental awakenings, a person would be inclined to pay more attention to her or his more bizarre dreams, and thus spend more time and effort rehearsing them while still in the waking state. Such rehearsal could only interfere (the objection continues) with the more usual effects of dream content variables on dream recall. However, there is a comparable kind of evidence which comes from nights of sleep that are *not* experimentally interrupted. As noted in the last chapter, it appears that spontaneous morning dream recall systematically *over*estimates the bizarreness of experienced dreaming. That is, dream bizarreness seems to favor, rather than preclude, later recall. Moreover, as we have seen earlier in this chapter, there are whole classes of non-REM ideation which are highly plausible and waking-like (e.g., "thinking" and "remembering"), but so *un*memorable that their existence wasn't even recognized until spontaneous morning recall was supplemented by experimenter-initiated awakenings during the night.

Thus, it does not seem that an argument just in terms of retrieval cues is very helpful to understanding our typical dream amnesia. However, it can be useful in thinking about why the laboratory REM-awakening procedure produces more dream recall than does spontaneous morning awakening at home. When (as in the laboratory) we are always awakened during the act of dreaming and someone quickly structures a retrieval situation for us, we generally can recall a dream. Part of the dream—the last part—remains within the boundaries of an immediate memory system, which has access to recently-processed conscious experience. That part generally will be—at least on REM awakenings—an effective retrieval cue for some or all of the rest of the dream. It will be effective because, as constructed, the dream will have been thematically interrelated.[68] The last moment of the dream (which research subjects in fact often do describe first in reporting an extended dream) provides a more effective retrieval cue for the rest of the dream than *any* experience we are likely to encounter in waking life. The laboratory dream reporting situation maximizes access to this cue, and hence to extended dream reporting more generally. How important this can be is illustrated by the finding described earlier that even several minutes of intervening non-REM sleep (with its shift away from full and continuing engagement of dream production processes) can drastically reduce the likelihood of REM-type dream recall.[69]

But if retrieval cues are of some help in thinking about why laboratory subjects' dream recall is as good as it is, how then can we understand why our typical (home) dream recall is so poor? Given, once again, the impressiveness of our dreams as we dream them, why aren't they recalled more often after we dream them? Here, I think, we need to consider what dreams are, how our minds are organized as we dream them, and the kind of *encoding* we consequently are able to give these new patterns of conscious mental organization.

First, (as was suggested in the Introduction) it may be useful to think of dreaming as a kind of episodic recollection. From a content perspective, this sounds more than a little crazy, because we're generally not reliving in our dreams anything that ever really happened to us. Consider, however, some *processing* parallels between dreaming and episodic recollection. If all conscious recollection is reconstructive processing, rather than a simple activation of ready-made filmstrips in the mind, then it involves the construction of experience from memory. Under conditions of deliberate waking attempts at episodic recollection, mnemonic information is accessed reasonably appropriately in terms of one's conscious intention (e.g., to "remember" last year's office picnic). However, this information still has to be integrated and organized in consciousness, so that (with varying degrees of verisimilitude) we can now experience what some past event was like.

Among the features of our experience of episodic recollection are the following: we believe in the validity of our simulation as (past) experience; conscious knowledge is organized spatially and temporally rather than abstractly; knowledge is processed "firsthand" or from a personal-experiential viewpoint—we're "reliving" our past.[70] From a processing perspective, this kind of recollection approximates or matches certain properties of our experience of dreams (more so, for instance, than does our recollection of facts or general knowledge). There's a big difference, of course. Dreaming doesn't labor under the constraints of recapturing some one past experience in our life, but draws from a wider and less intimately related set of knowledge representations. Given this different sort of knowledge base, it, too, simulates firsthand experience by consciously integrating and organizing information. One need not believe that dreams are "memories," or that patients under focal brain stimulation are experiencing "recollections," in order to see that some of the same processes may be involved in experience simulations that vary in real-life "truthfulness" from scrupulous recollection to improbable imaginings.[71]

The point of this argument is a simple one. When we compare our habitual forgetting of impressive dream experiences with our reasonably serviceable recollection of impressive life experiences, we are comparing two different sorts of phenomena. The dream may *seem* as real as waking life experience, but it *isn't* such experience: it's more in the nature of a momentary recollection. The appropriate waking comparison for the recollection of dreams is not, therefore, a memory for life events, but a memory for *recollections* of life events.

In this respect, another possible parallel between episodic recollection and dream experience may be especially significant. *While evoking* recollections of life events, our minds do not seem to be organized to further process these *recollections* for later recall. There is nothing in the process of recollection itself that guarantees the effective encoding of recollective experience in memory. In wakefulness, however, we can alternate reasonably rapidly between a recollective mode and one in which we reflect and conceptually elaborate upon a prior recollection. But, especially to the degree that our episodic recollection is a rich and vivid one, the very act of conscious recollection seems largely incompatible with the simultaneous deep analysis of the specific content of our recollection. In dreaming, this incompatibility becomes especially important, for our experience in a (broadly-defined) recollective mode is nearly continuous. Thus, the organization of our minds as we dream may be as incompatible over the long run with later recollection of dream contents as the organization of our minds for episodic recollection is in the short run incompatible with the encoding of the contents of such experience for later retrieval.

Following this line of reasoning, *what* we're dreaming is largely irrelevant to its later memorability.[72] What matters is *that* we're dreaming, that our minds are organized in a recollective rather than an encoding mode. Whenever our minds are organized to simulate experience rather than to process events for memory, our recollection for that experience will be correspondingly impoverished. The best known cure for this kind of experience amnesia is to reorganize our minds, as by waking up or otherwise reinstituting processing that is devoted to information encoding rather than experience simulation.

We have substantial independent evidence that encoding processes *are* continuously impaired during dreaming. Our investigation of the properties of dream consciousness in Chapter 1 suggested a limited ("literal") kind of comprehension of dream events during the act of dreaming. *From the standpoint of memory for dreams, this limited comprehension is identical with a limited encoding of dream events during the act of dreaming.* Encoding is adequate to help us understand what is happening in a dream, but it is not sufficient to permit us to reflect on the origins or rationale of our conscious experience, or to relate and compare that experience with the broad body of our conceptual knowledge.

In the context of one popular model of waking mnemonic processing, our encoding (comprehension) of our dreams could be characterized as relatively "shallow".[73] But the particular mental organization that underlies this processing is not well-modeled by waking experiments, because it involves a peculiar kind of self-regulation that is unlikely to be evoked in any such experiment (or to characterize much waking episodic recollection). What is relatively unique in the dream processing of sleep states is the *continuous* absence of what is ordinarly taken to be self-mediated conscious processing. That is, when we're dreaming we're not *deliberately* selecting and organizing the contents of our conscious thoughts and we're not able to reflect on them in a *self-conscious* way.

Yet, as we've already noted (Chapter 1), despite the absence of what is ordinarily taken to be self-mediated conscious processing, there is unmistakable evidence of the persistence of *some* self-regulation in dreaming. Consciousness itself—where *we* are aware of events, real or imagined—presupposes some sense of self. That self is, in large degree, a continuation of our waking conscious self. For example, it brings many of the same values and expectations to bear on what it processes. Dream experience is *our* experience. And, with suitable retrieval cues, such experience is accessible to *autobiographical* recall. This fact alone implies that there is some self-mediated encoding of dream narratives for commitment to "long-term" memory.

These manifestations of residual self-mediated conscious processing, and of the limited memory for dreams that such processing seems to permit, suggest an interesting intermediate case between dichotomous possibilities defined by waking cognitive psychology: *conscious processing* (permitting later recollection) versus *automatic processing* (with no later recollection).[74] If we're not quite our waking selves as we dream, neither are we automatons. This intermediate case can and should be an instructive one because it involves naturally recurring forms of encoding heretofore relatively neglected in (waking) cognitive psychology.[75] And, since our typical comprehension during REM dreaming and our recollection of REM dreaming are, in principle, open to independent study, it should be possible to correlate the *relatively* involuntary encoding REM dreams receive with their mnemonic fate in various retrieval conditions.

What *can* be said, at present, about the mnemonic fate of the conscious mental organizations we call dreams? *First,* it's clear that at least certain of their features are encoded in long-term memory. We know this from the retrievability of extended dream episodes on REM awakenings, and from examples of delayed, cue-stimulated dream recall. We also know this from the way in which dreams return to interrupted themes (e.g., the dreamer in Chapter 1 who "remembered" to open the schoolyard gate after having been stopped by the girls). Finally, we know this from the (limited) comprehension we have of our dreams as we dream them.

Second, dreams should be thought of as *differently,* but not as more *weakly* or more *transitorily,* encoded than real-life waking experiences.[76] With appropriate cues, they can be recollected to a degree and at a temporal distance that may be little different from the conditions governing our waking recollections. This does not, of course, mean that dreams are permanently and inalterably "etched" in memory. It simply means that they are subject to precisely the same kinds of changes and recodings as are our episodic recollections more generally.

Third, as a function of the different quality of their encoding, dreams are likely to be *accessible* to recollection only when some fragment of recent dream organization persists as a retrieval cue in immediate memory. However, they are also retrievable in a very limited range of other cue contexts which are as yet very poorly understood. Naturalistic studies of when and how dreams are recollected well after their occurrence are needed to fill this gap in current knowledge. Such studies would also contribute more generally to addressing the problem raised by Tulving: What kinds of cues are necessary and sufficient to stimulate episodic recollection?

There is a sense, then, in which it seems that Freud was right. The everyday forgettability of dreams is intimately related to how our minds are organized as we make them. Specifically, it is related to the quality of encoding (comprehension) permitted by the organization of the mind for dream production. Because this organization is associated with a particular (and peculiar) kind of self-regulation, the study of dream amnesia may also have a lot to tell us about the functional properties of those various "selves" who make, experience, and (sometimes) recall dreams.

NOTES

[1] Eugene Aserinsky and Nathaniel Kleitman, "Regularly Occurring Periods of Eye Motility, and Concomitant Phenomena, During Sleep," *Science,* 1953, *118,* 273–274.

[2] For a refutation of reductionism, see Jerry A. Fodor, *Psychological Explanation: An Introduction to the Philosophy of Psychology,* New York: Random House, 1968, ch. 3. Fodor's arguments are basic to understanding, in a hardware-minded culture, the validity of mentalistic science.

[3] For economy's sake, I am not documenting well-known findings from REM dream research. Two excellent recent summaries of this research are: Arthur M. Arkin, John S. Antrobus, and Steven J. Ellman (eds.), *The Mind in Sleep: Psychology and Psychophysiology,* Hillsdale, N.J.: Lawrence Erlbaum Associates, 1978; and David B. Cohen, *Sleep and Dreaming: Origins, Nature and Functions,* Oxford, England: Pergamon Press, 1979.

[4] For a lucid review of the body of research relating physiological changes to dream activity, see R. T. Pivik, "Tonic States and Phasic Events in Relation to Sleep Mentation," in Arkin et al., *op. cit.,* pp. 245–271.

[5] Allan Rechtschaffen, "The Single-Mindedness and Isolation of Dreams," *Sleep,* 1978, *1,* 97–109.

[6] For example: Robert D. Ogilvie, Harry T. Hunt, Christine Sawicki, and Jaroslav Samahalskyi, "Psychological Correlates of Spontaneous Middle Ear Muscle Activity During Sleep," *Sleep,* 1982, *5,* 11–27; David Foulkes and Richard Pope, "Primary Visual Experience and Secondary Cognitive Elaboration in Stage REM: A Modest Confirmation and an Extension," *Perceptual and Motor Skills,* 1973, *37,* 107–118.

[7]On earlier studies of non-REM dreaming, see references in David Foulkes, "Dream Reports from Different Stages of Sleep," *Journal of Abnormal and Social Psychology,* 1962, *62,* 14–25, and on earlier observations of sleep-onset dreaming, see references in David Foulkes and Gerald Vogel, "Mental Activity at Sleep Onset," *Journal of Abnormal Psychology,* 1965, *70,* 231–243.

[8]The sleep-onset figure is based on: Foulkes and Vogel, *loc. cit.;* David Foulkes, Paul S. Spear, and John D. Symonds, "Individual Differences in Mental Activity at Sleep Onset," *Journal of Abnormal Psychology,* 1966, *71,* 280–286; and David Foulkes and Marcella Schmidt, "Temporal Sequence and Unit Composition in Dream Reports from Different Stages of Sleep," *Sleep,* 1983, *6,* 265–280. The non-REM figure is based on: Foulkes, *loc. cit.;* David Foulkes and Allan Rechtschaffen, "Presleep Determinants of Dream Content: Effects of Two Films," *Perceptual and Motor Skills,* 1964, *19,* 983–1005; Terry Pivik and David Foulkes, "NREM Mentation: Relation to Personality, Orientation Time, and Time of Night," *Journal of Consulting and Clinical Psychology,* 1968, *32,* 144–151; and Foulkes and Schmidt, *loc. cit.*

[9]See, for instance, the discussion in Allan Rechtschaffen, "The Psychophysiology of Mental Activity during Sleep," in F. J. McGuigan and R. A. Schoonover (eds.), *The Psychophysiology of Thinking: Studies of Covert Processes,* New York: Academic Press, 1973, pp. 153–205.

[10]Foulkes, *loc. cit.*

[11]*Ibid.* Chapter 1 contained, for didactic purposes, a few hypothetical dream examples. *All* of the examples in this paragraph—and henceforth—are genuine ones, collected on laboratory awakenings.

[12]*Ibid.*

[13]Foulkes and Schmidt, *loc. cit.*

[14]Donald J. Foss and David T. Hakes, *Psycholinguistics: An Introduction to the Psychology of Language,* Englewood Cliffs, N.J.: Prentice-Hall, 1978, pp. 189–200.

[15]*Ibid.,* p. 193.

[16]During non-REM as well as during REM sleep, episodic or phasic cortical activation has been shown to be related to dream discontinuity. See David Foulkes, Elizabeth A. Scott, and Richard Pope, "The Tonic-Phasic Strategy in Sleep Mentation Research: Correlates of EEG Theta Bursts at Sleep Onset and During Non-REM Sleep," *Richerche di Psicologia,* 1980, *16,* 121–132.

[17]Foulkes and Schmidt, *loc. cit.*

[18]David Foulkes, *Children's Dreams: Longitudinal Studies,* New York: John Wiley and Sons, 1982, pp. 146–148; Allan Rechtschaffen, Paul Verdone, and Joy Wheaton, "Reports of Mental Activity during Sleep," *Canadian Psychiatric Association Journal,* 1963, *8,* 409–414 (see esp. p. 411).

[19]Foulkes, *op. cit.,* pp. 144–145.

[20]Foulkes and Schmidt, *loc. cit.* One systematic test of the derivational complexity argument, as described in Foulkes, *op. cit.,* p. 147, would be to compare the associations people give to their non-REM and REM reports. The prediction would be that non-REM associations would be less numerous and complex than REM associations, even where dreams were equated for their length.

[21]Foulkes and Schmidt, *loc. cit.* Using different methodology, John Antrobus has also found that, with control for report length, REM and non-REM reports are *not* qualitatively different. See John S. Antrobus, "REM and NREM Sleep Reports: Comparison of Word Frequencies by Cognitive Classes," *Psychophysiology,* 1983, *20,* 562–568.

[22]Lawrence J. Monroe, Allan Rechtschaffen, David Foulkes, and Judith Jensen, "The Discriminability of REM and NREM Reports," *Journal of Personality and Social Psychology,* 1965, *2,* 456–460.

[23] Foulkes and Vogel, *loc. cit.*

[24] Foulkes, Spear, and Symonds, *loc. cit.;* Gerald W. Vogel, Barbara Barrowclough, and Douglas D. Giesler, "Limited Discriminability of REM and Sleep Onset Reports and its Psychiatric Implications," *Archives of General Psychiatry,* 1972, *26,* 449–455.

[25] The judging study was by Vogel et al., *loc. cit.* The comparison with REM versus non-REM discriminability is somewhat suspect, because it may have reflected differences in judge competence rather than in report quality. See the review by Steven J. Ellman, and Vogel's reply, in *Sleep Research,* 1973, *2,* 369–371.

[26] Foulkes and Schmidt, *loc. cit.*

[27] The findings in this and the previous two paragraphs are from Gerald Vogel, David Foulkes, and Harry Trosman, "Ego Functions and Dreaming During Sleep Onset," *Archives of General Psychiatry,* 1966, *14,* 238–248.

[28] Robert D. Ogilvie, Harry T. Hunt, Paul D. Tyson, Melodie L. Lucescu, and Daniel B. Jeakins, "Lucid Dreaming and Alpha Activity: A Preliminary Report," *Perceptual and Motor Skills,* 1982, *55,* 795–808.

[29] Foulkes and Schmidt, *loc. cit.*

[30] For evidence that this is the succession of the loss of sense of self at sleep onset, see Foulkes and Vogel, *loc. cit.;* Vogel et al., *loc. cit.;* and Elizabeth Gibson, Franklin Perry, Dana Redington, and Joe Kamiya, "Discrimination of Sleep Onset Stages: Behavioral Responses and Verbal Reports," *Perceptual and Motor Skills,* 1982, *55,* 1023–1037.

[31] Gerald W. Vogel, "Mentation Reported from Naps of Narcoleptics," *Advances in Sleep Research,* 1976, *3,* 161–168.

[32] Foulkes and Vogel, *loc. cit.;* Gibson et al., *loc. cit.*

[33] Foulkes and Schmidt, *loc. cit.*

[34] This is a very old idea, one exploited by Freud's associate, Herbert Silberer. See D. Rapaport (ed.), *Organization and Pathology of Thought,* New York: Columbia University, 1951. One step forward in conducting such research, indeed in dream research more generally, would be to go beyond characterizing images, or image sequences, or image contents as being merely "bizarre." Such terminology almost inherently directs attention to something's effect on us, rather than to its own constituents. The questions should be what are the features of the dream that strike us as bizarre, and what do these feature reveal about peculiarities in the processes by which the dream is organizing its mnemonic sources?

[35] Foulkes, Spear, and Symonds, *loc. cit.*

[36] For suggestive, but not conclusive, evidence on this point, see Foulkes, Scott, and Pope, *loc. cit.*

[37] Vogel et. al., *loc. cit.;* Gerald W. Vogel, "Sleep-onset Mentation," in Arkin et. al., *op. cit.,* pp. 97–108.

[38] David Foulkes and Elizabeth Scott, "An Above-Zero Waking Baseline for the Incidence of Momentarily Hallucinatory Mentation," *Sleep Research,* 1973, *2,* 108.

[39] David Foulkes and Stephan Fleisher ("Mental Activity in Relaxed Wakefulness," *Journal of Abnormal Psychology,* 1975, *84,* 66–75) report an hallucination rate of 19%. The same figure was observed in daytime testing of 16 of the subjects studied by Foulkes and Schmidt, *loc. cit.,* although the article in question does not report these findings.

[40] Foulkes and Fleisher, *loc. cit.* This also was the case in the Foulkes and Schmidt series (see the preceding footnote).

[41] Foulkes and Scott, *loc. cit.*

[42] As in the research of Foulkes and Schmidt, cited above.

[43] Foulkes and Fleisher, *loc. cit.,* p. 72.

[44] Vogel et al., *loc. cit.*

[45] Foulkes and Fleisher, *loc. cit.* These figures are very much like the percentages of *all* reports that were nonhallucinatory (81%) and nonregressive (75%).

[46] *Ibid.* The five subjects with the largest number of regressive reports included none of the four subjects with the largest number of hallucinatory reports. Only 6% of subjects' waking reports were both regressive and hallucinatory.

[47] *Ibid.*

[48] These figures come from previously unpublished analyses of the data of Foulkes and Fleisher, *loc. cit.*

[49] See the preceding footnote.

[50] In three studies (Foulkes and Scott, *loc. cit.*, Foulkes and Fleisher, *loc. cit.*, and Foulkes and Schmidt, *loc. cit.*) 52 subjects had their "relaxed waking thought" sampled on 5 or 6 different occasions; exactly half (26) never reported an hallucination.

[51] Francis Galton, *Inquiries into Human Faculty and its Development,* New York: Macmillan, 1883. Other references are given in Foulkes and Fleisher, *loc. cit.* Related research can be found in Kenneth S. Pope and Jerome L. Singer (eds.), *The Stream of Consciousness: Scientific Investigations into the Flow of Human Experience,* New York: Plenum Press, 1978 (see especially the chapters by Eric Klinger, Kenneth S. Pope, Daniel F. Kripke and David Sonnenschein, and Mihaly Csikszentmihalyi).

[52] Foulkes and Fleisher, *loc. cit.*, p. 71.

[53] Sigmund Freud, *The Interpretation of Dreams,* New York: Basic Books, 1955 (originally published, 1900), p. 517.

[54] The repression hypothesis is inadequate conceptually because it proposes a content-specific mechanism for phenomena of forgetting, which we now realize (since the discovery of REM sleep) are pervasive and general. A particular problem is that it seems to be our most innocuous dreams which we are most likely to forget. Empirical evidence regarding the repression hypothesis has been reviewed by Donald R. Goodenough, "Dream Recall: History and Current Status of the Field," in Arkin et al., *op. cit.*, pp. 113–140 and by Cohen, *op. cit.*, ch. 6.

[55] On individual differences, see Goodenough, *loc. cit.*, and Cohen, *loc. cit.*

[56] Goodenough, *loc. cit.*, p. 114.

[57] Edward A. Wolpert and Harry Trosman, "Studies in Psychophysiology of Dreams. I. Experimental Evocation of Sequential Dream Episodes," *Archives of Neurology and Psychiatry,* 1958, *79*, 603–606.

[58] In the terms of our previous discussion, "immediate memory" is roughly synonymous with consciousness as a system. During dreaming, long-term memory units are activated, then organized in a novel and coherent way. The organizing system is the "involuntary", limited capacity processor whose activity is experienced as (dreaming) consciousness. The memory question is whether (and in what conditions) the particular organization imposed on memory units during this active processing *itself* becomes a permanent feature of long-term (episodic) memory.

[59] Goodenough, *loc. cit.*, p. 129. The italics are mine.

[60] For a brief discussion of the concept of state-dependency, its problems, and some references, see Roberta L. Klatzky, *Human Memory: Structures and Processes,* 2nd ed., San Francisco: W. H. Freeman, 1980, pp. 321–325.

[61] Goodenough, *loc. cit.*, p. 133.

[62] Foulkes and Fleisher, *loc. cit.*

[63] Or, to put it another way, it permits us to avoid specious physiological models of human memory and possibly unwarranted generalizations (e.g., "consolidation") from nonsymbolic memory to symbolic memory.

[64] Endel Tulving, *Elements of Episodic Memory,* New York: Oxford University Press, 1983.

[65] *Ibid.*, p. 169.

[66] E.g., Marigold Linton, "Transformations of Memory in Everyday Life," in Ulric Neisser (ed.), *Memory Observed: Remembering in Natural Contexts,* San Francisco: W. H. Freeman, 1982, pp. 77–91.

[67] E.g., C. A. Meier, H. Ruef, A. Ziegler, and C. S. Hall, "Forgetting of Dreams in the Laboratory," *Perceptual and Motor Skills,* 1968, *26,* 551–557.

[68] Sometimes on laboratory awakenings, experimental subjects recall earlier dream contents that are so different from the most recently remembered dream event that the subjects describe these contents as having been "a different dream." It remains to be demonstrated whether these dreams are so wholly different from the immediately preawakening dream sequence that the latter could not have served as a plausible retrieval cue for them. The self-character, for example, is so pervasive in dreams that it typically will be involved in both or all the "separate" dreams reported on a single awakening, and there generally is *some* carryover of nonself characters, settings, or thematic concerns from one dream report to the next on such occasions. To the extent that *no* such continuities exist, a case might be made for state dependency, i.e., for retrieval cues tied to the form of one's mental organization rather than to the specific materials being processed.

[69] Wolpert and Trosman, *loc. cit.*

[70] Tulving, *op. cit.,* ch. 3.

[71] This analogy of dream experience to episodic recollection is probably not one that Tulving would accept. Indeed, in his discussion of patients' fantasies under brain stimulation, Tulving denies that these fantasies are episodic memories, since they "do not contain descriptions of temporally dated and spatially located personal experiences (*op. cit.,* p. 62)." But this rather restrictive definition of episodic memory, focusing on the attribution of conscious contents to some particular time and place in one's past experience, seems to overlook a possible similarity in the processing modalities involved in stimulated fantasies and episodic recollection—and in dreams.

[72] Except insofar as certain kinds of contents are more likely than others to be associated with spontaneous (reflection-permitting) dream interruptions—e.g., mid-night arousals.

[73] Fergus I. M. Craik and Robert S. Lockhart, "Levels of Processing: A Framework for Memory Research," *Journal of Verbal Learning and Verbal Behavior,* 1972, *11,* 671–684. See also Alan D. Baddeley, "The Trouble with Levels: A Reexamination of Craik and Lockhart's Framework for Memory Research," *Psychological Review,* 1978, *85,* 139–152.

[74] E.g., Richard M. Shiffrin and Walter Schneider, "Controlled and Automatic Human Information Processing: II. Perceptual Learning, Automatic Attending, and a General Theory," *Psychological Review,* 1977, *84,* 127–190.

[75] Ulric Neisser, "Memory: What are the Important Questions?" in Neisser, *op. cit.,* pp. 3–19.

[76] Tulving, *op. cit.*

3 When and How Dreaming Begins

The adult's dream-production system *reprocesses* and *consciously* organizes activated *mental representations* (i.e., memories, knowledge). Thus, the presence and nature of dreaming in early childhood must be constrained both by what the child knows (i.e., the mental representations available for processing) and by how the child is able symbolically to process or transform what he or she knows (specifically, by the child's ability *consciously* to process knowledge from symbolic memory.) In this chapter, we look at evidence relating children's dreaming to the quality of their waking memory and thought.

There are obvious difficulties in studying the inner mental life (either sleeping or waking) of children. The typical methods of psychophysiological dream research can be applied equally well to children as to adults. You can monitor children's sleep and awaken them from some designated state of sleep to inquire about remembered dreams. However, you might feel less confidence in the *results* of these methods as applied to children. Maybe children cannot remember their dreams as well as adults can; maybe they can't describe them as well as adults can; surely they might be less interested in, and scrupulous about, describing dreams accurately. These problems in interpreting children's laboratory dream reports will be considered at appropriate points later in this chapter. For the time being, however, it can be said that, despite all of these real or imagined interpretive problems, children studied in the laboratory have described dreams that conform to an orderly and predictable pattern. Specifically, the pattern is predicted by the hypothesis that the experience of dreams changes over time in conformity with changes in waking mental development.

Not many children have been studied in the laboratory; at early ages of particular interest, their numbers are very small indeed. Thus, any dream observations described in this chapter should be considered tentative. For several reasons, however, I think that the limited observations currently available still deserve extended consideration.

(1)   As noted above, the data conform to a pattern which makes good theoretical sense.

(2)   Although not studied as frequently as adults, children have been the object of a fair amount of laboratory research—at least 150 children aged 3–15 have been awakened to report dreams from physiologically monitored sleep on at least 4000 separate occasions.[1]

(3)   Although a certain age range (2–7) is underrepresented in this sample, what we know about that age range is qualitatively rich, coming from the most extensive and systematic dream research ever conducted with any human subjects.[2]

(4)   Publicizing what is currently known (and not known) about the early development of dreaming may stimulate more research on children's dreams.

As we'll see, such research does not promise to be significant because of what children's dreams will tell us about their waking behavior. Children's dreams grow out of what they know, rather than out of what they do. Young children's behavior may be different from ours precisely by virtue of its lesser symbolic mediation.[3] That is, there are lags between when the child knows behaviorally how to act intelligently in given situations and when the child knows symbolically what is going on behaviorally. By symbolic knowledge, I mean knowledge that can be abstracted out of particular situations that are physically present, and that can then function independently of those situations. That's the sort of knowledge on which dreams would have to draw, because the external world no longer exists for us as we dream. Dreaming is a purely mental act.

The real significance of children's dreams lies in this fact. Their dreams reflect something that is, in the long run, much more important than what they are doing, something that is also much more obscure to waking observation. Specifically, the dreams reflect how children can represent and organize in their own minds what is happening in their lives. The diagnostic value of their dreams is in the area of cognition, rather than that of behavior. Children's dreams can tell us how youngsters mentally represent themselves, others, and the world. They also indicate the kinds of transformations children mentally can perform on what they know— how they are able to "operate on" their knowledge and consciously experience it. Thus, the real story children's dreams have to tell is one about the development of mind, which is the central question of child psychology—just as the nature of mind is the central question of psychology more generally.

1. THE WAKING GROWTH OF MIND

Before we consider evidence on children's dreaming, let us review some trends from *waking* studies of symbolic development. Following this review, and a look at the available dream data, we'll then be able to coordinate dreaming and waking observations in a more unified portrait of symbolic activity in the developing human being.

Because dreaming is a *complex* symbolic activity—one involving a number of different mental systems—our survey of waking studies of cognitive development must necessarily be multidimensional. First, because dreaming is a symbolic process, we must ascertain the origins of symbolic activity in early childhood. Next, because dreaming imposes organization on its mnemonic sources, we must consider the kinds of conceptual processing that are available in various periods of early human development. Because dreaming is a form of consciousness, we'll need to look at evidence bearing on children's ability to consciously process information, both perceptual information and knowledge from symbolic memory. This evidence perforce will be indirect; in fact, one of the unique aspects of children's dream reporting is that it speaks relatively more directly than any waking evidence to the issue of children's conscious states. Finally, because dreaming processes knowledge, we'll have to understand when and how children accumulate the sorts of knowledge it would seem that they would have to have to create dreams of the rich contents and fluent formal organization with which we associate our own dreaming.

Representational Intelligence.   What is a symbolic "representation"? As this term is used by cognitive psychologists, it refers to an internalized ("mental") structure, which can re-present some event in its literal absence. Mental "trial and error," the process by which we evaluate ways to solve a problem without ever actually performing them, takes place in a representational medium. We can mentally manipulate representations of the various possibilities; we are not limited merely to performing these possibilities overtly to determine their probable consequences. There is a symbolized, in-the-mind world, as well as an out-there world, on which we can act, and we can act on the symbolic world even when we are not stimulated by its counterparts in the real world. I can think about how I want to plan my days next summer at the beach even while the snow flies outside my office window. Representations make possible symbolic activity.

It's important to reiterate, in the context of a book on dreaming, this use of the word *symbolic*. In this sense, dreaming is symbolic behavior because it involves the evocation of representations of objects or events in the absence of their real-life counterparts. I can dream of the beach although there is no sand coursing between my toes and no sound of waves while I lie inert in my bed.

There is, of course, another sense in which dreams are alleged to be symbolic: innocent dream events are thought really to mean something else, something more "deep" and "meaningful." This kind of symbolism depends on supposed substitutions among symbols in the first sense. The dream representation of water, for instance, may be alleged to carry the meaning of the concept of the mother's womb. It's my assumption that no symbolism of this sort is in fact involved in the production of dreams. Interpreters are free, of course, to read whatever deep meanings they wish into dreams, but it should be understood that they most likely are not decoding meanings that were put into the dream as it was formed. They are, rather, adding something to it, in the same way that I add something to a random ink blot when I call it "butterfly" (see Chapter 5). The only sense in which dreams unequivocally can be characterized as symbolic is the first sense: They are the results of activity performed on mental representations in the absence of the real-world objects or events they represent.

In this sense, dreaming can occur no earlier in human development (nor in the development of species) than does symbolic activity. When, in waking life, does the child first evidence such activity? By most accounts, purely symbolic activity is first reliably demonstrated by children in the second half of the second postnatal year (18–24 months of age). Before this time, signification is tied to a context of perception and action. The child may search for an object which has just been removed from her or his sight, but gives no clear evidence that an object long gone can be represented symbolically.

Piaget, to whom we owe much of what we know of the child's mental growth, describes five newly appearing phenomena in the second half of the child's second year, which together suggest the beginnings of symbolic activity:[4]

1. Delayed imitation. Well after an observed event, the child imitates it. She stamps her feet, for example, in imitation of a playmate's earlier temper tantrum.

2. Verbal evocation of absent events. She says "Granpa bye-bye," pointing to a path by which the man earlier had left.

3. Drawing or other artistic reproductions of absent objects or events.

4. Other behaviors that seem to be guided by "mental" imagery of absent objects.

5. Symbolic play: the child "pretends," for example, to be a train.

Delayed imitation and symbolic play are forms of imitative action that are now capable of being instigated mentally. They no longer require the environmental stimuli to which they earlier were tied. Likewise, "seeing" no longer requires environmental objects or events for its elicitation. One can imagine objects or events in their absence. Piaget views mental imagery as an internally initiated process by which perceptual experience is "imitated" (i.e., simulated). In fact, he and his associates see imitation as the key underlying the development of a symbolic capacity. In a presymbolic ("sensorimotor") period of development (0–18 months), the child acquires immediate knowledge of action and objects. This immediate knowledge serves as the basis of the child's later (symbolically) "mediated" knowledge.[5] That is, there is first a mastery of perceptual and motor acts that are directly tied to external events. These acts can then be "imitated" in the absence of the events.

Speech, which we might want to take as the most obvious form of human symbolic activity, is also acquired partly through imitation. In fact, the child's earliest speech likely is purely imitative vocal behavior, rather than an index of any kind of symbolization. But speech acts become, as children move from single-word to multiword utterances, increasingly mediated by symbolic knowledge. Speech itself can also be imitated internally, and these "imitations" can be detached from their original eliciting contexts. It is in this way, we suppose, that words become one way in which we consciously "think," as well as a means of interpersonal communication.

Another way in which Piaget characterizes the development of representational intelligence is the formation of what he calls *evocative memory*.[6] Evocative memory is contrasted with what Piaget has designated *recognition memory*. Toddlers show recognition memory when they respond to the appearance of a pet with a standard repertoire of responses: running to it, petting it, and even repeating its name or some approximation thereto. Children treat dogs as something they know (and indeed do know). But this knowledge (memory)—which is both perceptual and motor—is tied to the appearance of its referent. Evocative memory exists when knowledge can be evoked in the absence of the referent and of any action toward it—when children can, for instance, in the dog's absence, think of it.

Recognition memory is widely distributed throughout the animal kingdom; it is the kind of memory Piaget imagines to be developing in the human infant's presymbolic (sensorimotor) stage of development. Evocative memory, on the other hand, depends on symbolic activity. It is, in fact, synonymous with what I've called "symbolic memory." Such memory is largely absent in other species and in the human infant. However, evocative or symbolic memory is the kind of memory on which dreaming must depend, since dreaming re-presents symbolic knowledge to conscious awareness without cuing from the environment. Even 2-year-olds give little evidence of such memory.[7]

Many of Piaget's observations on cognitive development have been called into question by succeeding generations of researchers, who have subjected his evidence and theories to the sort of scrutiny that is merited by the work of any scientific pioneer. By and large, however, Piaget's evidence on the timing of the development of representational intelligence has survived this test. For instance, recent research by Susan Sugarman produced findings in general accord with Piaget's demarcation of 18 months as the point where such intelligence emerges.[8] In her study, Sugarman was more scrupulous than most developmental researchers about discriminating what a child does from how the child does it. Her process analyses permitted determination of whether children's performances were in fact symbolic ones. She studied both children's spontaneous (nonverbal) organization of arrays of blocks and other objects and their use of language. In both domains, children demonstrated symbolically-mediated behavior at about the time Piaget would have predicted.

Sugarman's study highlighted another fact that is sometimes overlooked in interpreting Piaget's observations. Children do not access symbolic activity at exactly the same time, and they also do not consistently perform symbolically once they have demonstrated the potential to do so. That is, one needs (particularly in the early stages of symbolic development) to distinguish between symbolic competence and symbolic performance. Competence is defined by the most accomplished performance of which a person is capable; performance is defined by the *typical* level of accomplishment the person demonstrates. Thus, just because the typical 2-year-old is symbolically competent, it does not follow that he or she is an inveterate symbolizer. Neither the child's nor our own symbolic activity routinely can be inferred from the theoretical capability for such activity. Probably, the actual incidence of symbolic activity increases gradually in early childhood.

Conceptual Processes.   Piaget characterized the earliest stage of human symbolic functioning, evident from roughly ages 2 to 6, as a "preoperational" phase of representational intelligence. This term defines the phase not in terms of what is newly present—symbolic activity—but in terms of what remains absent: "operations."[9] Roughly, one can think of mental operations as symbolic acts that provide a stable, logically consistent, wholly internalized organization of mental representations. More precisely, Piaget defines operations as reversible mental transformations.[10] The concept of reversibility most often is illustrated with conceptual "conservation" problems.

To understand what is involved in such problems, it may be useful to consider a *perceptual* form of conservation demonstrated at the end of the sensorimotor (presymbolic) period. The child evidences perceptual conservation when an object is treated as a constant entity, despite (according to different angles of regard) its varied patterns of stimulation on visual receptor organs. Looking straight down at a plate, for instance, produces an optical pattern that is approximately circular; looking at it as you walk away from the table on which it lies, its pattern of optical information becomes elliptical. Yet perceptually it remains the same plate, both for us and for very young children. Even when the plate is *momentarily* removed (e.g., hidden underneath a blanket), presymbolic children may search for it at the place where they saw it hidden.

During the early symbolic (preoperational) period, this sort of conservation or preservation must now be mastered, according to Piaget, at the level of concepts—mental representations more than momentarily detached from their eliciting stimuli in the real world.[11] In a typical *conceptual* conservation task, for instance, the child watches as the water from a wide-mouthed short beaker is poured into a narrow-mouthed tall vase, and is asked whether the vase now contains the same amount of water as did the beaker, or more, or less. The preoperational child is likely not to conceive that quantity has been preserved in this perceptual transformation of the water. The higher water-line in the vase will be used, for example, to justify the judgment that there is *more* water in the vase than there was in the beaker.

This judgment reflects, according to Piaget, interrelated features of preoperational reasoning. The child "centers" on a momentary perceptual configuration—the water-line of the vase—rather than thinking beyond what her or his eyes now see. The child does not conceptualize in terms of inversions or reciprocity. That is, there seems to be no recognition of the fact that the vase water could be poured back into the beaker, where it once again would assume (approximately, of course) its old water-line, and there is no recognition of the fact that while the vase is taller than the beaker, this is compensated for by the fact that it is also narrower. Pouring, itself, is not conceptualized as a metric act: It is an incalculable qualitative performance. The child's mental representation of actions, including her or his own actions, is imprecise.

By ages 7 and 8, when what Piaget calls "concrete-operational" reasoning appears, all of this is changed. The child's judgment is that the quantity of water is preserved, despite its variable perceptual appearances. This judgment is justified on one or more of several grounds: it is *known* to be identical; if it were poured back from vase to beaker, it would be at the same level it originally had; the vase, although taller, is narrower, and this compensation explains the varied appearances of a common amount of water. Momentary *perceptual* differences are overridden by the child's internally organized *knowledge* of objects and their transformations. The child mentally can take an end point of a transformation, and reverse that transformation to achieve a representation of its beginning. From a fuzzy and imprecise understanding of actions, centered in their appearance, the child has moved toward a precise understanding of actions, based on an understanding of their logical properties. The transition from preoperational to operational reasoning is gradual, and it is manifested for different real-world phenomena at different ages. But, once it is achieved, the child has arrived at a pragmatic *conceptual* understanding of her or his world, on the model of the pragmatic understanding she or he achieved at the level of immediate *perception and action* toward the end of the sensorimotor period.

A still later achievement occurs, according to Piaget, during early adolescence. Operations can then be applied not only to situations one actually encounters, but also to those one merely imagines. The child can think not only as does the empirical scientist but also as does the theoretical scientist or philosopher. In line with the competence-performance distinction introduced earlier, it should not be imagined that the adolescent is perpetually immersed in a realm of pure ideation, only that this now is a possibility. The adolescent stage of "formal operations" will be of lesser concern in the present account of children's mental growth, not because it's unimportant or uninteresting, but because observations reviewed later in this chapter indicate that dreaming changes most dramatically during earlier periods of waking cognitive growth.[12]

In this regard, several features of Piaget's description of children's earliest (i.e., preoperational) symbolic thought deserve further attention. According to Piaget, the preoperational child does not demonstrate much internal planning of symbolic activity. Perceptual configurations are thought to drive what symbolic activity does occur. Where these configurations are relatively stable, the child's symbolic activity (as, for instance, in symbolic play) may also seem to be relatively stable over time. But, where real-world circumstances are subject to repeated change, the child's activity will seem to be highly distractible. Internal structure that is capable of overriding environmental flux in the service of symbolic stability does not, as yet, exist. Generalizing this observation to the realm of dreaming, one would have to predict highly episodic forms of dream representation, with little or no narrative planning. That is, mnemonic activation might evoke some sort of momentary "dream" imagery, but in the absence of the kinds of internally driven planning that must be responsible for coherent sequences of imagery in adults, there probably could not be any kind of coherent dream story built around changing patterns of mnemonic activity.

Piaget has argued that the symbolic play of preoperational children provides the nearest waking parallel to their (and our) dreams.[13] While there are, in fact, many compelling differences between these two creative phenomena,[14] in some respects the parallel is at least superficially appealing. One of them is the self-centeredness of the child's play. Indeed, a frequent, although often imprecise, characterization of preoperational reasoning more generally is that it is "egocentric," a term Piaget himself came to regret having applied to this period.[15] As we've already seen (in Chapter 1), egocentrism is susceptible to a variety of often quite different interpretations. One that does seem to apply to much preoperational reasoning (but *not* to narrative dreaming) is the way in which the young child's mental life is bound by her or his current environmental context. When snow flies, the child is not likely to think of the beach and next summer, but of making snow figures right now in the front yard. Piaget relates the demonstrated absence of logical thinking in the young child to the child's inability to decenter from an often very narrowly defined current perception: what she or he sees right now. The water-line I see is high; therefore there's more water than before. I'm looking now at a subset of beads that are red, therefore there are more red beads than beads. Or, at a more ideational level, phenomena are explained by my relation to them: we have night so that I can sleep.

Piaget thought that the preoperational child's social behavior demonstrates an equivalent centration on her or his own current state. He observed that the conversation of young children often has the quality of parallel monologs: Neither child seems to be addressing the other in any particular way, nor to be interested in the response of the other to what is said.[16] While the individuality of others may be respected at a physical level, their minds and interests are assumed to be just like the child's. Thus, an appropriate Christmas gift for father might be a doll or a toy truck.[17] On Piaget's account, we might therefore make another prediction about preoperational children's dreams: The contents of these dreams should be centered either in children's momentary states or on their more general personal interests. Even more so than seems to be true of our own dreams (cf. Chapter 1), young children's dreams should be "egocentric."

Piaget's characterization of the preoperational period has not gone unchallenged. As developmental psychologists have pursued leads developed by Piaget, it has become evident that there are respects in which his portrait of the period is overdrawn. The idea that preoperational children are primitively egocentric has been heavily criticized, as it has become apparent that there are conditions in which such children can and do adopt a viewpoint other than their own.[18] Still, as a matter of relative emphasis, few would doubt that Piaget's interpretation has caught the substance of an important difference between preoperational children's thought and our own.

A more general objection to Piaget's thinking relates to his whole concept of "stages" of intellectual development. The stage concept seems to imply relatively little development within stages, followed by massive discontinuities at the junction between them. Here, too, many contemporary researchers feel that Piaget's account is overdrawn, specifically that it detracts attention from ways in which children late in a stage are clearly different from those early in the same stage. There are many differences one easily can observe between the symbolic activity of 3-year-olds and 5-year-olds even if they both "fail" tests of conceptual conservation. Does Piaget allow adequate scope in his system for the number and nature of those differences? That's a theoretical question beyond the scope of this brief survey, so I won't pursue it here, other than to note that Piaget was a sophisticated observer of children's intelligence and that his theories are highly subtle ones (thus, objections to Piaget also run a considerable risk of being overdrawn).

For present purposes, however, it is important to note some respects in which conceptual processes do seem to be developing *during* the "preoperational" period. Some significant clues come from observations of children's linguistic growth in this era. Where the 2-year-old may be limited to fragmentary utterances designating unitary concepts, by age five the child can use language to express complex semantic relationships in much the same way as an adult can.[19] One cognitive basis of this difference lies in the increasing amount of conceptual processing the child can perform at the same time.

For example, observations have been made of the sequence in which linguistic rules are first applied in early development. Two such rules involve the placement of auxiliary verbs and of negatives in "wh-" questions. A reliable observation is that the child who imposes these rules on a question form is likely, at a certain stage of speech development, to invert the auxiliary in a positive question form correctly ("Why did you?"), but is unlikely to do so in a negative question form ("Why you didn't?"). One interpretation of this phenomenon is that the simultaneous planning of questions, negativity, and auxiliary verb forms exceeds the amount of planning the child can perform at one moment: "there is a limit on the number of processing operations the child can perform and . . . *this limit is raised as language development progresses.*"[20]

Likewise, in the study mentioned earlier, Sugarman found that children's spontaneous structuring of blocks and other objects revealed increasingly powerful conceptual strategies from ages 1½ to 3, i.e., during the early preoperational period. The quality of the organization the children imposed on objects changed as they were better able to coordinate conceptual classifications simultaneously. Moreover, there was a parallel between this development and the development of increasingly complex semantic reference in children's speech. Sugarman suggests that these developments also indicate that children's symbolic activity is not so much perceptually driven as Piaget imagined. Compared to the thought processes of still older children, preoperational thought may be more dependent on environmental cues, but to some extent preoperational children *are* developing increasingly sophisticated forms by which the purely symbolic regulation of mental activity can be accomplished.[21]

Thus, in its broad outlines, Piaget's picture of the symbolic life of the young child seems to have portrayed accurately some significant differentiating features of preoperational children's processing of information. However, more recent evidence suggests that conceptual processing in early childhood is less egocentric, better organized, and more susceptible to systematic internal regulation than Piaget might have allowed. This evidence also suggests significant changes in conceptual processing capacity and organization during the preoperational stage, changes that presumably have implications for how well children are able to put together those dreams which, as possessors of representational intelligence, they are now able to experience.

Consciousness.   As we have already seen, consciousness does not seem to be the keystone of human symbolic activity. In one sense, it seems more like a medium in which results of such activity sometimes are displayed, analogous to a computer print-out, which does not reveal computational processes but only some results generated by these processes. The dream is one form in which the outputs of human symbolic activities are consciously experienced; thus the development of dreaming must depend on our development of consciousness.

What do we know about the way in which young children consciously experience whatever it is they experience? How can we know anything about something as ultimately private as others' conscious experience? We can ask them, of course, and hope that the terms they use bear some resemblance to concepts we use in understanding ourselves. But suppose, as is the case for young children (or chimpanzees), they can't seem to understand our questions or to frame what we take to be coherent answers to them. What then?

Our first inclination may be to assume that consciousness is something we share with young children, infants, and even dogs and cats. But there's an uncomfortable degree of egocentrism in such an assumption. Just because we "have" something, should we assume that many other organisms, often otherwise quite different from us, have it too? What kind of "thing" is it that we have? Is it the sort of thing that plausibly could be shared across age and species boundaries? Or is it something which itself has cognitive prerequisites, such that we wouldn't expect to find it where symbolic activity itself was largely or wholly absent? These questions obviously are major ones for psychology, but they also obviously are the sorts of questions for which definitive answers are least likely to be available. The ways in which psychologists have sought to avoid thinking about them, while philosophers have swarmed around them, gives us every reason to believe that they are good questions for provoking arguments, but bad ones for uncovering relevant evidence. My strategy here is a limited one: first, to attempt a simplified analysis of what consciousness is, so that we might better estimate whether it could or could not be present in various forms of life, and second, to review several kinds of evidence that may give indirect readings of the quality of young children's consciousness. There's no pretense that this approach can do much more than jog our own thoughts a little. But even that might be helpful for something as nebulous and mysterious as consciousness.

Consciousness is something that exists in degrees or levels, and the first need in thinking about it is to try to distinguish these amounts or kinds of consciousness. At its most *elementary* level, consciousness is inferred from responsiveness or sensitivity to external stimulation. "Unconsciousness," by this criterion, is when you're in a coma, and "nonconsciousness" is when you're dead.

For our purposes, however, the responsivity criterion of consciousness is inadequate. There are at least two major problems with it. *First,* symbolizing organisms can experience consciousness in the absence of overt behavior. They can be conscious of their own symbolic activity, as well as of world events. Dreams are a prime example. They occur in states where external responsivity is absent or greatly attenuated, yet there is no doubt but that they are consciously experienced. In fact, dreaming could be defined as the kind of consciousness we typically experience during sleep. *Second,* response-defined consciousness seems to be too generous a concept when applied to primitive living things. Sensitive plants of the genus Mimosa have leaves that fold up as you touch them. Are they conscious?

At its most *advanced* level, consciousness is inferred from verbal reports. Because, on awakening from sleep, a person claims to have been dreaming (and describes the dream in question), we assume that, however inert he or she may have been before we performed our awakening, the person was conscious. By this definition, people often are *un*conscious of contingencies that can be demonstrated to have independently influenced their behavior.[22] That is, they don't know (can't tell you) why they're acting the way they are.

The verbal report criterion of consciousness, however, is too restrictive a concept. It seems arbitrarily to prejudge just the kinds of questions that interest us, for example, whether human infants or chimpanzees are capable of consciousness. Are we to conclude, simply from the fact that such organisms literally can't tell us otherwise that they aren't conscious?

Thus, another criterion must be sought somewhere between the primitive sort of consciousness implied by overt responses and the advanced sort of consciousness implied by verbal reports. Although this intermediate criterion will not presuppose verbal competence, it must suppose specific kinds of cognitive competence. We need now to consider what those forms of cognitive competence might be.

In the response-criterion model, one can think of consciousness as a kind of mental blackboard that instantaneously "displays" (is the awareness of) external stimuli.[23] In this model, consciousness itself is not so much a processor as a receiver of information. Interestingly, although Freud's concept of consciousness extends this model so that the blackboard also can display (or be our limited awareness of) internal or symbolic stimuli, his construct of consciousness retains the passive characteristics of the response-inferred model. Freud thought of consciousness as a kind of primitive perceptual system, which can be turned either outward (to the world) or, as in dreaming, inward (to the mind). We can sense what's in the world, or what's on our minds, or both.[24] But even in Freud's extension of the blackboard model, consciousness involves an automatic or passive kind of representation of information currently being processed. Consciousness itself is a system with few distinctive cognitive properties or prerequisites. (Accordingly, Freud seemed to take it for granted that dogs dream.[25])

More contemporary thinking about consciousness, however, stresses that consciousness is no sort of passive, automatic registration of stimuli (external or mental). Rather, it is a system which (a) selectively organizes information currently being processed, and (b) actively regulates both its own activities and those of other symbolic processes that do not achieve conscious realization.

Consciousness as a system is a limited-capacity processor. We cannot be conscious of an infinite or even a very large number of world events or mental acts at one and the same time. Thus, consciousness is inherently selective, and in the face of the array of information to which it is potentially responsive, it inherently involves an active imposition of coherence and organization on information. As can be recalled from the discussion of modular perceptual processing in Chapter 1, even *conscious perception of world events* does not seem to be a passive, automatic awareness of the modular processing of external stimuli.

Based on his studies of visual word recognition, Anthony Marcel has distinguished *unconscious* processes, which automatically analyze stimuli through rapid activation of an associatively organized body of word knowledge (e.g., "king–queen"), from *conscious* perception, which segments and organizes the outputs of modular processing based on a slower and more volitional access of a logically organized body of world knowledge (e.g., "king" refers to the concept of a male, hereditarily determined head of state.)[26] Marcel's proposal, then, is that conscious perception does not only reflect unconscious modular processing; rather, it adds structure and organization to the preconscious processing of sensory information. In support of his unconscious–conscious distinction, Marcel has described experiments demonstrating that "masking" a briefly presented visual stimulus (i.e., following it almost immediately with another stimulus) blocks conscious perception of that stimulus, but not the "subliminal" associative effects of its presentation on subsequent performances.

In Marcel's model, consciousness depends on the application of cognitive categorization to unconscious perceptual input analysis. A developmental implication of this model is that, until the child has acquired a certain quality of conceptual knowledge, perceptual behavior may not be accompanied by perceptual experience. Marcel does not shrink from this implication and proposes that "quite apart from verbalization, the child cannot have a phenomenal experience unless he or she has a construct for it."[27] That is, even conscious *perceptual* experience in childhood is not automatic: it depends on the development of appropriate categorical knowledge.

Another respect in which consciousness must have cognitive prerequisites has to do with its self-regulative properties. These properties refute the concept of consciousness as any kind of passive registration. Consciousness is associated with an active organization both of its own processing and of unconscious symbolic activity (as when we consciously pose a problem for our "mind" to solve). In this sense, consciousness can be defined as a higher-order symbolic process, namely as a symbolic competence in relation to other symbolic activity.

These aspects of consciousness are directly accessible to waking awareness. We have a sense of an Active-I,[28] which can call up to consciousness what it wants, can monitor and regulate the flow of whatever is processed by it, and can direct unconscious symbolic activity as well. We also have a direct sense of the duality (or multiplicity) of symbolic activity in consciousness. *We* are aware of what *we* are aware of. What may be distinctively human about this kind of consciousness is that it presupposes complexity in symbolic processing. Specifically, it presupposes higher-order symbolic activity (one symbolic system orienting itself with respect to another); organization (consciousness integrates and regulates both itself and the underlying symbolic acts it reflects); and the presence of double or multiple selves and some measure of active self-regulation (I can decide what I want consciously to think about).

You may well be wondering how this account of consciousness and its prerequisites could be relevant to dreaming, where both voluntary self-regulation and multiple self-awareness generally seem to be lacking.[29] The answer is that, although the cognitive prerequisites of consciousness may not be manifest *in dream experience,* they are no less implied *by the act of dreaming* than by any other conscious state. Dreaming is a conscious integration of unconscious cognitive activity, and it requires specific kinds of self-regulatory processing (Chapter 1). In these respects, dreaming is no different from any other form of conscious experience.

This brief analysis of the concept brings us to the realization that consciousness may indeed presuppose a certain level of symbolic development. It is neither guaranteed by differential responsiveness to external stimuli, nor necessarily precluded by an absence of language. The suggestion is that consciousness depends specifically on symbolic skills of the sort the child begins to demonstrate during the preoperational period. As these skills are accessed gradually, so too the evolution of consciousness must be gradual. From the competence/performance distinction, we might further conclude that consciousness is still only intermittent, even when its requisite conditions are capable of being satisfied.

It's easy, of course, to speculate about consciousness and its evolution. At this point, we clearly need some empirical ballast to keep us from soaring too far into the clouds. Let's turn our attention, therefore, to several lines of indirect evidence on the growth of consciousness in early childhood.

1.   One index of consciousness comes from measures of immediate memory. Presented with a fast-paced but brief list of single-digit numbers, for instance, how many can you repeat or recognize in their original order? Immediate-memory span for external stimuli in preoperational children apparently is lower than it is for older children or adults. Young children seem spontaneously not to use organizing strategies (rehearsal or grouping of the materials), and they do not profit from being instructed in the use of such strategies.[30] To the degree that the memory measures reflect the degree of children's immediate awareness, there is the suggestion both of a smaller capacity system and of the lack of ability to consciously regulate and organize what is processed there.[31]

2.   Analysis of the use of "mental" verbs (think, know, remember, etc.) indicates that they begin to appear in children's spontaneous speech between the ages of 2 and 3. Interestingly, they first seem to be used in contexts where they do not have a clear mental reference (e.g., "I think I want . . ." may function merely to soften the insistence of a child's

request, rather than to indicate a mental state). This suggests that the earlier lack of reference to mental states can't be due to a linguistic deficiency, since the linguistic behavior is present *before* the act of self-reference. Young children apparently lack an awareness of their own symbolic activity.[32]

3. Marcel has noted that studies of drug effects on children's conscious states produce results that are anomalous when compared to those of comparable studies with adults. Amphetamines, for instance, make adults euphoric while, at best, they merely make children "feel funny, not like myself." Marcel concludes that "it is a real possibility that autonomic [physiological] processes can have no issue in phenomenal experience or in modulating even the tone of behavior unless an appropriate cognitive, phenomenological category has been acquired."[33]

4. Another way of investigating children's conscious states is to study the apparent evolution of those concrete contents which we find most often in our waking conscious awareness: imagery and inner speech. How adept are young children at imaginal and inner-speech processing?

It has sometimes been argued that, until they master overt speech and then internalize language, children's ability to represent knowledge in consciousness must be more visual-imaginal than verbal.[34] The idea is that visual-imaginal coding in consciousness is somehow a more developmentally primitive system than is inner speech. If this argument were correct, it clearly would have important implications for the development of dreaming and dream reporting. For example, preoperational children might be able to dream in images much better than they could describe these dreams in words. However, the argument does not seem to be correct.

Mental imagery in early childhood probably is much more primitive than either overt or inner speech. Piaget and his collaborator Bärbel Inhelder performed a number of experiments suggesting that preoperational children can't imagine continuous visual transformations.[35] They can't, for example, either draw or select an appropriate drawing of the transformations that take place when an upright bar is allowed to fall to the horizontal plane. They know where the bar started from and where it ended up, but they can't seem to reconstruct mentally what happened to it in between. Piaget and Inhelder use such findings to suggest that preoperational children can't reproduce visual movement in their mind's eye, i.e., they lack kinematic or movielike mental imagery. These children can and do describe the fact of movement verbally, but they can't recreate the sequence of it imaginally.

Piaget and Inhelder further use their observations to make the point that what children can image depends on what they know, rather than on what they see. Preoperational children *see* movement all about them, but they don't yet *know* about continuous transformations and their reversals. In fact, Piaget and Inhelder showed that only when children get that kind of (operational) knowledge can they imagine movement at all; when they do get that knowledge, they can imagine movements equally well whether or not they've had extensive perceptual experience of the movements in question. Mental imaging thus seems to be a symbolic skill separable from perceptual experience, and one at which preoperational children are characteristically deficient. Piaget and Inhelder's observations can be interpreted as showing that a flexible and autonomous imaging system first appears between the ages of 5 and 7, an interpretation consistent with the observation (cf. Chapter 1) that it is only when persons are blinded after these ages that they retain the use of such a symbolic system.[36]

Those psychologists who continue to believe in the primacy of visual imagery in children's conscious mental life have doubted that Piaget and Inhelder's experimental observations are adequate to justify their conclusions.[37] But there are two independent kinds of evidence to suggest that Piaget and Inhelder are, in fact, largely correct. One comes from developmental studies of mental rotation, the phenomenon described in Chapter 1 in which you have mentally to rotate a figure (e.g., the letter "J") back to an upright position for comparison with a standard figure. In adults, one index that a continuous spatial transformation has been performed mentally is that there is a linear relationship between how many degrees the test figure is displaced from the upright and how long it takes a subject to make the comparison. The farther the figure has to be rotated to get it back to the position of the upright comparison figure, the longer it takes the subject to say whether the two figures are the same or different. Preoperational children, however, do not show this relationship.[38] Interestingly, congenitally blind adults *do* show linear relationships between how many degrees apart figures to be touched are, and how quickly they can be compared.[39] Therefore, the linear relation observed with adults and concrete-operational children for visually presented stimuli probably indicates something more general than the ability to manipulate representations *visually*. It reveals the ability to impose continuous mental transformations on any kind of *spatial* representations. Preoperational children seem defective in this ability, and that defect must severely constrain how and what they can imagine.

The second kind of independent evidence suggesting static and unversatile mental imaging in preoperational children comes, as we see later in this chapter, from the dreams such children report. Taken together, the evidence at hand suggests that young children are not "naturally" talented in creating mental imagery. Mental imaging apparently involves the reconstruction in consciousness, from what we *know*, of what things look like or of what their spatial relationships are.[40] Preoperational children are not adept imagers because they lack both substantive knowledge (about events) and procedural or operative knowledge (how to manipulate event knowledge so as to recreate in consciousness an appearance that mimics that of waking perception).

Thus far, only one dimension of preoperational children's imagery has been stressed: its static vs. kinematic quality. Is there reason to believe that it is defective (by our standards) in other respects as well? The preoperational child's understanding and representation of spatial relationships tends not to be metric in a Euclidean sense. Objects and spatial properties of objects may be represented, but it is difficult for the child to decenter from one position in representational space to establish a larger frame of reference in which perspective is maintained. Children's drawings typically reflect their spatial misunderstandings. It's important to realize that the spatial defects in young children's art aren't just deficiencies of the hand, which can't draw well, but also are tokens of larger defects of the mind, which doesn't understand spatial relationships very well. Children's art also nicely reflects the early relationship between mental imagery and conceptual knowledge. Preoperational children's drawings (guided by their mental imagery) represent what is known rather than what could be seen. Thus, if a man has just eaten potatoes, he's drawn with potatoes clearly visible in his stomach. It's only, apparently, in the concrete operational period that the general demand to be realistic in one's drawings begins to be defined as a demand to be perceptually realistic in Euclidean space coordinates.[41]

If children's imaging skills seem not to be highly developed, what about their capability for generating conscious speech representations? It might seem that any such capability would be less immediately relevant to dreaming, since our dreaming seems to be so highly visual (cf. Chapter 1). But speech simulation is a salient aspect of adult dreaming, and we should not foreclose the possibility that it plays a leading role in young children's dreams. Two ways of evaluating this possibility are establishing how much specifically *linguistic* information is reflected in children's early speech and concurrent nonverbal behavior, and determining how effectively young children seem to be able to use this information in purely symbolic (intramental) processing.

One question to which developmental psycholinguists have devoted much attention is the relative role of linguistic and world knowledge in shaping children's earliest speech behavior. For example, when young children show a preference for describing an event in the order subject-action-object (e.g., "I hit the ball"), does this reflect a conceptual understanding of the priority of agents to objects, or does it indicate the child's internalization of language, in particular, her or his use of the syntactic form for simple declarative sentences? Does the child's acquisition of language help her or him mentally organize events in the world, or does the child's understanding of what goes on in the world predate and help to shape the child's use of language? At different points in early language development, from the child's first single-word utterances to her or his first sentences, the evidence is fairly clear that conceptual understanding predates linguistic understanding. Thus, for example, the agent term always precedes the object term, even in the speech of children learning languages in which adults employ varying overt word orders. Children's earliest speech seems to reflect their way of understanding the world, rather than the way adults speak.[42] Specifically linguistic understandings only gradually come to be reflected in the child's speech. Presumably, at least in early childhood, the relative lack of systemization of knowledge at a specifically linguistic level would place some limits on the linguistic organization of consciousness. At the very least, we might conclude that language fares no better than imaging as a candidate for the role of providing a developmentally primitive system for consciously coding information in a relatively sophisticated way.

One of the major ways in which adults seem to regulate their own behavior is through inner speech. When we consciously plan and manage our activities, we say things to ourselves, we verbally rehearse, we verbally remind ourselves, etc. Indeed, it has been proposed that inner speech processes of these sorts play a critical role in the child's development of *self*-control.[43] Preoperational children's demonstrable deficiencies in effective self-regulation (e.g., their relative inability to use rehearsal or other verbal strategies in memory tasks) presumably are just another indication, then, of limitations in their ability to structure their conscious experience.

In general, the available evidence suggests that young children are probably not very talented either in thinking in pictures or in thinking in words, the two ways in which we seem most often *consciously* to think. The evidence should not be read as necessarily implying a comparable lack of talent in carrying on symbolic activity. Such activity may occur but it may not achieve conscious representation or a very effective realization in conscious experience. Rather than thinking of consciousness as being primary, and of unconscious mental acts as those that have passed (through routinization) to an unconscious level, we might better think of unconscious symbolic activity as primary, with a slowly evolving capability for reflecting some small part of this activity in conscious processing. This capability probably largely depends on the accessibility of visual-imaginal and verbal-symbolic processing systems, which seem to evolve correspondingly slowly. The consciousness system does not seem, from the evidence of introspective experiments or our own experience, to play a large role in solving complex problems. In fact, there are good reasons to believe that most of our "thinking" could not possibly be performed either on or through verbal or imaginal representations.[44] So, when we talk about consciousness and conscious forms of mental representation, we're not talking about the core level of our symbolic competence.

We are, however, talking about something highly relevant to dreaming, because the dream is an organization of consciousness. As such, the dream presumably depends on (and to some extent reflects) the underlying symbolic activity of our mind. But it also depends on and must reflect the kind of conscious mental organization we are able to impose on the symbolic processing we are performing. Data suggest that preoperational children are not able to construct elaborate or versatile mental imagery, and that they do not yet have highly developed skills in the realm of conscious inner speech. This does not mean that they are perpetually unconscious of what's happening to them or of the symbolic acts they are capable of performing. But it does suggest a considerable limitation in the possibilities of conscious representation.

5.   It was mentioned in the Introduction that there is some evidence that young children may have relatively inefficient episodic memory. Because episodic recollection is a "*(conscious)* experience of remembering,"[45] such evidence might well reflect limitations in children's conscious experience more generally. Two sorts of observation, one indirect and the other more direct, have been made regarding young children's ability to recollect discrete events in their past experience.

The indirect observation is the phenomenon known as "childhood amnesia." Adults have very few discrete recollections either of infancy or of large portions of the preoperational period. As has also been alluded to earlier, those few memories adults do seem to have from early years of life may be pseudo-memories, later confabulations of plausible events that they only imagine to have happened. Clearly, adults still know many things that they learned during the first years of life; speech is a prime example. But adults don't seem to have many (if any) reliable memories for particular events as opposed to general knowledge.

Based on the fact that adult amnesiacs seem primarily to show a loss of memory for particular episodes rather than for more generalized knowledge, and on the principle that the most recently acquired accomplishments are the first to disappear under duress, Daniel Schacter and Endel Tulving recently proposed that autobiographical memory must appear later in human development than does memory for generalized knowledge.[46] This would, of course, be consistent with adults' general failure to remember the personal history of their early childhood.

The more direct line of observation bearing on the development of episodic memory comes from the study of children's memory for life events. For example, Katherine Nelson and Gail Ross observed a bias in toddlers' and preschoolers' recollections toward general rather than specific (one-time) features of recurrent events.[47] This finding is particularly significant because it supports the idea that, from the very outset, human information processing is inherently abstractive, searching for general meanings at the expense of particular contextual details. Further, it suggests that the ability to recontextualize knowledge in conscious experience (as in episodic recollection or dreaming) is a special, slowly acquired processing skill, rather than the basis of human symbolic memory.

Later research from Nelson's laboratory, while supporting the preschoolers' bias toward more effective general than episodic recall, has qualified the earlier findings in some respects.[48] General retrieval questions (e.g., "What happens at dinner?" or "What happens when you go to the zoo?") elicit more information than do specific retrieval questions (e.g., "What happened at dinner yesterday?" or "What happened one time when you went to the zoo?"). The more familiar an experience (e.g., the more times the child actually has been to the zoo), the more activities a child can recall, even when asked to remember one particular occasion. It is as if general knowledge (which increases with familiarity) helps to provide a structure in terms of which the recall of particular events can better be organized. This dependence of particular recall on general knowledge is further demonstrated in the observation that some 3-year-olds cannot give *any* specific reports. When asked what happened "one time" at the zoo, they can only report what generally happens on zoo trips; this was particularly true when going to the zoo was a familiar event for the child. However, children did demonstrate some episodic recall, particularly for novel events and when a greater number of retrieval cues were provided. Novel events could not be incorporated in generalized activity "scripts," and hence were later accessible (with appropriate retrieval cues).

It should not be surprising that children have some particularized memory for events. It clearly would be unrealistic to imagine an all (generic) versus none (episodic) situation for children's earliest event memories. On balance, however, the evidence does suggest that children's episodic recollection is generally less accomplished than their generic recollection, and that it may be general knowledge which helps structure discrete knowledge, rather than vice-versa. To this extent, the evidence is consistent with the idea that young children are less capable of consciously recontextualizing knowledge than they are of directly accessing generalized knowledge.

Many questions remain, however, about how children do encode and retrieve their particularized event knowledge. One important distinction may be between memory for events one has observed and memory for events in which one has participated. Both kinds of events are *episodic,* in Tulving's terminology, but the latter are more *autobiographical* than the former. Still another important distinction might be between the episodic recollection of one's overt acts and the episodic recollection of one's entire "mental field," including not only the acts but the interpretations and ongoing commentaries one supplied for them. Both forms of recollection are autobiographical—the latter more richly so. To the degree that children's encoding of discrete events is not self-involving and is not associated with rich self-elaboration, their event memories may be both less susceptible to later retrieval and less a part of an autobiographical *system* in symbolic memory.

Based on Piaget's evidence, only the child who can decenter from self (i.e., the concrete-operational child) can view the self as a stable object— a "me." To conceive of a "me" means being able to take another's point of view. To experience an Active-I depends on the realization that there is a distinctive self who can be a causal agent in the same sense that others seem to be causal agents.[49] Tulving has referred to "the person's 'me-ness', his personal identity" as "the ultimate 'control-element' . . . that subsumes all the information in episodic memory and that must be 'activated' before personalized knowledge can be remembered. . . ."[50] To the extent that this control element is as yet inoperative in young children's event memory, it is not surprising that such memory is as sketchy as it seems to be, and that events of early childhood are largely inaccessible to later recollection by a fully self-regulated episodic memory system.

The major point to be drawn from evidence and reasoned speculation about young children's episodic recollection is *not* that children will simply have poor memory *for* dreams. Rather, a relative inability to consciously recontextualize knowledge, and to consciously organize and experience knowledge as *personal,* must have dramatic consequences for the ability to *create* dream experience and to create dream experience which has the immediate personal involvement characteristic of most adult dreaming. As we see later, young children do seem to have difficulty in generating dream experience and in creating experience which is momentarily autobiographical.

We've looked at several different lines of indirect evidence on children's ability to consciously experience life events and their own mental states. In general, the evidence indicates that it would be foolish to assume that consciousness as we know it is something shared by other species or very young children. Because dreaming is a particular kind of consciousness, the evidence suggests that conditions for the production and experience of dreams may generally be either lacking or relatively unfavorable even after children begin to be capable of symbolic activity.

Consciousness itself seems to be a complex kind of symbolic processing, and, as such, its development probably lags behind that of more elementary forms of symbolic activity.

It's a shame, of course, that we can't communicate more directly with young children to find out about their waking experience of their world and themselves. Perforce, we're limited to such strategies as analyzing what consciousness is, of determining what its mental prerequisites might be, and of then trying to establish to what degree these prerequisites are present in early development. We're limited also to the indirect evidence of those performances which are deficient in ways which might index deficiencies in consciousness and conscious self-regulation.

As we see later in this chapter, one of the most powerful performances from which to index children's ways and means for organizing awareness is the very kind of dream children can experience, insofar as their dream reports reflect their dream experiences. Young children may think that, in giving dream reports, they're describing real events,[51] but what they're really describing (if they're describing anything at all well) is the structure and organization of their consciousness. By inference, they're telling us about the possibilities they have for conscious experience. If they tell us their dreams over time, they're telling us about how these possibilities expand and are transformed as they grow to be more like us.

For the present, however, we might bear in mind the likelihood that our difficulties in more directly determining what children's conscious states and capabilities are like lie precisely in the fact that they're different from our own. Not only different, but impoverished. Such impoverishment would have to affect any mental process which makes relatively strenuous demands on consciousness.

Knowledge. So far, we've considered the early development of the kind of knowledge representations of which we can become directly aware—those that we experience consciously. But when knowledge is experienced consciously, it is no doubt altered from its state when we're not conscious of it. Specifically, for us to be consciously aware of things we know often means putting these things into particular words or images. But the underlying form of our latent knowledge may not exist in those words or images, or in any words or images at all.

Leaving aside the difficult (and perhaps impossible[52]) problem of specifying what the ultimate form of human knowledge representation might be, a couple of general points can be made about children's symbolic memory—that is, about what they know in a form rendering it accessible to a process such as dreaming. *First,* as we've already had occasion to observe, there seem to be some fairly considerable gaps in early childhood between knowledge children can demonstrate behaviorally and knowledge on which children themselves can reflect symbolically. For example, Piaget has shown that preoperational children are, in general, little aware of their own overt behaviors and are incapable of successfully deploying conscious attention toward them.[53] They know, for instance, at a motoric level how to crawl on "all fours," but they're not consciously aware, and are not easily led to conscious awareness, of the organization of that activity.

Second, bearing in mind the information-abstracting nature of the conceptual processes that permit us to determine and mnemonically encode the meaning of events, it should not be at all surprising that children's exposure to events does not necessarily lead to effective symbolic memory for those events. To determine the meaning of events presupposes that we have performed at least two sorts of conceptual processing: First, we have analyzed the features or properties of these events, and second we have related the results of such analyses to our representation of other events. Analysis and context give meaning to events. Thus, children's symbolic memory for events can only be as good as their skills of analyzing and interrelating mental facts. In fact, the cognitive change that seems to underlie both children's first symbolic speech and their passage into the preoperational period of reasoning more generally is precisely "a change from dealing with objects and events as global, undifferentiated wholes to dealing with them as collections of properties."[54] As we've already seen, preoperational children aren't (by our standards) initially very good at analyzing and interrelating information. Thus, because their memory depends on their skills of symbolic analysis, it must, at different points in early development, be (by our standards) specifiably deficient. The point here is that young children's relative inability to analyze and synthesize information not only limits how knowledge can be reprocessed (i.e., consciously experienced, as in dreaming) but also imposes considerable constraints on the very kinds of knowledge available for such reprocessing in the first place.

Consider, for example, some of the kinds of knowledge on which accomplished dreaming might be imagined to depend. There is, first of all, *self*-knowledge, because in our dreams a self character is the most frequently appearing, and often the leading, character. Although perceptual self-recognition is achieved during the sensorimotor period, preoperational children's ability to tell about themselves (to evoke symbolic knowledge of the self) is severely limited. Comprehension passes only slowly from the "me" that is differentiable by its body characteristics or physical activities to an "I" who is capable of thinking thoughts, feeling feelings, and deliberately initiating activities. These changes in self-comprehension are predictably related to changes in the child's waking mental development, and they are completed only during the concrete-operational period (ages 7–12).[55]

There is, next, the child's knowledge of other people, because our dreams, with rare exceptions, simulate *interpersonal* experience. Early in the preoperational period, children's ability to characterize others, and to describe how others' activities might be related to their own, is demonstrably poor. The other is differentiable from the self at a physical, but not at a psychological, level. Later (age 5 and following), there seems to be some conception that others might not think exactly as you do or want exactly what you do, but their acts and states are filled in more by stereotype than by any rich understanding. Self-reflectivity is not as yet conceived as a possibility for either self or other. Comprehension of others and the ability to adopt their perspective are also predictably related to the child's waking mental development, and they are also beginning to assume minimally acceptable adult standards only in the concrete-operational period.[56]

Consider, finally, some of the more "technical" knowledge a child would need to possess to be able to dream dreams like ours. If her or his dream imagery were momentarily to simulate what reality *looks* like, then the child would have to know how things look. Such knowledge has been called "depictive."[57] Since dreams don't "re-play" events we've actually experienced, but invent new ones, the depictive knowledge used in dream formation would have to have been abstracted out of the child's waking experience. That is, the sort of depictive knowledge used in generating dream imagery would require a fairly sophisticated analysis of the appearance properties of real-world happenings. It's not enough that the child can *recognize* the appearance of familiar objects or events; rather, these objects or events must also be subjected to a conceptual analysis of appearance properties so that appearance knowledge later can be used in the symbolic generation of realities heretofore never encountered. As we've already seen, Piaget's data suggest that preoperational children don't do this sort of analysis very well.[58] Some of his evidence indicates that mentally representing the sequence of others' acts may be easier than representing the sequence of the child's own acts, but neither seems to be at all easy. Piaget's point is that, until the concrete-operational period, the child's conceptualization of event appearances is rather poor.

Likewise, if her or his dream imagery were to portray *narrative* or storylike sequences of imagined events, then the child would have to have some knowledge of the constituents and properties of such sequences. The waking stories children tell can give some indication of their comprehension of the narrative form and of their ability to use this knowledge in symbolic creation. Children's earliest stories are not stories at all, but seemingly unrelated descriptions. By age 2 or 3, some minimal comprehension of sequence may be present, but there is a stereotyped centration on one character or act (for instance, "I gave a candy to Mommy, and I gave a candy to Daddy, and I gave a candy to Jimmy . . ."). Still later, complementary activities may be described, that is, activities which go together in real life (for instance, "Danny took a candy, and his Daddy spanked him"), or the chaining of one character's activities may be less stereotyped (he or she does different things with the same or with different people). It is only when children approach the concrete-operational period, however, that genuine narratives are produced. Predictably, these narratives have a kind of "reversibility." That is, having heard the whole story, you can see that the end is entailed by the beginning.[59]

In related research, Nelson has been studying the development of what is known as *script* knowledge.[60] A script is a generalized representation of an ordered sequence of events. The most widely cited example probably is the "restaurant" script. What typically happens when you go to a restaurant? Note that the question is not "What happened the last time that you went to a restaurant?" It is generalized over different individual occasions, and even 3-year-olds recognize that difference. An adult's restaurant script might include the following sequence: enter, choose seat or be seated, get menu, order meal, have courses brought out in the order salad-entree-dessert, eat, get check, pay waiter/cashier, leave. Children, too, have generalized script knowledge, but compared to adults' it is different in three ways. First, children have fewer scripts. That is, their knowledge of regularities in environmental and interpersonal situations is less broad than adults'. Second, what scripts they do have contain fewer steps than adults' ("You go in and you eat"). Third, children have more stereotyped or less flexible notions of concepts that can fill any given slot in a script. In a "visiting a friend" script, for instance, there may be only two peers who are conceived of as being eligible to fit the friend role. Thus, although the preoperational child is not without some generalized knowledge of event sequences, that knowledge is rudimentary, and it only later evolves into the kind of event knowledge that adults take for granted.

Another kind of knowledge, which children only slowly acquire, is that concerning the kinds of situations associated with particular kinds of *feelings* for particular kinds of people.[61] Little is known about the child's earliest understanding of her or his own feelings, or even about whether those feelings are in any way comparable to our own. We can observe that 3- and 4-year-olds behave emotionally (e.g., throw tantrums when someone takes away their toys), and that this overt behavior is accompanied by certain forms of physiological activation. We know much less about the third aspect of emotion in early childhood—subjective state. However, the picture of development we've elaborated thus far suggests that children's emotional experience must be limited in some of the same ways as is their other experience.

Although scanty on this point, the evidence is suggestive. Recall, for example, Marcel's description of the anomalous affective consequences of amphetamine administration in children. Investigators have also recently reported that kindergarten-age children (but not second-graders) denied having experienced sadness.[62] The researchers interpreted this finding as showing that younger children "distance" themselves from emotions such as sadness. The simpler interpretation is that they do not experience them. Finally, there is the intriguing observation made by Helen Keller that, before she attained the idea of a language system, she had sad and angry behavior, but not sad or angry feelings.[63]

"Feeling" emotional, in our (adult) sense, may depend first on some mental differentiation of a self to whom feelings may be ascribed or by whom they may be felt, and second on symbolic knowledge and processes, which permit us to elaborate behavioral and body-state stimulation so that they can be interpreted in consciousness as certain kinds of feeling states. On this account, young children's inner worlds of feeling must not be very well developed. A sense in which children must be even more restricted, however, is in the ability to generate feelings purely symbolically (without environmental provocation or its accompanying physiological activation). It's this kind of feeling competence, of course, that's most directly relevant to the experience of feeling in dreams.

My presumption is that such competence is not a matter of simply being able to reactivate feelings that are "stored" somewhere as if they were whole memory units that could be wheeled out of storage on demand. Rather, feelings are stored in precisely the same way as other symbolic memories. That is, the affective properties of events are abstracted from them just as are the appearance properties of events. In neither case is a replica of the event stored. Rather, in both cases knowledge is abstracted from events which is relevant to an experiential domain and which can later be used to consciously reconstruct experience in that domain. Just as there is depictive knowledge, knowledge of what things look like which can be used in the construction of dream imagery, so too there is affective knowledge, which can be used in the symbolic generation of feelings that simulate how we feel when emotion is externally provoked.

If this argument is correct, then the young child's ability to create another aspect of what we take for granted in our dreams—their feeling accompaniments—must be very restricted. First, the feelings to be imitated must themselves be relatively primitive and undifferentiated. Second, the child's ability to abstract knowledge from externally-provoked emotional behavioral encounters must be quite limited. Third, the child's ability to operate on this affective knowledge so as to recreate felt feelings purely symbolically must also be quite limited; at any age, it is probably much less well developed than the child's ability to recreate observed scenes.[64]

Thus, there seem to be many respects in which young children lack the knowledge to enable them to construct, purely in their minds, rich simulations of their waking experience. Indeed, such simulations would require a rich waking experience of self and world in the first place. This, in turn, would presuppose interpretive abilities children largely lack, but which would be critical to abstracting knowledge from waking life experience for use in any later symbolic simulation. Dreaming is precisely this kind of symbolic simulation. Given the identifiable respects in which preoperational children's experience and knowledge are different from our own, then children's dreams should be different from our own in these very same respects. Also, as children's waking experience and knowledge move toward forms more like our own, so too should their dreams. Finally, the picture of what children know and experience, which we have had tortuously to extract from all sorts of indirect waking observations, may emerge much more clearly and directly in children's dreams. That is, it may be in their reported dreams that children offer us the best single picture of what their personal experiences are like.

2. THE GROWTH OF DREAMING

Most of the observations to be described here come from two studies in which children's dream reports were collected on laboratory awakenings 9 nights a year over 5-year periods. One group of children studied ranged in age from 3 to 9, the other from 9 to 15.[65] The former group is of primary interest, because their dreams were reported during years of major changes in waking mental development, and because their dream reports also showed correspondingly striking changes. During the course of these two studies, a number of "control" experiments were also conducted. These experiments were meant to detect possible bias in the main data due to the way in which the children were studied (for example, were dreams changed because the children were studied in a laboratory or because the children were observed repeatedly?). The results indicated little such bias,[66] hence, we can turn our attention directly to the primary findings of the main studies.

Preoperational Period (Ages 3–5). The first significant observation was how *seldom* children reported a dream on REM awakenings, and how *little* dreaming they reported when they were able to remember a dream. To be precise, only 27% of REM awakenings yielded any dream report at all, and the typical dream report was 14 words long. No report ever exceeded 50 words in length.

The other major finding was how *different* the children's reported dreams were from adult dreams, and even from the same children's dreams collected at later ages (i.e., 5–9). The differences can be described in terms both of "expected" features which were absent and of "unexpected" features which were present in the preschoolers' dream reports. Absent were: narrative quality or storyline (unsurprising, in view of how brief the reports were), active self-representation (a self character actively doing anything in the dream), known human characters (other than a few references, mainly to family members), movement or physical activity (only a quarter of the reports described any locomotion by any dream character), human "strangers" (including bogeymen or frightening figures more generally), feelings (positive or negative), and portrayal of interpersonal (or intercharacter) interaction. With such a list, you may well wonder what remains for the children to have dreamed. Present in their reports in amounts generally uncharacteristic of later dreaming were themes revolving around body states (sleep itself, interestingly enough, as well as hunger) and animal characterization. Thus, for example, we have reports in which a child imagines himself to be sleeping some place other than where he is (e.g., in a bathtub, at a refreshment stand) and in which animals are relatively statically portrayed (e.g., chickens are eating, a fish is in a bowl by the side of a river).

What are we to make of such reports? Are they believable? If so, what do they have to say about the place of dreams in children's mental development?

One way to estimate the credibility of dream reports is through the examination of other variables with which such reports are correlated. For example, if children with the largest numbers of reported dreams and of dreams with animal characters could be shown to have had the poorest accuracy in tests of waking memory, we probably wouldn't place much faith in their dream reports or in the phenomenon of animal characterization. In the studies reviewed here, extensive information was collected for each child on her or his cognitive competency and typical waking performances. Thus the correlated-variable strategy can be used to evaluate the children's dream reports.

At ages 3–5, the correlational data have a mixed story to tell about the children's "dreams." The reporting of dreams was strongly related to differences in children's general expressiveness and in the degree of their orientation to adults. This pattern makes sense, of course, because the child's nighttime task in the laboratory was to talk about dreams to an adult experimenter. However, this pattern presumably means that some relatively unexpressive children may have had dreams they chose not to talk about and that some highly adult-oriented children may have made up dreams just to have something to be able to tell the experimenter. Possibly these two tendencies might have canceled each other out (leaving the 27% estimation of dream occurrence relatively accurate). Differences in reporting dreams were not, however, related to other variables that might be expected to influence report rate, such as how quickly and how well children awaken, the level of their understanding of what dreams are, and their ability to remember and describe pictures from memory.

The distinctive positive features of children's reports, on the other hand, emerged as relatively credible ones by correlational criteria. Children who reported animal characters to the relative exclusion of human characters scored high on measures of verbal comprehension and visuospatial cognitive skill. Children who reported sleeping-self themes to the relative exclusion of overt activity by nonself characters also were high on similar traits, as well as being relatively advanced in their level of preoperational reasoning. They also were older than their peers. Thus, the most characteristic dream reports of 3- to 5-year-olds (sleeping-self, static-animal) seemed to be credible, coming as they did from the relatively brightest children. Furthermore, these children had talents in specific areas (visuospatial reasoning) that can more plausibly be associated with making dreams than with describing them. That is, there is some reason to think that the differences in dream reports aren't just a function of some children attending to or describing their dreams better than others: They may also have to do with genuine differences in the quantity and kind of dream experiences the children could have.

What do children's reports at ages 3–5 have to say about the possibility of children's dreaming at still earlier ages? Because even the most talented 4- and 5-year-olds reported dreams that were very meager intellectual accomplishments (static imagery, no narrative quality, no social interaction, etc.), it does not seem likely that there can be much dream accomplishment—or much dreaming at all—in the earliest part of the preoperational period (ages 18 months–3 years).

The sleeping-self reports of the 3- to 5-year-olds have several properties that obviously reflect preoperational reasoning: episodic and static mental imagery, absence of narrative planning, failure to decenter from the self. The animal reports generally also involve static imagery and an absence of narration but they seem, on the face of it, to have achieved a more competent portrayal of nonself characters.

Because animal reports seemed to be more characteristic of younger children in the 3–5 group, however, it appears likely that the animal character is the first form in which children's own interests are vested. Several bits of evidence support this hypothesis. First, there were correlations between children's own assertiveness and aggressiveness and their portrayal of animal characters. Second, independent observations of children's waking stories in the early preoperational period suggest that children frequently intermix self and animal descriptions: "Stories which name an animal as a character at the beginning may end by assuming that the child himself is the animal; the essential continuity seems to lie in the action rather than in the nature of the character."[67] Third, children's recourse to animal characterization later declines precisely when they first seem able to portray an active human-self character. The key to the prevalence of animal characters in children's earliest dreams (as well as in their waking mental life) may lie in: (1) murky boundaries between self and animal models, and (2) the more objectified nature of these models. When you don't as yet know yourself very well (either depictively or conceptually), then animal characters (and also stuffed toy animals) may serve as transitional concepts through which the self's interests can be expressed. It's not mere chance, then, that the cautionary fairy tales (and cartoons, etc.) we address to children do so using animal role models.[68]

The particular kind of animal children dream about is also indicative of their self-investment in the dream. Typically, dream animals were neither highly familiar and individualized (their own pets, for example) nor very exotic or frightening. Dream animals tended most often to come from two classes: domesticated farm animals or relatively familiar and unaggressive undomesticated animals (frogs, birds, deer, etc.). They were, in short, the type of animals that probably best lend themselves to self-identification.

The absence of frightening animals is part of a larger pattern (no bogeyman, no victimization of the self, no feelings) that offers little support to psychiatric theories ascribing complicated emotional representations to young children. It should be readily apparent that 3- to 5-year olds' dreams are just about what you'd expect were the production of dreams to be viewed as a cognitive achievement, and were Piaget's description of the cognitive attainments of 3- to 5-year-olds approximately correct. The picture that emerges is one of children who can only organize their consciousness in sleep in the same limited ways and to the same limited extent that they can organize their waking thought. Preoperational dreaming, no less than waking preoperational reasoning, is constrained by defects both in knowledge and in procedures that flexibly organize and transform that knowledge.

It seems reasonably clear that dreaming, and not just reporting dreams, is constrained in this way. Three- to five-year-old children, for example, have the skills both to observe and to describe activities and other people. That their dream reports are singularly lacking in verbs of motion and human nouns cannot reflect poverty in children's ability to observe or describe. Rather, it must indicate peculiarities in the phenomenon under description, peculiarities which can sensibly be related to known waking limitations in their ability to reconstruct interpersonal reality symbolically.

The peculiar nature of dreaming in 3–5-year-olds, then, seems to be attributable to well-known defects and limitations of preoperational reasoning more generally. An interesting question, in view of the many ways in which preoperational dreaming is so *different* (and so predictably different) from our own, is whether there are any respects in which the two are the same. Is there some essential aspect of dreaming which remains constant despite far-reaching differences in how effectively it can be accomplished? As it turns out, there is:

> from its apparent outset, dreaming is not a "play-back" of undifferentiated global units from one's past experience. Children's earliest REM reports represent a *creative recombination* of memory and knowledge. In this sense, the children are *dreaming,* and not merely remembering discrete events or retrieving self-contained packages of knowledge. Dreaming seems inherently to involve the analysis of objects and, particularly notable even in early childhood, of events, as collections of detachable features, features whose recombination in dream imagery rarely if ever corresponds to their most familiar waking constellation.[69]

From this consistency in the nature of dreaming, in the face of otherwise striking differences between its earliest and its later forms, we may draw two tentative conclusions. *First,* a critical feature of dream consciousness is that it synthesizes otherwise unrelated or discrepant mnemonic elements. I suggest that the need for this kind of synthesis results from relatively diffuse and widespread mnemonic activation occurring in the absence of voluntary regulation. To make conscious sense of such activation implies the fusion of disparate mnemonic units. *Second,* insofar as mental skills enter into dreaming, they should be skills of analysis and synthesis—abilities to analyze concepts into parts and to fuse such parts together into novel wholes. It's already been suggested that the beginning of analytic reasoning marks the start of the preoperational period, in which dreaming first becomes possible. As we'll see shortly, individual differences in mental analysis and synthesis also seem to explain later differences in levels of dream experiencing (reporting) among children.

What are we to make, finally, of the majority of REM awakenings, which produced no dream report at all? No doubt the children might have had dreams, but then forgot them. That sometimes seems to happen to adults, and there's no reason why it shouldn't happen to preschoolers, too—and probably more often. But can it account for a 73% rate of "no-dream" awakenings? I think not. From the apparent cognitive requirements of dream production (which seem only rudimentarily satisfied by preschoolers), and from the dreams they do report (which are so notably lacking in most of the features we consider characteristic of dreaming), I think the wiser conclusion is that much of children's REM sleep may be unaccompanied by the conscious mental synthesis we know as dreaming.

This, in turn, may have a good deal to say about the quality of consciousness 3- to 5-year-old children can achieve in wakefulness. The whole quality of thought and behavior during the preoperational period is such that it's difficult to imagine that consciousness could be present to the degree or in the form that we know it. Indeed, Piaget's earliest descriptions of preoperational reasoning suggest the relative absence of consciousness. Verbal reasoning, for example, is not yet internalized. As Piaget notes, the child may talk incesssantly about what he or she is doing or going to do. It's almost as if there are no means by which children could keep their thoughts to themselves, even if they wanted to. According to Piaget, the child's "attention is wholly turned toward the external world, toward action, in no way directed toward thought as a medium interposed between the world and himself."[70] Elsewhere, Piaget speaks of "the faint degree of consciousness present" in preoperational reasoning, and of the "unconsciousness" which preoperational "egocentrism entails."[71]

In the context of such statements and of the evidence on which they rest, it would not be surprising if consciousness (i.e., dreaming) were largely absent during REM sleep in the earliest years of human symbolic thought. Both the incidence and the nature of dream consciousness from ages 3 to 5, as these may be guessed at from children's dream reports, may be still one more bit of evidence in favor of Piaget's hypothesis that consciousness, too, depends on mental growth. Children's dreams may, in fact, be our best evidence as to the episodic quality and rudimentary nature of early human consciousness, for when children are telling their dreams they're doing something it's just about impossible to get them to do when they're awake: Unwittingly, they're directly describing their conscious mental state.

Transition to Concrete Operations (Ages 5–7).   When the same children were studied 2 years later, they did not report dreams significantly more often than they had at ages 3–5, although their reported dreams were significantly longer than they'd been at those younger ages. Specifically, while the overall rate of reporting dreams was only slightly changed (up from 27% to 31%), children's reports of their dreams were, on the average, three times as long as earlier (from 14 to 41 words).

But the most dramatic changes were in the *content* of children's dream reports. The major changes were these: (1) a significant increase in the portrayal of physical movement such as locomotion, probably indexing the onset of kinematic (continuous, movielike) mental imagery in children's dreams; (2) a shift in focus from the portrayal of body-state concerns (sleep, in particular) to the portrayal of social interaction; (3) a relative shift from animal dominance to human dominance in dream characterization (animals remained relatively frequent, but human characters now were more so); (4) the appearance of primitive storylines linking dream events together in a linear sequence; and (5) a significant increase in (i.e., the first appearance of) novel or wholly invented human characters—people not otherwise known to the child.

Thus children ages 5–7 describe, and apparently can visually image, activities with continuous movement. Dream reports can include such events as a man swimming or cows running around in a field. Along with the possibility of successive imagery, children also demonstrate the possibility of linear storylines. There's nothing very fancy about the "plots" children describe: they're like the storyline that accompanies unedited home movies, which simply show what happened next (and still next after that). These storylines do indicate, however, sequential planning of imagery, which was largely absent at ages 3–5. There also are indications of reduced egocentrism in the kinds of events portrayed in children's dreams at this stage. Drawing on their increasingly organized knowledge of others and the social world, children's dreams seem to have shifted from a dominant concern with the self (and its body states) toward the representation of social interactions among human characters. Perhaps drawing on children's increased analytic skills, it's not just events but now also persons who can be portrayed in ways that intermix or generalize across the features of particular known instances. The people in children's dreams now may correspond to no one literally known to them.

The correlates of children's reports at ages 5–7 suggest, moreover, that these *reports* were generally credible accounts of children's dream *experiences*. Children who reported relatively many dreams were particularly talented, for instance, at tasks requiring visual or spatial analysis, as were children who showed significant increases in dream reporting from ages 3–5. One such task is the Block Design test of the Wechsler intelligence test battery. Here the child must look at models or pictures of red and white patterns, and then recreate those patterns with blocks. Some of the block faces are all red, some are all white, and some have one color above the diagonal and the other color below it. To match the demonstrated pattern, the child must be able to analyze its components, and thus reconstruct it, on a block-by-block basis. The mental analysis and synthesis skills measured by this test are evidently important to effective dream construction, because Block Design scores were the most reliable predictors of dream reporting on REM awakenings from ages 5–7 through early adolescence. Because these skills don't seem to have much to do with memory or with verbal description, the most plausible interpretation of this relationship is that it involves real differences in making and experiencing dreams, rather than just differences in remembering or describing them.

Interestingly, Block Design scores also predicted the frequency of non-REM dream reporting at ages 5–7. Such reporting was, overall, relatively rare: only 8% of non-REM awakenings produced dream reports. But on correlational criteria, at this and later ages (when non-REM dream reporting was generally increasing), children's non-REM reports were as credible as their REM reports. This finding is not surprising given another one: At ages 5–7, children who reported the most REM dreams also tended to report the most non-REM and sleep-onset dreams. This evidence bolsters arguments from the previous chapter that the same dream-production system is used in different physiological states.

Another interesting observation is that, despite children's evidently greater talent in making reasonably well-formed dreams, they didn't report dreams significantly more often at ages 5–7 than they did at ages 3–5. A few children showed striking increases in the frequency with which they told dreams on REM awakenings (e.g., from 8% at ages 4–5 to 60% at ages 6–7), but most did not. At minimum, this negative finding suggests that dream reporting can't be increased just by socialization at school. During the study year described here, all the children were attending school, and presumably learning to acquiesce to requests from adults other than their parents. But this training apparently didn't increase the children's ability to attend to or describe their dreams. Possibly, then, the problem wasn't attention or description after all, but the fact that dreams often just weren't "there" to be remembered and reported. Children's continuingly low frequency of dream reporting from REM sleep at ages 5–7 suggests that they still find it difficult to consciously organize their own symbolic activity.

Considered separately, a number of the changes or new features in children's dreams at ages 5–7 seemed credible by correlational criteria. The reporting of human strangers, for example, was predicted by waking measures of cognitive skill. The length of children's dream reports (and the story development increased length permits) also seemed to be related to their waking mental abilities.

Several features of adult dreaming still were largely absent, however, in the reports of 5–7-year-olds. Children's reports still were not as long as adult reports collected under comparable conditions (the same amount of REM sleep before awakening) and they did not have the narrative complexity of adult dream reports. Active participation of a self character still was generally lacking in the children's reported dreams. (Perhaps in consequence of this fact, reliable reports of feelings accompanying dreams still were absent.) The self seems to have been left behind in the shift from passively portrayed body-states to actively portrayed social interaction. At ages 5–7, there's movement and social interaction in children's dreams, but the children aren't participating in it "themselves."

Given the fact that 5–7-year-olds are only beginning to function at Piaget's concrete-operational level of reasoning, it's not surprising that their dreams are not yet as accomplished as adults'. Nor should it be surprising, given the survey of waking mental development earlier in this chapter, that active and accurate self-representation in conscious imagination still is a particular problem. Some findings, in fact, suggested that the children still were using other characters—animals, and, now humans as well—as means for expressing their own interests. For example, immature and impulsive children were most likely to dream of animal characters, and the overt physical activity of *other* dream characters was related to the *dreamer's own* level of waking activity.

Thus, imagining activities by others—a new achievement at ages 5–7— seems to precede, and in some sense to preclude, active self-portrayal. From the point of view of its cognitive prerequisites, it would seem inherently more difficult to have a dream in which you act than merely to "watch" dream events enacted by others. If the self-participatory dream is seen from the perspective of an omniscient overview, it requires a splitting of the self such that one self watches while another acts. If it is seen "through the eyes" of the self character, it involves rapid shifts in perspective as the self moves about, shifts not required from the perspective of a global overview of self and others.

Much remains to be learned about how children experience their earliest activity dreams, and about why self-representation is a particularly difficult achievement in them. Thus far, the questioning of children about these matters has been relatively crude, and our knowledge is correspondingly meager. There is the promise, however, that future research can fill in some of the missing facts, and that these facts will contribute to a better picture not only of how dreams change with cognitive maturation but also of the development of conscious self-representation and of the self more generally.

Early Concrete Operational Period (Ages 7–9).   When the same group of children previously discussed was studied still 2 years later, their REM dream reports again showed both quantitative and qualitative changes. The quantitative changes included (as from ages 3–5 to 5–7) an increase in typical report length (from 41 to 72 words). Unlike the previous transition period, however, this one was also marked by a significant increase in the rate at which children reported a dream on REM awakenings (up from 31% to 48%).

From ages 3 to 9, growth in dreaming was not similarly reflected in how frequently children reported dreams, and in how long a dream they described when they did report one. The two indices were essentially uncorrelated with one another. One reason for the independence of these two measures of dream "potential" probably is that as children increase in their ability to experience dreaming during periods of REM sleep, these increases are in the form of initially rudimentary (brief) dream episodes. It also seemed to be the case that the length of children's reports better reflected children's steadily developing skills at verbalizing, while their frequency of dream reporting may better have reflected their actual production of dream experience. For example, increases in report length were observed throughout early childhood, while significant increases in report frequency occurred only when children entered the period of concrete operational reasoning (i.e., when they may have acquired the skills through which effective dream construction becomes possible). Likewise, correlates of individual differences in dream length never included measures like the Block Design test, which, as we've seen, did predict individual differences in report frequency, presumably through mediation at the level of dream production rather than at that of dream description. However, at ages 7–9, even report length had some correlates suggesting real differences in the amount of dream experienced. In particular, measures of visual thinking and narrative skill predicted report length.

By ages 7–9, in fact, children's REM reports were not much different in length than those of children studied at later ages, nor even than those of adults studied under the same conditions. Thus, as indicated by report length, competence at dreaming was well-developed by these ages. As indexed by report frequency, however, children's dream competence still was somewhat inferior to that shown by older children and by adults. Once again, the frequency measure may be the better reflection of the underlying dream process. Specifically, if that process depends on general cognitive development, then the 7–9-year-olds probably had not yet developed or generalized all of the critical features of concrete operational reasoning.

Children's reporting of dreams on non-REM awakenings also increased significantly from ages 5–7 to 7–9, from 8% to 21%. This result supports the ideas both of a general increase in dream competence with the onset of concrete-operational reasoning and of a common dream-production system for REM and non-REM sleep. Once again, it was observed that children with relatively high rates of dream reporting on REM awakenings also had relatively high rates of dream reporting on non-REM (and sleep-onset) awakenings. Non-REM report rates were also correlated with Block Design scores, further suggesting a common process underlying REM and non-REM dreaming.

Children's increases in REM and non-REM dreaming showed a common pattern in another respect. Both occurred predominantly on awakenings made later in the night, i.e., toward the time of spontaneous morning awakening. In addition, the non-REM reports came predominantly from awakenings made in portions of non-REM sleep with higher cortical activation (i.e., "lighter" stages of non-REM sleep). These data agree with the supposition made in earlier chapters that dreaming depends not merely on the presence of an effective dream production system but also on relatively diffuse or intense activation of mnemonic elements. That is, there needs to be both a system to make sense of what's happening mentally and a state in which relatively many things *are* happening.

The changes in children's dreams from ages 5–7 to 7–9 were not, however, merely quantitative. In three significant respects, they were also qualitative: narrative quality, self-representation, and character "psychology." The change in narrative quality was roughly like that found at a certain stage in the development of children's waking stories: from stories which are merely sequentially ordered events ("I did this, and then I did that, and then she did this") to stories unified by a common theme or plot. Such a theme or plot oversees the unfolding of dream events at ages 7–9 in the sense that events are part of a larger pattern, rather than merely things that just happen one after the other, and in the sense that the portrayal of that pattern may involve joining together events occurring in different contexts. Organization is by thematic coherence, rather than merely by temporal succession. In effect, the child's dream now can be more like an edited, professional film than like a home movie.

A second qualitative change in children's dreams at ages 7–9 is that they involve significantly more participation in the dream by a self character. Compared to ages 5–7, the dreamer character is more likely to move around and to initiate and receive social interaction. Probably, these increases reflect the first genuinely active self-participation in children's dreams. The incidence of such participation was correlated with measures of waking cognitive skill, as would be expected for a feature of dream representation implying (as we've already noted) relatively complex cognitive mediation.

Interestingly, coincidental with this rise in self-representation there was a decrease (by about one third) in the number of dreams with animal characters. It is especially interesting that the children still reporting such dreams were those with poorer test performances on mental skill tests. One of these tests determines how successfully the child can discriminate living from nonliving objects, and assesses the maturity of the child's reasoning about this distinction. These observations support the idea discussed earlier that animal characters in preoperational dreams may, in fact, be primitive forms of self-representation.

Another sign of the appearance of mature self-representation at ages 7–9 lies in the pattern of correlation for particular acts in which the self character engages. Recall that, at earlier ages, what the child was actually like was likely to be reflected in which *non*self characters appeared and what they did in the dream. At ages 7–9, however, friendly acts by the *self* in dreams were initiated by children independently determined to be friendly, and aggressive acts by the *self* in dreams were initiated by children independently determined to be aggressive. Such findings suggest the child's development not only of a reasonably coherent self-concept, but also of a reasonably accurate one. That is, the dream self is continuous with the kind of self *others* see. The child now must be capable of taking another's point of view toward her- or himself, and of incorporating that perspective in self-representation.

Qualitative changes in the "psychology" of dream characterization are reflected in the first reliable appearance in dream reports of ascriptions of thoughts and feelings to dream characters. That is, the dream now can proceed on a psychological as well as on a physical plane. The rates of appearance of both thoughts and feelings in children's dreams were related to waking cognitive skill. Thus, it was not the more "emotional" children who reported dream feelings, but the children who were more cognitively talented. Once again, this indicates that new achievements in dream representation arise as evolving cognitive skill permits them to. Since the correlates of having characters think and feel were similar, it seems that feelings first occur in dreams in response to increased comprehension of inner mental life in general, rather than as a function of any specifically emotional characteristic of the dreamer.

The particular feeling to which the prior summary applies, and the one children most generally reported, was happiness. The character to whom this feeling was ascribed was, almost invariably, the self. Likewise, the significant increases in social interaction by the self at ages 7–9 occurred specifically in the area of friendly social exchange. As reflected in their dreams, children's earliest coherent self-representations in consciousness are relatively benign. Studies of children's waking comprehension of feelings also indicate that happiness is the earliest and most easily identified human emotion.[72]

One finding about children's dream reports at ages 7–9 deserves mention, for it qualifies a finding reported earlier for 5–7-year-olds. You'll recall that, at ages 5–7, children first reported unfamiliar characters ("strangers") in their dreams, and that, at this age, the frequency of dreams with strangers was highest in the brightest children. At ages 7–9, however, dreaming of strangers occurred most often for the least gifted children, whereas dreaming of known persons from outside the child's own family occurred most often for the most gifted children. One interpretation of these findings is that the "strangers" at ages 5–7 weren't really that, but rather were poor imaginal approximations to known persons whom the dreamer in some sense "meant" to portray. The brightest children recognized them as poor approximations to known persons, but the duller children did not (at ages 5–7, it was these children who claimed most often to have dreamed of friends and acquaintances). Following this reasoning, by ages 7–9 the brightest children could now really imagine friends and acquaintances, whereas the duller children still could not (but now recognized this to be the case, hence claiming more often to dream of strangers).

This interpretation is, of course, highly speculative, but it does point out a potential problem in discerning the growth of versatility in characterization in dreams. Changes in representational skill may be obscured in early development by differences in how scrupulously dream characters are identified in waking reports. Several bits of evidence are consistent with the interpretation, however: (1) At ages 5–7, frequent dreaming of *highly* familiar persons (family members) was predicted by waking cognitive skill, as if dreaming of even intimately known humans was still a difficult achievement; (2) at ages 9–11 (in another group of children), dreaming of friends and acquaintances no longer was predicted by waking mental ability (this "hurdle" having been mastered by all), but dreaming of strangers was (this hurdle now being surmounted only by the brightest children); (3) most of the "strangers" children reported at ages 5–7 must have been vaguely portrayed, because children typically could not identify their approximate ages (e.g., child or adult).

Underlying this interpretation is the idea that the ease with which children should be able mentally to image other persons should be a function of how familiar those persons are (i.e., of how much knowledge the children have of such persons). Family-member imagery should be easiest, and come first; images of friends and acquaintances should be somewhat more difficult, and come later; and images of mostly or wholly unfamiliar persons should be most difficult, and come last. The problem with this idea is that "strangers" of some sort seem to come relatively early (at ages 5–7). The interpretation previously advanced preserves the hypothesis of a relationship between person-knowledge and ease-of-imaging by supposing that these strangers are, in effect, poorly imaged acquaintances, and that it's only later that strangers as such can be imaged. The interpretation clearly might be wrong. But discussing it has perhaps indicated not only some pitfalls in studying how children acquire and use knowledge by way of their dreams, but also some of the ways in which children's dreams permit us to ask (and may someday permit us to answer) some very interesting questions about their development and conscious portrayal of interpersonal knowledge.

For those who have followed the presentation of this chapter in its entirety, there can, again, be little occasion for surprise in the data presented in this section. At ages 7–9, as was true also of ages 3–5 and 5–7, the nature and evolution of children's dreaming follows predictably from what is known about their waking mental development. But you have seen once again some ways in which dreaming is a special part of mental development. For example, at ages 7–9, children's dreams may contain especially rich reflections of how they come to organize and to be able to consciously represent their knowledge of themselves and of their social world.

Later Concrete Operational Period (Ages 9–13).   Later in the period of concrete operational reasoning, children's REM dream reports are not only comparably long to those of adults, they are also volunteered at a comparable rate. Moreover, these two indices of "dream potential" (length of report, frequency of report) are now positively correlated with one another. Children who give longer reports now also give reports more often. Thus, there is reason to believe that dream development has stabilized, and that it has reached stabilization at a level comparable to that of adult dream competence.

There seem to be few new distinctive accomplishments in the form and content of children's dreams in this period. Rather, achievements imperfectly accomplished at earlier ages now seem subject to consolidation. Specifically:

1.   The participation of a self character in children's dreams increases to relative parity with that of nonself dream characters. Animal characterization decreases correspondingly.

2.   Feelings in dreams become increasingly diversified. Fear and anger, for instance, now seem to be genuine possibilities as feeling accompaniments in children's dreams. However, most dreams are still experienced without feeling, and happiness is still the most frequently reported dream feeling.

3.   In line with the interpretation of human character development in dreams given in the preceding section, at ages 9–11, relatively bright children reported human strangers most often. That is, for the first time, it may be possible for some children at ages 9–11 to synthesize human depictive information in the creation of genuinely novel characters. Children high in novel characterization at ages 9–11 also scored high on the same Block Design test which elsewhere has been a predictor of new achievements in dream quality.

4.   Predictably, children's dreams reached new high points in concrete portrayal of physical activity and social interaction.

5.   Perhaps as a consequence of this high-level stabilization of dream competence at ages 9–13, children's dreams seemed to reflect their waking interests and behaviors even better than they did at ages 7–9.

Sex differences in children's dreams may be used to illustrate this last point. You've perhaps been wondering, in reading about children's dreams, whether it's really justifiable to group together observations from boys and girls. By and large, however, children's dreams do not seem to differ markedly in form or substance according to the gender of the dreamer (at least for the sort of dream features we've been discussing here). This observation surprises many people, who imagine that boys' and girls' dreams should be very different because their waking behaviors seem to be so different. Two points need to be made here. First, against a baseline of their similarities, boys' and girls' waking behaviors probably aren't as different as we imagine, particularly in earlier childhood. Second, children's dreams can't be affected by the sex differences we think *we* observe, but only by those which the children themselves think *they* know. That is, if dreaming is based on the dreamer's knowledge of self and world, then the relevant factor in predicting sex differences in dreaming is the *knowledge* that boys and girls are acquiring and organizing about sex roles.

Turning this argument around, one can look at children's REM reports for reflections of sex differences in mental organization. That is, dreams may be of special value in indicating the "inner" side of what it means to be a boy or a girl. From this perspective, from ages 7–13 the difference between being a boy and being a girl is first and foremost a matter of being more interested in same-sex peers than in opposite-sex peers. That is, the earliest and most reliable sign of differentiation between boys' and girls' REM dreams was in the gender of the friends or other age-mates they contained as characters. Boys dreamed more of boys, and girls more of girls. This tendency was most marked at ages 11–13. But, by these ages, boys' and girls' dreams were beginning to diverge in other respects as well. Specifically, the girls' dreams were containing less aggressive behavior than were the boys', as if being female now reflected differences in ideas about *how* to interact with others as well as about *who* these significant others are.[73] Later, in early adolescence, girls' dreams also would retain greater ties to their family (as characters) and to their home (as a setting) than would boys' dreams. Our understanding of when and how boys' and girls' dreams begin to diverge in this way is as yet rather meager. But the promise here is considerable. Once again, children's dreams may provide a unique viewpoint on an important problem in human development: the origins and nature of sex differences in interpersonal knowledge and in the organization of conscious experience.

Early Formal Operational Period (Ages 13–15)   Just as many people expect large sex differences in children's dreams, many also expect major changes in dreaming in adolescence. These expectations derive from the observation that adolescence seems to have momentous psychological consequences in waking life, and from theories that stress the centrality of sexual development in human experience. Once again, however, the evidence does not fit these expectations. Specifically, although children's dreams seem to show some characteristic changes in early adolescence, these changes aren't large. They seem, moreover, to stem not so much from children's new social or sexual status as from their new mental status.

Specifically, in several respects, the form of children's dreams seems to become more abstract in early adolescence. (1) There are fewer dreams with concrete portrayals of physical activity. Most sensitive to this change are forms of action (locomotion) and interaction (friendly social exchanges) that develop relatively early in dream maturation and that had become staples in dream representation by ages 11–13. Relatively well-preserved are later developing and more "mental" forms of dream activity (speech, perception, thought). (2) There are corresponding decreases in the portrayal in the dream of body-states such as sleep, hunger, and thirst, which reach new developmental lows in dream representation. (3) There are increases in the creation of novel dream characters and settings, relative to known ones, suggesting an increased ability to abstract properties of the known world in the conscious creation of a heretofore unknown one. Correlational evidence suggests, moreover, that this increased dream "distortion" depends on levels of cognitive skill. That is, growth in mental ability permits dream distortion, rather than (as clinical dream theories might predict) personality disturbance compelling it.

Correlational evidence also suggests three additional ways in which children's dream worlds are beginning to differ in early adolescence. (1) Active self-representation (as at ages 7–9) seems to be a relatively difficult achievement. It is reduced in frequency, and more gifted children (on Block Design and other measures) report the most dream self-participation. (2) It now seems to be possible for children to have dreams without a strong narrative component; dreams, for example, in which they "zoom in" on some object and have no sense of a larger setting or narrative context for that object. (3) The relationship between children's waking behavior and their dream portrayals seems to become increasingly complex. The first two of these observations suggest new representational possibilities in the dream medium; the third probably reflects a new quality of organization in children's waking knowledge. Let's consider each in a little more detail.

Both the reduction in active self-representation and the relationship between residual levels of such representation and mental skill suggest some new difficulty in portraying the self. The difficulty is new because by ages 11–13 active self-portrayal, as we've seen, becomes about as frequent as the portrayal of active others. A possible basis for this difficulty may be found in waking observations that it is only toward adolescence that children can think of self–other exchanges from the perspective of a third party (rather than from that of the self, other, or self-and-other).[74] Perhaps in their dreams, too, early adolescents are beginning to experiment with new modes of representation in which a third-party vantage point is being adopted toward all dream characters, including the self. Direct evidence on this point is at present meager, and more systematic questioning of children regarding *how* they apprehend the events of their dreams will be required to confirm this line of explanation. However, what little evidence is available does seem to suggest that the kind of active self-representation which first appears in dreams at ages 7–9 is one in which the child sees the dream "through the eyes" of the self character, while that kind of self-representation may not be so typical for early adolescents, who may be beginning to experiment with the perspective of the detached, sideline observer.

More REM dreams have vague or unclassifiable settings in early adolescence than formerly. This seems largely attributable to dreams with a peculiar new format, in which an object is the focus of interest and that object has little background or narrative context. One girl, for instance, dreamed of manipulating a green-tipped pen. Another time, she dreamed of dragging a great big ribbon bow around with her. In each instance, the dream seemed to focus on the object, with little narrative development and no sense of any particular setting. Such dreams, which seem very primitive, were not in fact reported at earlier ages, and were reported most often at adolescence by children who were mentally talented (e.g., at Block Design and other tests of visuospatial analysis). Thus they are, despite their seemingly primitive form, new *achievements* in dream construction.

As noted in the previous chapter, isolated object-imagery is most typically experienced by adults during non-REM sleep. Children's non-REM reports, however, begin as scaled-down versions of their REM narratives. That is, "thought" and "isolated image" reports are no more characteristic of non-REM sleep than of REM sleep in early development. Evidently, it's only when children approach the stage of formal operational reasoning that they begin to experience the more fragmentary images and thoughts that help to define typical non-REM ideation for adults. The evidence regarding both when such ideation appears (relatively late in childhood) and for whom it appears (children with high analytic abilities) suggests that more fragmentary kinds of non-REM mental experience are the ones that require more ability to elaborate. Apparently, when the ability to organize consciousness in this way is first present, it is exercised not only in non-REM sleep (to which it seems to be largely confined in adults) but also in REM sleep.

More generally, if one had to make a summary statement about children's REM versus non-REM reports, it would be that they seem less different than do adults'. Initially, REM and non-REM (and sleep-onset) dreaming seem to start out with the same general format: a small-scale dramatization of events. Qualitative differences of dreams from different sleep stages seem to emerge only slowly, as REM reports lengthen and become more complex narratively, and (later) as non-REM reports begin to show some of their distinctive *non*narrative forms. It's interesting that this latter development initially is not limited just to non-REM sleep, but spills over into REM dreaming as well. All this evidence strongly supports the main conclusion of the previous chapter, that there is basically just one dream-production system.

In addition to the new representational possibilities dreams assume at adolescence, possibilities that permit greater diversity of ideation within and across sleep stages in adults, there also seem to be new ways that dreams can reflect waking life experiences in adolescence. The relation of waking aggressiveness to dream portrayal of aggressive acts illustrates this change. At ages 7–9, for example, children who received a high rating in unprovoked physical aggression to their peers dreamed most often of aggression by the self character. Presumably this relationship depended not only on children's ability to represent themselves in consciousness (first generally apparent at these ages) but also on their inclusion in their self-concept of traits that other observers would also use to describe them. That is, they were portraying themselves as they "really were." At ages 13–15, however, children who were aggressive most often in their dreams were not aggressive, but anxious and insecure, in waking life. This association also makes sense, but of a different kind. It suggests the elaboration of a mental world in which the conscious self is less constrained by objective reality, yet is better able to redress or compensate for that reality. In addition to the reality others see, there is now a mental reality, which is related to the objective world, but different from it.

Children's dreams at this point can begin to portray these systematic mental representations of the world. Because the dream reflects what the child thinks he or she knows rather than what's "real," it now assumes importance as an index of a new plane of inner reality. Since the hallmark of adolescence is the way in which inner reality transcends—and sometimes distorts—the more mundane world of everyday activity, the adolescent's dreams may be especially revealing of the evolution of such a reality. That is, just as younger children's dreams can reveal their increasing understanding of what is, adolescents' dreams can reveal their increasing mental elaboration of what might or should be.

3. THE GROWTH OF MIND, DREAMING, AND CONSCIOUSNESS

Children's dream reports change over time in ways that might have been predicted from what is known more generally about their symbolic maturation. If one takes children's *reports* of their dreams as reflecting what their *dreams* are like, then certain conclusions seem inescapable.

Dreaming is a symbolic act, a conscious organization of mental representations. As such, it is limited throughout childhood by defects in what children know symbolically and in how well they are able consciously to represent and organize this knowledge. Children can dream only as well as they consciously can think. Piaget's observations suggest that competence in waking conscious reflection is slow to develop. Here, we have seen that the same seems to be true of competence in dreaming. This means that children's dreams can't, in general, be very accurate reflections of how children behave. Rather, the importance of children's dreams lies in the fact that they reflect the quality and organization of children's symbolic knowledge of self and world and children's ability *consciously* to organize and reprocess that knowledge.

While it might have been imagined, a priori, that sleep (i.e., a dreaming mode of cognitive organization) would afford a more restricted environment in which reflective consciousness could be experienced, the data indicate a relatively close relationship between progressions in dream development and the development of waking symbolic competencies. In fact, it has been shown that, for the younger (preoperational to early concrete operational) children whose dreaming has been described here, there are "stages" of dream development which individual children reliably pass one after the other, and that the precise age at which they reach a new stage is at least partly predictable from independent measures of their waking cognitive growth. Furthermore, the dream stages correspond both in time and in substance to comparable stages in waking mental development.[75]

The stage-dependence of children's *earliest* dreams, specifically, the very rudimentary quality of image processing which they evidence, argues strongly against any theory of dreaming which supposes that dream experience is simply a by-product of autonomous physiological activation in sensory systems in the brain.[76] Children's dreams are not nearly so accomplished imaginally as their waking perceptual behavior would lead us to expect. Nor are they nearly so accomplished imaginally as we might even suppose children's waking perceptual experience to be. Rather, the imagery of children's dreams seems equally as limited as is their waking "mental" imagery, that is, the imaginal processing they are able deliberately to instigate in wakefulness from a knowledge base in symbolic memory. This observation has something very significant to say about dreaming: It is a process by which *symbolic* control is exercised over modular input systems and over conscious processing of modular-system activity.

In this sense, stages of dream development are phases in a slowly evolving capability to exploit modular systems for other than sensory processing and to use consciousness to process symbolic as well as sensory information. Although consciousness is not synonymous with thinking or symbolic ability, this sort of capability is clearly a part of what is so interesting and so distinctive about the human mind. The unique value of a cognitive-developmental approach to dreaming is that its data are the most likely basis on which we'll understand when and how this capability emerges.

But the nagging problem of report-experience correspondences still threatens the validity of all these conclusions and suggestions. Can we be sure that what children tell us about their dreams is what their dreams are actually like? No, we can't be sure. But the kinds of dream evidence at which we've been looking don't offer much refuge for the skeptic. If 3–5-year-olds are having fancy dreams, just like adults', why don't we see more indication of that fact in their reports? That the children don't describe movement, for instance, is (as we've seen) hard to understand if they are experiencing it. The very nature of the changes observed over time in children's dreams—from no movement to movement, from animals to humans—is difficult to reconcile with the hypothesis that their dream consciousness is not simultaneously changing as well.

Likewise, consider the kinds of waking cognitive variables most strongly related to dreaming and to the appearance of new features in dreaming in early childhood. If it is only children's descriptions of their dreams, and not the dreams themselves, that are changing over time, then why is it that dream-report changes aren't correlated with demonstrated changes in verbal skills or memory performances? Why, instead, does a test like Block Design predict these changes? That's more easily understood if you imagine that the analytic skills and strategies measured by this test actually help children dream better dreams.

It seems more likely, then, that the developmental changes we've been reviewing here *are* changes in the dreams children make and experience. That is, we've been looking at how the human dream-production system develops in early life. Among the other interesting observations we've been able to make is one that relates to our concern in the previous chapter: whether we have one or several ways of making dreams. In early development, the evidence seems relatively clear. There is one system, which generates the same kind of dream experience no matter the state (REM or non-REM) in which it's activated. Another significant result of our look at the development of a human dream-production system is heightened appreciation of how closely connected dream development is with the growth of the potential for symbolic consciousness, consciousness of our own symbolic activity. In the next chapter, I try to synthesize the results of our researches thus far by describing what the components of the human dream-production system must be, how they are interrelated, and how "consciousness" fits into the mode of their organization.

NOTES

[1] David Foulkes, "Children's Dreams," in Benjamin B. Wolman (ed.), *Handbook of Dreams: Research, Theories and Applications,* New York: Van Nostrand Reinhold, 1979, pp. 131–167.

[2] David Foulkes, *Children's Dreams: Longitudinal Studies,* New York: John Wiley and Sons, 1982.

[3] Graeme S. Halford, "Introduction: The Structural Approach to Cognitive Development," in John A. Keats, Kevin F. Collis, and Graeme S. Halford (eds.), *Cognitive Development: Research Based on a Neo-Piagetian Perspective,* Chichester, England: John Wiley and Sons, 1978, pp. 1–25.

[4] Jean Piaget and Bärbel Inhelder, *The Psychology of the Child,* New York: Basic Books, 1969 (originally published, 1966), ch. 3.

[5] B. Inhelder, I. Lezine, H. Sinclair, and M. Stamback. "Les débuts de la fonction symbolique," *Archives de Psychologie,* 1972, *41*, 187–243.

[6] Piaget and Inhelder, *op. cit.,* pp. 80–83.

[7] Katherine Nelson and Gail Ross, "The Generalities and Specifics of Long-Term Memory in Infants and Young Children," in Marion Perlmutter (ed.), *Children's Memory,* San Francisco: Jossey-Bass, 1980, pp. 87–101. In a study of recollections by two-year-olds, "there was no evidence from any report of a spontaneous (uncued) memory (p. 95)." Yet, "This process is essential to independent thought and imaginative activities . . . (p. 100)."

[8] Susan Sugarman, *Children's Early Thought: Developments in Classification,* New York: Cambridge University Press, 1983.

[9] John H. Flavell, *Cognitive Development,* Englewood Cliffs, N.J.: Prentice-Hall, 1977, p. 62.

[10] Piaget and Inhelder, *op. cit.,* p. 97.

[11] Monique Laurendeau and Adrien Pinard, *The Development of the Concept of Space in the Child,* New York: International Universities Press, 1970, ch. 1.

[12] The account of cognitive maturation in this and the preceding paragraphs is largely based on Piaget and Inhelder, *op. cit.* For data on dream changes in early adolescence and their possible relationship to formal operational reasoning, see Foulkes, *op. cit.,* ch. 8.

[13] Jean Piaget, *Play, Dreams and Imitation in Childhood,* New York: W. W. Norton, 1962 (originally published, 1946).

[14] See David Foulkes, "REM-Dream Perspectives on the Development of Affect and Cognition," *Psychiatric Journal of the University of Ottawa,* 1982, *7*, 48–55.

[15] Piaget and Inhelder, *op. cit.*, p. 61*n*.

[16] Piaget and Inhelder, *op. cit.*, is the basis of this and the preceding examples.

[17] Robert L. Selman, *The Growth of Interpersonal Understanding: Developmental and Clinical Analyses*, New York: Academic Press, 1980.

[18] E.g., Marilyn Shatz and Rochel Gelman, "The Development of Communication Skills: Modifications in the Speech of Young Children as a Function of Listener," *Monographs of the Society for Research in Child Development*, 1973, *38*, No. 5 (Serial No. 152).

[19] Donald J. Foss and David T. Hakes, *Psycholinguistics: An Introduction to the Psychology of Language*, Englewood Cliffs, N.J.: Prentice-Hall, 1978, ch. 8.

[20] *Ibid*, p. 261 (italics added).

[21] Sugarman, *op. cit.*

[22] Robert E. Nisbett and Thomas D. Wilson, "Telling More Than We Can Know: Verbal Reports on Mental Processes," *Psychological Review*, 1977, *84*, 231–259. The more general argument on levels of consciousness is similar to that of Eric A. Lunzer, "The Development of Consciousness," in Geoffrey Underwood and Robin Stevens (eds.), *Aspects of Consciousness*, vol. 1, New York: Academic Press, 1979, pp. 1–19.

[23] Thomas H. Carr, "Consciousness in Models of Human Information Processing: Primary Memory, Executive Control and Input Regulation," in Underwood and Stevens, *op. cit.*, pp. 123–153.

[24] Sigmund Freud, *The Interpretation of Dreams*, New York: Basic Books, 1955 (originally published, 1900), ch. VII.

[25] Paul Roazen, *Freud and His Followers*, New York: New American Library, 1976 (originally published, 1974), p. 58.

[26] Anthony J. Marcel, "Conscious and Unconscious Perception: An Approach to the Relations between Phenomenal Experience and Perceptual Processes," *Cognitive Psychology*, 1983, *15*, 238–300.

[27] *Ibid*, p. 291. Human neuropsychological evidence suggests that while unconscious visual discrimination may be mediated at the thalamic level, cortical mediation may be "necessary for the *conscious experience* of visual phenomena" (Muriel Deutsch Lezak, *Neuropsychological Assessment*, 2nd Edition, New York: Oxford University Press, 1983, p. 65, [italics added]).

[28] William James, *The Principles of Psychology*, vol. I, New York: Dover Books, 1950 (originally published, 1890), ch. X.

[29] Allan Rechtschaffen, "The Single-Mindedness and Isolation of Dreams," *Sleep*, 1978, *1*, 97–109.

[30] Roberta L. Klatzky, *Human Memory: Structures and Processes*, 2nd ed., San Francisco: W. H. Freeman, 1980, pp. 98–100; Peter A. Ornstein (ed.), *Memory Development in Children*, Hillsdale, N.J.: Lawrence Erlbaum Associates, 1978.

[31] The more limited capacity of children's immediate memory has been demonstrated for other than verbal materials (e.g., for geometric forms). See Marshall M. Haith, Frederick J. Morrison, Karen Sheingold, and Paula Mindes, "Short-term Memory for Visual Information in Children and Adults," *Journal of Experimental Child Psychology*, 1970, *9*, 454–469.

[32] Marilyn Shatz, Henry M. Wellman, and Sharon Silber, "The Acquisition of Mental Verbs: A Systematic Investigation of the First Reference to Mental State," *Cognition*, 1983, *14*, 301–321.

[33] Marcel, *loc. cit.*

[34] For example, Jerome S. Bruner, "On Cognitive Growth: I, II," in Jerome S. Bruner, Rose R. Olver, and Patricia M. Greenfield (eds.), *Studies in Cognitive Growth*, New York: John Wiley and Sons, 1966, pp. 1–67; Stephen Michael Kosslyn and Jerome Kagan, " 'Concrete Thinking' and the Development of Social Cognition," in John H. Flavell and Lee Ross

(eds.), *Social Cognitive Development: Frontiers and Possible Futures*, New York: Cambridge University Press, 1981, pp. 82–96.

[35] Jean Piaget and Bärbel Inhelder, *Mental Imagery in the Child*, New York: Basic Books, 1971 (originally published, 1966).

[36] Joseph Jastrow, *Fact and Fable in Psychology*, Boston: Houghton, Mifflin, 1900, pp. 337–370.

[37] For example, Stephen Michael Kosslyn, "The Representational-Development Hypothesis," in Ornstein, *op. cit.*, 157–189.

[38] Nancy H. Kerr, Raymond Corbitt, and Gregory J. Jurkovic, "Mental Rotation: Is it Stage Related?", *Journal of Mental Imagery*, 1980, *4*, 49–56; Jane E. Platt and Sophia Cohen, "Mental Rotation Task Performance as a Function of Age and Training," *Journal of Psychology*, 1981, *108*, 173–178.

[39] Patricia A. Carpenter and Peter Eisenberg, "Mental Rotation and the Frame of Reference in Blind and Sighted Individuals," *Perception and Psychophysics*, 1978, *23*, 117–124.

[40] Zenon Pylyshyn, "The Imagery Debate: Analog Media versus Tacit Knowledge," in Ned Block (ed.), *Imagery*, Cambridge, Mass.: MIT Press, 1981, pp. 151–206.

[41] Piaget and Inhelder, *The Psychology of the Child*, pp. 63–68.

[42] Foss and Hakes, *op. cit.*, ch. 8–9.

[43] See the discussion of Soviet theory and research in Flavell, *op. cit.*, pp. 64–72.

[44] Jerry A. Fodor, *The Language of Thought*, Cambridge, Mass.: Harvard University Press, 1975.

[45] Endel Tulving, *Elements of Episodic Memory*, New York: Oxford University Press, 1983, p. 126 (italics added).

[46] Daniel L. Schacter and Endel Tuving, "Amnesia and Memory Research," in Laird S. Cermak (ed.), *Human Memory and Amnesia*, Hillsdale, N.J.: Lawrence Erlbaum Associates, 1982, pp. 1–32.

[47] Nelson and Ross, *loc. cit.*

[48] Judith Hudson, "Children's Memory for Real World Events," Psychology Department Colloquium, Emory University, 1984.

[49] Shelley Duval and Robert A. Wicklund, *A Theory of Objective Self Awareness*, New York: Academic Press, 1972.

[50] Tulving, *op. cit.*, p. 99.

[51] Jean Piaget, *The Child's Conception of the World*, New York: Harcourt, Brace, 1929, (originally published, 1926); Monique Laurendeau and Adrien Pinard, *Causal Thinking in the Child*, New York: International Universities Press, 1962.

[52] John R. Anderson, "Arguments Concerning Representations for Mental Imagery," *Psychological Review*, 1978, *85*, 249–277. Commentary on this article appeared in the same journal, 1979, vol. *86*.

[53] Jean Piaget, *The Grasp of Consciousness: Action and Concept in the Young Child*, Cambridge, Mass.: Harvard University Press, 1976 (originally published, 1974).

[54] Foss and Hakes, *op. cit.*, p. 241.

[55] William Damon and Daniel Hart, "The Development of Self Understanding from Infancy through Adolescence," *Child Development*, 1982, *53*, 841–864.

[56] Selman, *op. cit.*

[57] Stephen Michael Kosslyn, *Image and Mind*, Cambridge, Mass.: Harvard University Press, 1980.

[58] Piaget, *op. cit.*; Piaget and Inhelder, *Mental Imagery in the Child*.

[59] Arthur N. Applebee, *The Child's Concept of Story: Ages Two to Seventeen*, Chicago: University of Chicago Press, 1978.

[60] Katherine Nelson, "Social Cognition in a Script Framework," in Flavell and Ross, *op.*

cit., pp. 97–118. The concept of script is owed to Roger Schank and Robert Abelson (*Scripts, Plans, Goals and Understanding: An Inquiry into Human Knowledge Structures*, Hillsdale, N.J.: Lawrence Erlbaum Associates, 1977).

[61] Carolyn Uhlinger Shantz, *The Development of Social Cognition*, Chicago: University of Chicago Press, 1975, pp. 20–26.

[62] Rhoda Glasberg and Frances Aboud, "Keeping One's Distance from Sadness: Children's Self-Reports of Emotional Experience," *Developmental Psychology*, 1982, *18*, 287–293.

[63] See Joseph P. Lash, *Helen and Teacher: The Story of Helen Keller and Anne Sullivan Macy*, London: Allen Lane, 1980, pp. 43–62.

[64] Foulkes, *loc. cit.*

[65] Foulkes, *Children's Dreams: Longitudinal Studies*. This source is largely the basis of the remainder of Chapter 3, and it will not be further cited on a piecemeal basis.

[66] David Foulkes, "Home and Laboratory Dreams: Four Empirical Studies and a Conceptual Reevaluation," *Sleep*, 1979, *2*, 233–251, as well as Foulkes, *op. cit.*

[67] Evelyn Goodenough Pitcher and Ernst Prelinger, *Children Tell Stories: An Analysis of Fantasy*, New York: International Universities Press, 1963, pp. 168–169.

[68] Bruno Bettelheim makes this point in his book, *The Uses of Enchantment: The Meaning and Importance of Fairy Tales*, New York: Alfred A. Knopf, 1976.

[69] David Foulkes, "Goal and Method in Dream Research," in *Sleep: Proceedings of an International Colloquium*, Milan, Italy: Carlo Erba, 1982, 147–157. The quote is from p. 155.

[70] The quote is from Howard E. Gruber and J. Jacques Vonèche's Piaget "reader," *The Essential Piaget*, New York: Basic Books, 1977, p. 97.

[71] *Ibid.*, pp. 96, 98.

[72] Shantz, *op. cit.*, pp. 20–22.

[73] Eric W. Trupin, "Correlates of Ego-Level and Agency-Communion in Stage REM Dreams of 11–13 Year-Old Children," *Journal of Child Psychology and Psychiatry*, 1976, *17*, 169–180, and Foulkes, *Children's Dreams: Longitudinal Studies*, ch. 7.

[74] E.g., Selman, *op. cit.*, ch. 2.

[75] Patricia Maykuth, "Individual Development in Dreams: A Longitudinal Study of 3- to 8-year-olds", Ph.D. Dissertation, Emory University, 1984.

[76] A "neurobiological" theory of dreaming proposed by Hobson and McCarley (J. Allan Hobson and Robert W. McCarley, "The Brain as a Dream State Generator: An Activation-Synthesis Hypothesis of the Dream Process," *American Journal of Psychiatry*, 1977, *134*, 1335–1348) has been interpreted in this way, but it actually hedges its bets on the issue at question. It proposes that *"specific stimuli"* (p. 1346) for dream imagery are provided by brain-stem stimulation which lies outside "cognitive areas of the cerebrum" (p. 1347), but it seems to imply that the "integrated dream image" *(ibid.)* may not be so free of symbolic constraints. The theory has been aptly criticized on other grounds: See Gerald W. Vogel, "An Alternative View of the Neurobiology of Dreaming", *American Journal of Psychiatry*, 1978, *135*, 1531–1535.

4 What Dreaming Is

In this chapter, the evidence and arguments of the previous chapters are brought together in a model of how our minds are organized when we dream. The word *model* implies a hypothetical portrait. No one "knows" for sure how mental systems are organized during dreaming (or, for that matter, at any other time). Nor are there any "direct observations" we can make that will reveal how the mind is organized during dreaming (or during any other mental act). In particular, no amount of painstaking observation of the brain will give us the answers we require, because the questions we're asking don't have to do with the structure or processes of any body organ. Rather, they have to do with the information-storage and information-processing *functions* in which the brain evidently participates. We don't observe and cannot know such functions and how they're organized in the same way that we can observe neural structures (e.g., the cerebral cortex) or events (e.g., spreading electrical activation in the cerebral cortex) and how they're organized.[1]

But this doesn't mean that psychology, the discipline that wants to understand a certain range of human functional accomplishments, is impossible. Demonstrably, it *is* possible. During this century, and particularly during the past several decades, we've learned a great deal about how human beings acquire and use knowledge. Models—sets of hypotheses about our informational functioning—have played and will continue to play a central role in this development. They summarize current knowledge, and they serve as stimulus to the gathering of new knowledge. Thus they are doubly constrained: They must be consistent with present data, and they also must be able to generate new observations consistent with their premises. But new observations do not always fall so neatly into line with old ideas. And so models change. This is not a sign of weakness in a discipline, but one of strength. The more we poke about nature, the more suspicious we become of timeless truths. Our understandings are always relative to the context of our current knowledge. Because we are not gods, that knowledge is always partial. As knowledge inches forward, so too do our models. And models are, in fact, the essence of the scientific quest. We don't want more knowledge simply for knowledge's sake, but for the sake of understanding. Models synthesize and organize knowledge so that we may better understand the phenomena they (at some distance) "describe."

This introduction may seem rather grandiose for a discipline as ill-developed as the cognitive psychology of dreaming. However, considerable experience has led me to believe that it's not inappropriate. People frequently ask me such questions as: "How do you *know* that this (or that) way of thinking about dreaming is right?" (I don't); "How then do you justify it?" (It looks as if it fits the current facts, and it suggests some interesting further research); "But aren't other, quite different models possible?" (Certainly, particularly at the present state of our understanding, which is meager); "What's so special, then, about this one?" (It seems to fit the available data better than any other model, and it's spelled out or "formalized," making it possible to test it in certain ways; its formalization also may encourage others to spell out *their* ideas, and to test them); "Could you tell, then, which model was better?" (Theoretically, yes: By evaluating the range of current data covered by each and by judging their relative usefulness in generating new observations. Practically speaking, probably not: Dream psychology may be so undeveloped that different models still can coexist without the immediate prospect of any definitive cross-evaluation); "Isn't model building all just a waste of time, then? Isn't it unscientific?" (No. It's precisely what we need to do to *make* dream psychology scientific).

In this vein, then, a model of dreaming will be presented.[2] This model isn't, in absolute terms, terribly well formalized. Its advantages, if any, are only relative: This may be a start toward thinking of dreaming the way cognitive psychology now thinks of such phenomena as remembering or speaking. Fortunately for you, because it *is* just a start, the model can be presented fairly simply. We'll consider the model in three stages: *Memory* (the knowledge representations reprocessed during dreaming and the "sources" of dream imagery); *Planning* (the nonconscious structures that begin to interpret and organize the mnemonic sources of the dream); and *Conscious Organization* (the imagery and feelings which we consciously apprehend and call the "dream" and which are the results of nonconscious planning at the second level).

1. MEMORY

Activation.   The model considers dreaming to be instigated by diffuse
activation in mnemonic systems. That is, it is provoked by elements of
memory and knowledge whose insistent and widespread activity calls up
the interpretive machinery of the dream-production system. Diffuse activation in memory may result from positive (excitatory) or negative (disin-
hibitory) influences. "Positively," it may reflect increases in general
cerebral activation (as during REM sleep). "Negatively," the diffuseness
of mnemonic activation may result from a release from inhibition.

For example, relinquishing voluntary self-control may cause increases
in the effective strength of mnemonic units whose influence previously
has been inhibited by self-regulation. That is, when you're consciously
planning your thought, there are many things you're keeping out of conscious awareness because they aren't relevant to whatever plan you're
following. Even while you are consciously planning your thought, you
sometimes are aware of dissociated images, words, or thoughts that lie at
the edge of the conscious mainstream of your more orderly and planned
thinking. Evidently these elements are relatively potent, because if you
relax your conscious vigilance even momentarily, they sometimes completely replace your orderly, planned thinking. Dreaming can't be explained simply *as being* this release of fringe ideas from active inhibition,
but such release might help to set in motion the more active planning
mechanisms that help to explain dreaming. And, as we've seen earlier, it
is precisely the relinquishment of voluntary self-regulation which seems
to be one cognitive precondition of dreaming.

It's clear from the multiple and sometimes weakly related mnemonic
sources of dream imagery, and from the odd fusions and juxtapositions of
knowledge in dream imagery, that mnemonic systems *are* diffusely active
during dreaming. It isn't clear, however, whether we should think of this
activation as just being a semi-random potentiation of mnemonic elements
or mini-networks or whether it also reflects some ongoing but nonconscious conceptual processing of these elements or within these networks.
While the evidence for diffuse activation suggests that there could be no
coherent *overall pattern* of nonconscious conceptual processing—that's
something which the interpretive system of dreaming itself must try to
provide during dream formation—this does not mean that there couldn't
be parallel but unrelated "pockets" of conceptual processing occurring
within the various networks of mnemonic elements that happen to be
activated.

Put another way, the question here is whether there's any evidence for
a *nonconscious adaptive reorganization of mnemonic elements or subsys-
tems* during REM sleep. Since the experimental deprivation of REM sleep

in humans has produced no clear-cut cognitive effects, it would seem that recurring periods of cortical and mnemonic activation during sleep play no adaptive role in our overall cognitive functioning (see the discussion in Chapter 5). Even if it were shown that the experimental deprivation of REM sleep did have dysfunctional adaptive consequences (either for us, or for animals that we'd have to assume [from the developmental evidence reviewed in Chapter 3] don't dream), that evidence would not necessarily imply that a *conceptual reprocessing* of memories typically occurs during REM sleep. The effect could be mediated in many other ways, and in organisms that otherwise give little indication of conceptual processing capabilities, the most economical assumption is that it must be mediated some other way. A performance deficit need not imply direct cognitive mediation. That is, it would take relatively strong evidence (much stronger evidence than we now possess) to justify the assumption that even "pockets" of conceptual processing are associated with the cortical and mnemonic activation of REM sleep.[3]

It's important to clarify precisely what sort of hypothesis the diffuse-mnemonic-activation proposal is. It is a psychological (mental) hypothesis, not a physiological one. This distinction is partly blurred by the fact that some correlations between physiological activity and mental activity can be used to bolster its plausibility. Because cerebral activation is relatively higher in REM than in non-REM sleep, it is plausible to propose greater mnemonic activation—and hence better developed dreaming—in REM sleep. The same arguments apply to sleep-onset versus later non-REM sleep, and to late-morning versus early-morning non-REM sleep.[4] At present, however, the correlation between mental and physiological activation is imperfect. One can at least imagine states of cerebral activation which are *not* accompanied by diffuse mnemonic activation, and vice versa. Therefore, dissociations of *cerebral* activation and dream reporting cannot refute the psychological hypothesis that *mnemonic* activation leads to dreaming. Simply put, this is because this hypothesis links mental systems to one another, rather than joining mental systems to physical states.

In what sense, then, could the hypothesis be tested—or refuted—by purely psychological evidence? Probably only in a weak one, because it is a hypothesis whose validity is almost self-evident. One cannot, for example, imagine dreaming in the absence of mnemonic activation. Of what could one be dreaming, if not of the contents of one's mind? Even if you proposed, on a 19th century model (Chapter 1), that dreaming interprets stimuli in the world rather than in the dreamer's own mind, those stimuli would still have to be interpreted in terms of one's accumulated knowledge of what the world is like. On the other hand, it *is* possible to imagine mnemonic activation during sleep that is unaccompanied by dreaming. On

REM awakenings, for instance, people could report their pre-awakening experience of a diffuse mnemonic flux—bits and pieces of various recollections following (or superimposed on) one another without any hint of "dreamlike" organization. But such reports are, in point of fact, about as rare as hens' teeth. And, even if they were moderately prevalent, it would only establish that mnemonic activation is not *sufficient* to guarantee dreaming. It would not refute the hypothesis that is *necessary* in order for dreaming to occur.

Thus, the proposal that mnemonic activation plays some role in dream production is relatively noncontroversial. What may be more controversial is the proposal that its role is that of dream instigator. At least two alternatives seem possible here.

You could propose that some more basic system is responsible for the selective activation of memories and knowledge, and that this system merely *uses* mnemonic activation as a means of provoking certain kinds of dreams. On this view, mnemonic activation is effect as much as cause. This view is something like some interpretations often given of Freud's dream theory.[5] These interpretations imply that some non-mnemonic factor (unconscious feelings, libido, instincts) sets dreaming in motion by activating memories or knowledge of a comparable "tenor" so that the non-mnemonic factor can gain access to consciousness. But these interpretations face numerous (and probably insuperable) difficulties. First, it is not clear how *non*-mnemonic Freud meant his instinctual concepts to be, nor how, if they are non-mnemonic, they establish an interface with memories and knowledge. Second, the history of Freud's theory, which is now well over eight decades old, suggests that it is impossible to marshal evidence about either the existence or the nature of any more "basic" force that lies behind the memories used in dream formation. Third, it is a formal deficiency of the basic-force model that it proposes still another level of explanation, when the possibilities of explaining dreams in terms of more accessible levels—such as memory—have not yet been exhausted; in fact, they have barely been scratched. This book is, in effect, an attempt to explain dreaming precisely in terms of these more accessible levels of mental functioning.[6]

The other alternative to mnemonic instigation of dreaming is that memories and knowledge are activated not so much "from behind" as "from in front." That is, the planning that evidently goes into dreaming (and makes dream imagery coherent and dream-image sequences narratively well-formed) may serve as the instigator of dreaming. On this view, the planning functions don't just synthesize whatever memories happen to be activated: they search out and selectively activate those memories in the first place, so that the dream can be well-organized and conform to their pre-existing plan. This alternative has the advantage of proposing a more accessible instigator of dreaming. The planning functions that go into dreaming are directly reflected in the dream itself. The question about this alternative, however, is whether it has the right direction of causation: Is it planner → memory, rather than memory → planner?

If so, we have an immediate problem, namely accounting for the peculiar plans that are executed during dreaming. On the memory → planner hypothesis, the unusual imagery and plots of our dreams can be seen as a "rational" planner's attempts to cope with diffuse mnemonic activation. Precisely because the nature of that activation is outside the planner's control, the ensuing dreams can be peculiar in just the way dreams typically are peculiar. The planner is doing the best it can, but the materials it is given to interpret aren't always compatible with (by waking standards) plausible images or image sequences. On the planner → memory hypothesis, however, we lose this way of explaining the peculiarities of dreaming. Now, we have to assume either that dreams are intentionally peculiar (that is, they're planned that way) or that there are defects in how a "rational" plan is executed. We thus have to explain either the peculiar intentions faithfully executed in the dream (no small chore), or how the planner can be simultaneously formally accomplished (almost always giving us well-formed imagery and internally coherent narratives) and substantively slipshod (the coherent images and stories can be of relatively implausible objects and events).

Thus, it seems preferable to imagine that whatever substantive unpredictability or oddness dreams possess derives from their mnemonic sources rather than from any faulty integration of those sources. That is, the memory → planner model provides us with a more reasonable explanation of the oddness of dreaming (as compared to the post-facto comprehensibility of much of our waking conscious experience). However, this model still leaves us with no explanation for random or diffuse mnemonic activation itself. That's precisely the breach into which Freudians are wont to jump, proposing some underlying (but unverifiable) rationale for how memories are activated during dreaming. Admittedly, there is something more satisfying about a theory which orders a process than about one which views it as being, for most intents and purposes, random. But the Freudians have purchased order at great cost, a cost that ultimately leaves them with explanations that are even more untidy than the random-process alternative. Perhaps we just have to accept that some degree of randomness is inherent in the explanation of a cognitive phenomenon like dreaming, and to assign it to that level of explanation where it most comfortably fits. That level seems to be one of mnemonic activation.

Moreover, we can use the evidence of our own experience to justify this choice. While a fit of a psychological theory with everyday observation isn't an infallible ground for evaluating that theory, outside observers are probably right in thinking that psychologists should use it more often than they do. In this case, the fit is simply that, when we relax our waking self-regulation of consciousness, we sometimes do experience unpredictable and/or odd images, thoughts, or image sequences. That these experiences, which just "pop" into consciousness, draw on sometimes diffuse or unrelated mnemonic sources is obvious. That they conform to some underlying plan or have some underlying meaning is not at all obvious (although the credulous always may find such a fit if they strain hard enough). Perhaps this is a case where we simply should refrain from embroidering the obvious. Obviously, dreaming is accompanied by an absence of the kind of Active-I self-regulation that is largely responsible for the retrieval to consciousness of memories and knowledge organized to conform to some meaningful intention. When such regulation is lacking, memories and knowledge seem to access consciousness in a more haphazard way. This may also happen in dreaming, although as we see in the succeeding sections of this chapter, dreaming also involves the imposition of distinctive forms of organization on activated or disinhibited mnemonic units.

Because these forms of organization are *selective,* they imply planner → memory relationships. These relationships qualify, but do not refute, the memory → planner hypothesis. As was noted in the last chapter, there are most likely many more mnemonic units that are sufficiently activated to be experienced consciously than there are mnemonic units that actually achieve consciousness. That is, the planning mechanisms, which are responsible for the formal organization and the specific contents of consciousness during dreaming, must select, from the diversity of mnemonic units available, those which will be processed for dream representation, and they must compose those units (or parts thereof) into comprehensible dream imagery. Thus, it certainly should not be imagined that the planner's role is in any sense a passive one. The planner is an active system continuously faced with decisions about which mnemonic units to process and how to process them. These decisions are one-of-a-kind decisions, because neither dream imagery itself nor the mnemonic activation which is its ultimate source probably ever literally repeats itself.[7] Thus the processor must be both selective and creative in its use of activated mnemonic units.

The point of the memory → processor hypothesis is that this selectivity and creativity must be constrained by the nature of the mnemonic units *potentially* available for use in dream construction. If this were not the case, there would be problems in explaining the peculiarities of dreams. Where the planner has to work within a constrained mnemonic context, these peculiarities can be seen as the result of a rational planner that does the best it can, given what it has to work with. If the planner were unconstrained mnemonically, then we would lose that way of explaining the peculiarities of dream representation.

That the planner is, in fact, constrained by mnemonic activation is suggested by cases where dream planning evidently breaks down. Here we must imagine that the activation of certain mnemonic units is so insistent that the planner has no choice but to process them. When dreams show sudden changes in direction, or when new elements appear which, by waking standards, cannot plausibly be related to what previously has happened in the dream, we have evidence that mnemonic elements sometimes simply cannot be refused a place in the dream, no matter how they may upset its evolving internal logic.

The argument thus far has been that mnemonic activation must have general priority over planning processes, which interpret this activation. But can the planner ever deliberately activate certain memories to facilitate coherent dream production rather than merely having to choose among those already "spontaneously" active? In lucid dreaming (Chapter 1) this may be the case, but being able to take the dream where you want it implies the return of voluntary self-regulation, whose presence makes lucid dreaming something rather different than unlucid dreaming. Furthermore, such control is difficult to achieve (and uneasily managed even when it is achieved), which makes it unlikely that it characterizes much garden variety dreaming, with its absence of voluntary regulation.

There is one sense, however, in which the planning processes already have direct access to specific memories that help them fulfill their function. The interpretive schemata through which these processes organize mnemonic activation are, themselves, components of symbolic memory. A particular schema will be selected for this role on the basis of its own activation and of its compatibility with the other mnemonic units in a simultaneous state of activation. The use of any such schema necessarily implies selective access to related mnemonic units. By analogy to the concept of script (Chapter 3), for example, once a certain script has been adopted (e.g., a restaurant script), there is a much higher probability of associative facilitation of certain concepts (e.g., food, dishes, etc.) than of others (e.g., bathtub). Thus, since any interpretive schema itself is an activated component of symbolic memory, the path has already been partly cleared by the selection of such a schema for the production of a relatively coherent dream scenario. In this sense, there *is* some interaction between mnemonic activation and dream planning, and this interaction can only facilitate the integration of mnemonic elements into an effective dream plan.

One final point should be made about the kind of mnemonic activation that underlies dream construction. I've used the phrase "some degree of randomness" to characterize the way in which particular mnemonic elements become activated during dreaming. This ambiguous phrase suggests that mnemonic activation during dreaming both *is* and *isn't* random. I think this suggestion is correct. Mnemonic activation probably *is* random in the sense that we typically can't predict the topic or theme of particular dreams we will experience. The particular mnemonic focus with which the dream begins, or upon which it settles, is largely unpredictable. (But randomness is not entirely present here: nagging, central concerns of our waking consciousness are probably more likely to be activated during dreaming than are other mnemonic units.) Mnemonic activation probably *isn't* random in the sense that it jumps around unpredictably over time. Specifically, any pattern of mnemonic activation, once initiated, is constrained by the structure of the dreamer's mnemonic network. While activation may be random, the system being activated is not. Thus, activation spreads according to pre-existing patterns in symbolic memory. (But randomness is not entirely absent here; sometimes, when the dream itself shows radical thematic discontinuity, we can assume that mnemonic activation has been initiated at a new site in symbolic memory, a site without obvious connections to the sites previously activated.) As this discussion indicates, we need now to turn our attention to what happens *over time* in memory during the course of dreaming any given dream.

Temporal Continuity in Activation.   During REM sleep (where dreaming gains its maximum momentum), what sort of temporal continuity exists in mnemonic activation? Can the narrative coherence of typical REM dreams be explained in terms of the fact that the same or "similar" mnemonic units are in a state of activation over relatively long stretches of the REM period? Conversely, can the typical choppiness of conscious ideation during non-REM sleep be explained in terms of a lack of moment-to-moment continuity in the kind of mnemonic units subject to activation outside REM sleep? *Explanation* may be too strong a term in these contexts, for it seems that there is no way of knowing about the state of activation of mnemonic units during dreaming except by looking at the dream itself. To say that the greater narrative momentum of REM dreams comes from more continuous activation of similar mnemonic complexes becomes circular: you only hypothesize that activation to be more continuous because the narrative momentum is greater. Moreover, as we've seen (Chapter 2), there is a serious factual problem with this explanation: Whether matched or unmatched for report length, non-REM dreams in one study didn't show any less moment-to-moment narrative continuity than did REM dreams (and both showed considerable such continuity).[8]

That same study *did* show reliable differences between REM sleep, on the one hand, and non-REM sleep (including sleep-onset) on the other hand, in terms of how lengthy the dream narratives were. Evidently, mnemonic activation is likely to be more continuous or sustained in REM sleep. Thus, although there may be no more moment-to-moment continuity in *what* memories are active in REM sleep than elsewhere, *some* memories will be continuously active in REM sleep more often than in non-REM sleep. REM sleep apparently guarantees more continuous mnemonic activation, but not necessarily that such activation will be of similar mnemonic units for longer periods of time, than does non-REM sleep. The constraining factor on the spread of activation over time presumably is the structure of the mnemonic system, which is invariant across states.

Is it true, though, that the dream itself is our only way of knowing about mnemonic activation during dreaming? Physiology cannot give us reliable, independent indices of which symbolic memories are in a state of current psychological activation. There is another psychological technique, however, which has been used to determine the mnemonic activation underlying dream production. Although this technique is not independent of the dream (and thus shares the same flaws as do dream observations), it does provide a somewhat different perspective than one gets from simply looking at the dream itself. The technique, already discussed in Chapter 1, is free association. Free association to dream episodes is supposed to recapture the mnemonic context from which these episodes originally derived. Whether this is literally true (something we have no way of knowing), free association can isolate some of the dreamer's most salient waking associations to elements in dream imagery. On the economical assumption that the structure of mnemonic organization is similar in sleep and wakefulness, these associations may provide some clues as to what is going on in memory during dream formation, and some clues are better than none at all.

How might free associations help us to judge the temporal sequence of mnemonic activation during REM dreaming? Suppose we line associations up in the chronological order of the dream episodes to which they refer. Consider the following example,[9] for instance.

The Dream	*The Dreamer's Associations*
1. A large hall—numerous guests, whom we were receiving.	Anticipation of seeing Irma, whom the dreamer recently has learned will be attending his wife's birthday party in this hall.
2. Among them was Irma. I at once took her on one side, as though to answer her letter and to reproach her for not having accepted my 'solution' yet. I said to her: "If you still get pains, it's really only your fault."	Irma has not accepted the dreamer's (sexual) formulation of her hysterical symptoms and remains unwell. The dreamer—her physician—is anxious not to be held accountable for her continuing symptoms.

3. She replied "If you only knew what pains I've got now in my throat and stomach and abdomen—it's choking me." I was alarmed and looked at her. She looked pale and puffy.

The symptoms are a blend of those of a hysteric friend of Irma's and of the dreamer's pregnant wife.

4. I thought to myself that after all I must be missing some organic trouble. I took her to the window and looked down her throat,

The dreamer had seen the patient's friend examined in precisely this position by his colleague and mentor, Dr. Breuer.

5. and she showed signs of recalcitrance, like women with artificial dentures.

The dreamer had not examined Irma's oral cavity, but recalls having examined a "youthful beauty" whose reluctance was related to her desire to conceal her dental plates. Irma is recalcitrant in accepting the dreamer's formulation of her symptoms.

6. I thought to myself that there was really no need for her to do that— She then opened her mouth properly.

Irma's friend would not have acted that way, and the dreamer would rather be treating her, but she, too, was recalcitrant; however, *in* therapy, she would have been more compliant, have opened her mouth properly, and have told the dreamer more of her problems than did Irma.

7. And on the right I found a big white patch; at another place I saw extensive whitish grey scabs upon some remarkable curly structures which were evidently modeled on the turbinal bones of the nose.

The white patch was reminiscent of diphtheritis, and hence of Irma's friend, but also of an illness suffered 2 years earlier by the dreamer's daughter, one which made the dreamer highly anxious. The nasal features remind the dreamer of (a) worry about his own nasal swellings, for which he is self-administering cocaine; (b) having heard recently that a female patient who'd followed his example had killed some of her own nasal tissue; (c) his long-time self-approach for having contributed to a male colleague's death by prescribing cocaine for him; (d) another highly-valued male colleague, whose specialty is diseases of the nose, who has operated on the dreamer's nose, who has examined Irma to see if her problems are nasal, and who recently botched an operation on another of the dreamer's female patients.

8. I at once called in Dr. Breuer, and he repeated the examination . . .

The dreamer is Freud, and the dream material consists of roughly the first half of his most famous dream, "Irma's Injection" (so called because its ultimate resolution is that one of Freud's colleagues is discovered to be responsible for Irma's symptoms—he thoughtlessly injected her with a substance from an unsterile syringe!). There are some risks in taking this material too seriously: Freud's theoretical bent no doubt has led him to proceed somewhat selectively in presenting the dream and its associations; in preparing the material for publication, he certainly has made both the dream and the associations more coherent than they originally were; and so forth. My concern here, however, is not so much with Freud's dream as with illustrating the more general potential that free associations may have in trying to track down the course of mnemonic activation during dream formation.

As Freud himself indicates, the precipitating event for this dream seemed to be an encounter he'd had on the evening of the dream day. A colleague—the same one the dream ultimately indicts for causing Irma's illness—had brought Freud news about the condition of his patient Irma: "She's better, but not quite well."[10] Freud thought he detected a note of reproach in that comment, and later in the evening he determinedly wrote out, for Dr. Breuer, a lengthy justification of his handling of Irma's case. As many observers have noted, more was at issue here for Freud than simply Irma and her continuing symptoms. Was Freud's theory—crudely presented to Irma—of the sexual causation of hysterical symptoms (and much else) correct? If so, why wasn't Irma getting any better? Beyond these concerns with the validity of Freud's theory, which he took to be the major achievement of his life, there also were questions about his scrupulousness as a physician and about whether he could justify his increasingly odd (i.e., psychoanalytic) professional conduct to his more orthodox colleagues.

Although we sometimes can take such fundamental and nagging concerns to bed with us, and later dream of something apparently wholly unrelated to them, Freud was not so lucky. His dream deals with reactivated representations of his presleep concerns, and, in fact, seems to come up with a conveniently self-serving resolution of them. Bearing in mind how many REM dreams Freud had, either of which he was unaware or which he was unwilling to present for publication, we may rightly wonder how typical a dream like "Irma's Injection" is, with its neat little resolution of one of the dreamer's central waking problems. A perennial problem with psychoanalysis has been how heavily its theory has rested on carefully selected examples, rather than on a wide-ranging investigation of any phenomenon—science by anecdote, rather than by systematic observation, as it were.

But Freud must be given great credit for having seen the major implication of the fact that the dream is a creation of the dreamer's own mind: You have to understand the mnemonic organization of that mind to understand how that dream came to be dreamed. By extension, to understand dreaming in general, you have to understand minds in general. Moreover, in free association, Freud gave us a technique for exploring mnemonic organization and mental processing that cognitive psychologists continue (without Freud's theoretical commitments) to use profitably today. Perhaps the technique can also help us to estimate the time course of mnemonic activation during dreaming.

From the relentlessness with which Freud's dream dealt with the same issue—Irma's continuing illness and who was to be held responsible for it—we already suspect that memories related to the prior evening and to his treatment of Irma were in a state of high activation throughout the dreaming of "Irma's Injection." But there seem to be interesting moment-to-moment variations in the way such activation fans out to related mnemonic material. If Freud's account is to be believed, for instance, thoughts about Irma (I'll be seeing her again at my wife's birthday party) seem to have predated her appearance as a central figure in the dream imagery. It's as if a director has decided that, even though the "movie" will be about Irma, he'll build up to her appearance by first supplying an appropriate setting and occasion, and then panning in on her as one of what originally seemed to be a large group of indistinguishable people. One can't be sure of this, of course, because Freud's transcription of his dream may not adequately reflect its actual imagery or temporal course, but there is a hint that this dream is not just bumping along as life sometimes seems to do but that it's being planned as a well-formed narrative.

Once Irma becomes a focal character (episode 2), it seems that Freud's most obvious concern about her—and his favorite line of self-defense—achieve dream representation. She's still ill and it's her fault, not his. Then (episode 3), it seems that the dream starts to run the risk of digressing, as mnemonically related symptoms of other women are introduced (Irma's friend, Freud's wife). However, since it is Irma who manifests or complains of these symptoms, she retains her position as the focus of the dream. In episode 4, mnemonic units referring to Irma's friend (in whom Freud seems to have some special interest) still seem to be active, but now in the context of her examination by Freud's senior colleague, Dr. Breuer. Once again, however, narrative continuity is preserved by letting it be Irma who assumes a posture more naturally associated with her friend. By episode 5, still other female patient memories seem to be active; once again they are assimilated to the Irma character, and narrative continuity is maintained.

In episode 6, Irma again seems to be acting partly for herself and partly as a foil for her friend. The "thought" element here—"no need for her to do that"—is interesting, because it almost seems as if the dreamer, through his self character, is monitoring the dream and has decided that Irma's recalcitrance is incompatible with the further development of the drama. Thus, "She then opened her mouth properly." While this probably wasn't any kind of *voluntary* self-regulation, it clearly reflects some sort of higher-order narrative planning in which, in effect, an error is corrected.

In episode 7, narrative continuity is again maintained as Irma assimilates at first oral, and then nasal, symptoms significant for Freud in other contexts. It is an especially considerable narrative achievement that the dream continues to tell a story about Irma at this point. In the documentation of her symptoms it seems that Freud has lost sight of the unique interest of her case. In the dream itself, there no longer seems to be a question of responsibility. By implication, of course, that question may have been answered: it's nobody's responsibility; the symptoms are physical (but how then did Freud miss them earlier?). One gets the feeling that the medical consultant to this little drama is, at this point, wielding a heavier hand than is its director.

Accordingly, in episode 8, the larger theme of the dream—assigning responsibility—is reinstated. Here, too, the dream begins to recruit its subsequently largely male-physician cast. It is suggestive that the appearance in the dream of its first focal male character other than Freud is anticipated by the associations to episode 7. That is, it seems as if the male-physician mnemonic elements newly activated at that point have led to the appearance of a male physician in the dream itself: i.e., memory → planning. Thus, the planning of episode 8 has retracked the theme of the dream by making use of mnemonic units which may have been in a state of relatively high activation.

A young man sleeping in a laboratory was once awakened just after the first eye movement of a REM period. He reported the following dream: he'd been washing his face at the apartment of a friend, Curtis. Just before he was awakened, he had said something to Curtis to the effect that Curtis really ought to have a two-bathroom apartment. His associations to being in Curtis's apartment were that he'd been there the previous evening, and had seen Curtis for the first time in a long while. When he was there, another person also present had mentioned to Curtis that the dreamer was becoming interested romantically in Sally. Sally called forth two episodic recollections: (1) 2 weeks earlier, he'd had a conversation with *her* about the desirability of two-bathroom apartments; (2) more recently, he'd told Sally he was going to be sleeping in the laboratory—she'd said, "Let me know what you dream," and he'd replied, "Only if I dream about you."[11]

Once again, it seems as if we can comprehend the narrative progress of the dream in terms of two sorts of influences. First, there is a narrative-planning influence, which says, in effect, "Hey, you were just dreaming of being at Curtis's, washing your face. Anything you want to say now, you'll have to say to *Curtis*." Second, there are shifts in mnemonic activation, such that reactivating memories about Curtis naturally enough is associated with reactivating memories about Sally. Because these Sally-memories may have been particularly active just before the elaboration of the second (speech) episode of the dream, it is a *Sally*-related speech which the dreamer ends up addressing to Curtis. Once again, narrative planning seems to have been constrained by the mnemonic units currently in a state of relative activation. But it is also notable that what the dreamer said to Curtis, although Sally-related, conformed to the earlier setting of the dream: Curtis's bathroom. Constraints of narrative continuity also were present here.

It is a fair charge that these two dream-association examples are selected anecdotes, and not any better evidence than Freud has been chastised for using. My point, however, is not that these examples themselves constitute evidence from which to draw any momentous conclusions. Rather, they are meant to indicate that the joint analysis of chronologically sequenced dream episodes and free associations may provide a useful way not only of charting the temporal course of mnemonic activation during dreaming but also of determining the ways in which mnemonic activation and thematic planning interact in dream formation. The implicit idea is that "what happens next" in a dream depends partly on what memories then are in a state of activation and partly on the narrative requirements that what happens next must be some sort of dramatic continuation of what happened last. Analyses of the sort outlined here may provide a way of investigating these relationships. That is, the method illustrated in these anecdotes *can* be applied systematically. In the tradition of empirical science, the results of such systematic research should force us to reevaluate any conclusions we might want to draw about mnemonic activation during dream formation.

Organization.   Various ideas have already been presented about the waking structure and organization of human symbolic memory. Distinctions have been drawn between memory for particular autobiographical episodes versus more generalized knowledge, and among conceptual knowledge (the abstract meaning of a phenomenon), depictive knowledge (the appearance properties of a phenomenon), and affective knowledge (what feelings, if any, are associated with that phenomenon). In a rather informal way, it has been noted that conceptual meaning may depend on analyzing phenomena by their component features, and on establishing networks of mnemonic relationships among phenomena and their component features. The notion of abstracted event representations—scripts—has also been introduced. But no attempt has yet been made to integrate these ideas in a unified portrait of human symbolic memory—and none will be.

There are two justifications for this disavowal of responsibility. *First,* with so many researchers working on so many different, specialized aspects of waking memory, and not wholly agreeing on how those aspects best may be characterized, it is premature to expect any grand synthesis of human memory. That has not yet been achieved in memory psychology, and it would be foolish for such a synthesis to be presumed by dream psychology.

Second, it seems to me that the most reasonable general position for cognitive dream psychology might be one of accepting whatever memory models and observations waking cognitive psychology has to offer, rather than having to worry about formulating memory models of its own. If dream psychology is to become an integral part of cognitive psychology, it cannot afford to strike out on its own at just that point where its interests most closely intersect with those of the rest of cognitive psychology. The unique aspect of dreaming may be the peculiar way in which memories and knowledge are being *processed* as we dream. We more than have our hands full trying to deal with the processing, so we needn't take on the onerous chore of characterizing precisely what it is that's being processed.

Having made these arguments, I'd now like to qualify each of them. Specifically, it seems to me that there are certain minimal requirements a memory theory must meet if it is to be useful in understanding dreams, and that there are certain ways in which the study of dreaming can and should *actively contribute* to the formation of general models of memory.

1.   As we've already seen, a major question in memory theory has been whether knowledge representation is quasi-pictorial (analog) or whether it's abstract, representing meanings in a nonpictorial, nonspatial format (such as in propositions or lists of features). The evidence of the previous chapter, on the early development and nature of dream imagination, seems to me to be inconsistent with any memory theory proposing developmental or any other kind of priority for "pictorial" rather than abstract representations of symbolic knowledge. Young children cannot evoke dream images of events which they have seen many times, which they can recognize facilely, and for which they can readily supply verbal labels. Neither perception, nor perceptual or verbal recognition, apparently guarantees accessible mental imagery. If event knowledge is stored "imaginally," it's very difficult to understand why this should be so: very little processing should be required to evoke that knowledge in consciousness. If, on the other hand, imagery is reconstructed from knowledge representations that have few or no imaginal properties, then the child's limited imagery becomes much more comprehensible. Image reconstruction would depend on the acquisition of abstract depictive knowledge in the first place and then on the ability to process that knowledge back into

imaginal "copies" of perceptual phenomena. That is, both processes of mental analysis and of mental synthesis are required: There is deconstruction and reconstruction. But this means that event knowledge is not represented in pictorial or analog form.

Dreaming has been described as the closest most of us ever come to symbolically recreating "raw sensory experience."[12] Given this description, it is remarkable how little the course of dreaming seems to be guided by the pictorial or spatial properties of its imagery. Image properties seem to play a subservient, rather than a leading role in the "raw sensory experience" of the dream. As the examples in the previous section illustrate, dream image follows dream image not because of the perceptual features they have in common, but because of linkages in meaning. Freud didn't take Irma over to the window because *her appearance* when she recited her complaints suggested that pose, but because *what she was saying* indicated the need for further examination of her symptoms. Freud clearly relied on depictive knowledge to portray Irma's pose by the window, but he wasn't moved to create that imagery by depictive associations with what had been dreamed before. The more general point is that the unity of the dream lies in its theme or meaning, which may require many different concrete depictions. It does not lie in common image depictions, which have the potential of portraying conceptually unrelated referents (spoked wheel looks like a flower looks like a bullet hole in glass, etc.).

2. Dream psychology could simply accept the current models of memory psychology and devote its time to studying the peculiar ways in which dreams process memories. However, there are certain dream phenomena whose study might actually contribute to making better models of symbolic memory. That is, there are some good reasons why memory psychology might want to pay attention to dreams.

One interesting dream phenomenon, for example, is dream imagery which blends the features of what, in wakefulness, we'd consider different concepts. In Freud's "Irma's Injection" dream, for example, when Dr. Breuer appears, he is not a literal replica of the real Dr. Breuer. The dream Dr. Breuer has the limp and the clean-shavenness of Freud's step-brother. Freud feels, in line with the preceding argument, that the basis for his fusion of these two people was conceptual rather than depictive: both had angered Freud by rejecting some proposal he had made. Furthermore, one general property of dreaming's image fusions, illustrated in this dream, is that they build upon an abstract conceptual analysis of object or event features. We analyze faces in terms of features like eyebrows (bushy/trim), facial hair (none/mustache/beard), or set of eyes (close together/far apart). Fusions in dream imagery seem to follow the kind of analyses we perform of perceptual information, such that person A gets person B's facial hair. As suggested in Chapter 1, we do not seem to perform facial analyses along a right/left dimension; thus, we do not dream that the right side of person A's face is juxtaposed with the left side of person B's face.

Further study of the image fusions people do report in their dreams is needed. To the extent that these fusions do follow a conceptual feature analysis, rather than doing something like juxtaposing slices of different photographs, (a) the conceptual (as opposed to analog or imaginal) basis of dreaming is supported, and (b) a conceptual feature-analysis model of memory is supported. But *which* conceptual feature analysis is supported may depend, in part, on what kinds of fusions are observed in dreams. That is, a catalog of detachable and intermixable features in dreams can contribute to a more general model of how information is analyzed and represented in symbolic memory.

Fusions in dreams are not limited to visual imagery. "Irma's Injection" provides another example: In episode 3 above, Irma describes her symptoms, which turn out in fact to be those of Irma's friend, and of Freud's wife. Here it's as if the dream is reading off a list in Freud's mind we might entitle "female symptoms." Highest up on that list seem to be particular symptoms of most recent acquaintance and interest to him—those most "on his mind," as we'd say. Observation of dream fusions of these sorts may also have something to say about how we organize our knowledge of objects and events.

Still another peculiarity of dreaming is observed when we realize, on awakening, that the person we had been interpreting as person A actually had the appearance in the dream of person B. Evidently our depictive knowledge of B has been connected with our conceptual knowledge of person A. Such instances, which also deserve systematic study as to their frequency and nature, support a distinction between depictive and conceptual knowledge and may help to illuminate how these two forms of knowledge are interrelated.

Other odd details of dreaming include *dissociations* (expected features are missing in dream imagery), *regressions* (one character appears as at an earlier age, while the rest are portrayed as they now are known), *faulty conclusions* (as in the hypothetical example of Chapter 1: because it's Saturday, I must hurry to work), and *reversals* (a friend becomes an enemy, or vice versa; I hate someone I love; etc.). In one way or another, they, too, should provide a rich set of data for memory models. Dissociations may indicate dimensions of featural analysis, here conspicuous by their absence in the dream. Regressions may indicate the ways in which we know the "same" people over time, even though their appearance changes (we have biographical memories of significant others, as well as autobiographical memory). Faulty conclusions suggest something about the kinds of inferences we associate with particular units of knowledge and about the interconnection of the units whose associated inferences are being confused in the dream. Reversals may prove explicable not from the old Freudian adage that "You *really* hate that 'loved' person," but from the fact that part of what we know about people, objects, and events is what they are not. We know whales are not fish not so much by inference (whale is a mammal, mammals aren't fish, ergo whale isn't a fish) as by direct representation.[13] We've been taught the nonidentity in question precisely because features (lives in water, swims) might otherwise mislead us into assuming an identity. Presumably, dream reversals indicate which information is directly encoded in memory as to what something *isn't,* information whose logical classification (not a . . .) is lost in dream formation.

As we've already observed (Chapter 1), dreaming probably involves a rather wider and less discriminating spread of activation in memory than is typically the case when our thought is voluntarily self-regulated.[14] Thus, the dream can fuse or otherwise join together knowledge that our waking judgment wouldn't imagine belonged together, and it can leave things out that our waking judgment would insist belonged together. The opportunity for memory theory lies in the strong likelihood that the structure of mnemonic organization is preserved during dreaming, and that the particular (and sometimes peculiar) ways in which activation spreads during dreaming can help to reveal what that structure is. Thus, when cognitive psychologists conclude that bird knowledge is organized in a certain way, because "robin" is a frequent waking response to "name a bird" while "penguin" is not, they are using memory-mediated outputs (responses) to construct models of mnemonic organization. The dream is also a memory-mediated output, and the ways in which it joins together or does not join together knowledge representations also may help us to map out the organization of memory.

This argument presupposes that things don't just "fall apart" during dreaming such that memory no longer has any real organization. There is good reason to think that organization *is* preserved in symbolic memory, even under conditions where mental processing is much less accomplished than it is during dreaming. For instance, one patient with dementia (a progressive and relatively global disease of cerebral cortical tissue) was unable to name pictures of common objects.[15] On multiple-choice testing, however, she could correctly select the appropriate response in many cases, and most of her errors involved the selection of choices semantically related to the correct response. The patient's tendency to overgeneralize categorical knowledge was shown to be lawful. For instance, she would label cats, but not birds, "dogs." The categorical overgeneralization was "not limitless or random."[16] Evidently the patient's systematic confusion was conceptual (having to do with features defining categories) rather than purely linguistic, "since in English we have no linguistic label that pairs only dogs and cats and excludes birds."[17]

Moreover, almost everything we know about dreaming, including its plausible simulation of reality and its high degree of internal coherence, is consistent with the presupposition that memory organization is preserved in conditions associated with dreaming. If empirical study confirms that even the odder moments of dreaming—e.g., some of the phenomena we've just been discussing—also are lawful products of an organized but rather differently activated memory system, then the case for the presupposition will be secured. At that point, an examination of *how* the oddities of dreaming are lawful can be used as supporting data in the construction of general models of memory.

At that point too, dream psychology will have reaped a rich harvest from its collaboration with memory research. It will have shown the possibility of explaining the peculiarities of dream expression—which most need explaining—in terms of psychological models of memory, which can be justified both by dream data *and* by the results of waking experimentation. Further, it will have shown that there is no need to assume that peculiarities of dream expression are merely random products of a "broken machine" and that there is no justification for assuming that these peculiarities must be dictated by deep, hidden motives of the Freudian sort. In the study of slips of speech (so-called Freudian slips), it has been demonstrated that puzzling outputs of symbolic processing can be understood as lawful occurrences in a standard cognitive system: You don't need to conjure up hidden motives to explain errors of speech.[18] When that demonstration is repeated for dreaming, dreaming finally will establish itself as a legitimate object of cognitive psychological study. We don't need to run to psychiatrists to find out how we think or speak; neither will we need to consult them about how we dream. The territory is, in each case, the same. There are no privileged observations that lie outside it. In each case, the territory is cognitive psychology.[19]

The earlier proposal, which this discussion has been "qualifying," says that dream psychology should study the *processing* of knowledge representations during dreaming and leave to memory psychology to figure out what those representations are and how they're organized. But the qualifications offered in this discussion have been far-reaching, so the plausibility of the earlier proposal is correspondingly diminished. It turns out that we probably can't understand the peculiarities of dreaming—how memories and knowledge are processed during dreams—without some clear hypotheses about how human beings represent and organize their symbolic knowledge. It also turns out that dreaming may have a special role to play in arriving at those hypotheses. Finally, since knowledge representation and organization are central issues in cognitive psychology, it seems that dreaming should be a central concern of cognitive psychology. This is not yet the case. It's a goal of this book to convince you that it should be, and to enlist your support in making it so.

2. PLANNING

Nature.   Dream planning is demonstrated by the dream's well-formed imagery and narratives. Despite the diversity of its mnemonic sources, the dream most often is well-organized. Its *momentary* imagery is immediately comprehensible: we know during the dream itself what's happening (though we might later wonder why our mind created those particular images). What happens typically makes at least an abstract kind of waking sense (it's possible that a person might have the nickname "Computer," even if you don't know anybody who does). Often, it makes much more sense than that (for instance, when Freud vented his frustration at Irma, telling her that her continued illness was her own fault). Moreover, the *sequence* of dream experience is well ordered. The dream seems to have a narrative form—like a story with an internally coherent plot. As we've seen (Chapter 3), the narrative quality of dreaming seems to appear at that point in human development when children begin to be able to effect a systematic internal regulation of their own cognitive activity. At this point, the dream seems to become something more than a simulation of random "slices of life"; it begins to have the same quality we find in professionally edited films. And, as we've also seen (earlier in this chapter), the good narrative form of dreams seems to persevere in the face of shifts in mnemonic activation which threaten its integrity. There can be no doubt that dreaming is a planned mental activity.

What is not so immediately clear is *what kind* of planning takes place in dream formation. Based on a seemingly plausible analogy from other organized cognitive acts (such as much of our waking speaking or thinking), many people assume that dreaming is planned in what I call a *semantic-intentional* sense. By this, I mean that these people believe that the dream is purposely formed to express certain underlying meanings. Just as in our waking speech we typically end up saying something we mean, so the dream, too, expresses some underlying meaning, and the process of dreaming—like that of language production—is organized so as to convey an underlying message or set of messages. In this view, dream interpretation is the process by which the message(s) can be reconstructed. It's how we find out what the dream really means.

However, dream interpretation is a troublesome business. It seems that interpreters find it difficult to agree on the meaning of particular dreams, or on the nature of the messages that dreaming more generally conveys. The reason for the proliferation of contradictory and sometimes highly implausible theories of dream interpretation seems to be that there's no way these theories can be empirically constrained or validated. It's like arguing how many angels can sit on the head of a pin: Depending on one's theoretical assumptions, the answer can range from none to infinity, and there's no conceivable evidence by which one answer can be judged superior to another. Let's consider, then, the possibility that what's sought in dream interpretation doesn't exist, that there's no more under-lying meaning in dreaming than there are angels who might sit on the heads of pins.

This possibility emerges as a strong probability when we consider why people ask to have their dreams interpreted in the first place. Usually, it's because they can't find a meaning (or meanings) in their dreams in the same way they can for their speech or for much (but as we've seen, not all) of their waking thought. There's no doubt in my mind about why I wrote the preceding sentence or about what it means. It means what I meant it to say. But I do doubt why I dream the dreams I do, or what they mean. When I'm dreaming, I have no sense of semantic intent—that I'm trying to achieve some particular sequence of dream happenings. Indeed, as we've seen, the kind of voluntary self-regulation that underlies seman-tic intent seems wholly absent during dreaming. While writing, I can think: "Good, that's what I meant to say," or "No, that's not what I meant." Imagine how odd it would be to think that way while dreaming.

And, to carry the argument outside of the immediate context of dream-ing itself, consider the oddness of someone waking up from a REM dream and saying, "Good, that's just what I meant." The typical case is that we awaken from REM dreams and are unable not only to see meaning in the dream but also to identify any intent to which its imagery might corre-spond. Nor does free association seem to be much help. It uncovers mnemonic material which might have *contributed* to particular imagery in the dream, but it does not uncover a previously unnoticed intent to con-vey some unitary meaning in that imagery. Granted, Freud can look at his imagery of Irma's oral-cavity symptoms and say, "That *must* mean that I'd rather have Irma's friend than Irma as a patient," but he doesn't verify that this is what he *did* mean. Moreover, the associative material is sufficiently diffuse that it doesn't permit unitary formulation even of what "must" have been meant. If Freud meant to say he'd prefer to treat Irma's friend, then why, for instance, was Irma also portrayed as having symp-toms similar to those of his pregnant wife? Here, the interpreter can synthesize some still higher-order (but more obscure) unitary meaning including both friend and wife, but it seems even more likely here that this is not a *recognition* of intention. Rather, it's a theoretical formulation of what Freud's intention might (must) have been. Or, the interpreter can say, as Freud himself often seems to, that different meanings are expressed in a "single" dream image (e.g., "I'd rather treat Irma's friend"; "I wish Irma's illness were organic so that it wouldn't be my psychoanalytic treatment which is responsible for her continuing symptoms"; "I'm concerned about my wife's appearance"; "I toy with the idea of being intimate with my lovely, unpregnant young patients," etc., etc.). But here the analogy to speech and ordinary waking thought totally breaks down, because semantic intent typically is unitary (you mean one thing, and this is what you say or think).

The interpreter's situation becomes even more desperate when the *sequence* of dream imagery is considered. When Freud's associations to Irma are laid out in the order of the dream episodes to which they correspond, they don't reveal any unitary sequential message corresponding to the sequence of his dream imagery. What they do reveal is meandering mnemonic activity which corresponds in no sense to the kind of intentionality that underlies speech production. Not only can't intentionality be recognized in this sequence, it can't even be forced upon it. Granted, the whole Irma dream might in some sense be viewed as reflecting the intention to find a reason other than Freud's theoretical or therapeutic incompetence for Irma's continuing symptoms. Still: (a) most dreams, as noted earlier, don't seem to end as neatly as this carefully selected Freudian specimen dream and (b) intention does not and cannot explain the meandering moment-to-moment texture of the dream in the same way a speaker's overall intention explains the inner texture of her or his speech. Freud is, at his very best, a highly distractible and distracted "speaker," veering this way and that in what he "says" in response to shifting patterns of diffuse mnemonic activation. That is, he's not really functioning as a speaker at all.

The case becomes even clearer when one considers typical laboratory reports. What sequence of intention corresponds to the sequence of the computer dream (Chapter 1) or of the two-bathroom dream (this chapter)? The dreamers themselves could recognize none, and their associations did not permit the forcible imposition of a specific intention on their dream material.

The simplest and most direct way of reading all this, and of interpreting the typical results of free association, is that there *is* no meaningful plan underlying the construction of particular dream imagery or of its narrative sequence. The reason why dreamers can't understand what their dreams mean, and why we have such difficulty in reconstructing adequate accounts of what they might have meant, is that they didn't mean anything. That is, unlike the case in speech production, no unitary message is momentarily or sequentially encoded during dream production. The dream isn't, therefore, any kind of translation of such a message, and if we persist in searching for one, we're in the angel counting business.

Thus, the only compelling evidence we have for planning in dreams is not for *what* is dreamed but for *how* it is dreamed. Semantic intent typically can't be recognized by the dreamer (who, if anyone, should know), either while dreaming or after having dreamed. We can't even come up with plausible plans of meaning corresponding to imagery or imagery sequences in the dream that can induce dreamers to say something like, "That *probably* is what I meant (even though I don't remember having meant it)." On the other hand, dreaming clearly does demonstrate what I'll call *syntactic intentionality*—the intent to "say" whatever is "said" in a well-formed fashion. We have evidence of this kind of intentionality in the "perceptual" well-formedness of dream imagery and in the narrative well-formedness of dream imagery sequences. Despite the diffusely active mnemonic activity that underlies dreaming, the dream does come out saying something that we can *literally* comprehend. We can understand, in the dream itself and later, what was dreamed, even if we don't comprehend why we chose to dream that specific event sequence. Dreaming, then, is the imposition of formal ("syntactic") organization on mnemonic activation, which is itself too diffuse and ill-organized to have expressive or thematic ("semantic") coherence.

Understanding the kind of processing that memories and knowledge receive during dreaming thus necessarily involves identifying the formal or syntactic organizing structures characteristic of the dreaming mode of mental organization. These structures are the heart of the human dream production system.

What can be said of these structures? From the previous chapter, it appears that they are only gradually acquired in early human development, and that their acquisition is part of human mental growth more generally. We know, too, that they function automatically, that is, without conscious awareness and without voluntary self-regulation. Putting these two observations together, we can think of these mental structures as being analogous to some of the grammatical or syntactic structures children acquire as they learn to speak. Children aren't aware they're acquiring or following grammatical rules, but they clearly are. When a young child who previously used the irregular past tense for the verb "go" (i.e., "went") begins instead to say "goed," he or she is demonstrating the acquisition and use (and overgeneralization) of a grammatical rule.[20] But there is no awareness of rule use. When children later are "taught" grammar in school, the teaching often consists of drawing children's attention (most often quite imperfectly) to rules their speech indicates they already "know," because they generally follow them. As adults, our speaking and writing are constantly constrained by internalized grammatical organizers that function quite automatically. An interesting question posed by this analogy between dream "syntax" and speech syntax is whether speech rules or speech production mechanisms might not play some role in dream formation. We'll consider some evidence bearing on this question shortly.

First, however, we might consider some unanswered questions about the kinds of imaginal and narrative planning that go into dream formation. They're unanswered because, as yet, there's very little systematic formal description of what dreams are like. So much effort has gone into trying to determine the particular contents and the "meaning" (or, more recently, the physiology) of dreams that there hasn't been much *formal description* of dreams. This clearly is an area begging for further study. How, for instance, does a typical REM-dream visual image compare to a typical nondream mental image? To a typical perceptual experience? At the planning level, such questions perhaps should be asked more about the informational content of imagery and its organization than about such surface features as grain or focus. What kind of narrative organization is evidenced in the dream? Given the apparent susceptibility of narrative planning to at least partial derailment by insistent mnemonic elements, this may not be easy to determine. But, can we, for example, identify some idealized narrative schemata in REM dreaming, which generalize over the imperfect realizations of narrative coherence in particular dreams?

Such schemata might be characterized in relatively formal (content-free) terms. For instance, "grammars" for describing stories have employed units such as characters' *goals, activities,* and how well characters' activities *fulfill* their manifest goals. Since subjects' comprehension and recall of stories have been demonstrated to be related to these structural descriptions, grammars are assumed to be describing not only the stories but also the cognitive structures that subjects employ in processing them.[21] To the degree that dream content is storylike, such structures clearly might also be used in the processing of mnemonic information during dreaming.

But is it correct to think of the dream as having storylike properties, as compared for instance, to merely lifelike properties? Most of our unedited waking experience probably wouldn't make a very good story, yet we can comprehend and recall much of what has happened to and about us during any typical day. We must also have even more general structures which permit us to organize life-events that often do not cohere as neatly as those in a story and that may not move along at all well toward any sort of dramatic resolution. How many dream narratives are structured in this way, rather than as tidy, self-contained, and self-resolving stories (such as Freud's "Irma's Injection" dream?) Here is an issue to which structural-descriptive research could well be addressed.[22]

The discrimination of storylike event progressions from lifelike event progressions has been a problem in waking research on "story grammars." Critics have wondered whether the so-called story grammars can in fact discriminate descriptive accounts of people engaging in mundane activities from more storylike narratives. Their suggestion is that such discrimination cannot be made in purely formal terms. There are goals and subgoals and activities and resolutions when I clean my nails, just as there are in "Little Red Riding Hood." But one event sequence does not make much of a "story;" the other does. Thus, waking research on narrative discourse has begun to focus on content (semantics) as well as on form (grammar).[23] Still, it seems that we have formal expectations in listening to stories more than in life that there will not be radical disruptions of event sequences. In REM dreaming, these expectations may also be satisfied.[24] But more precise comparisons are needed among dream reports, waking stories, and randomly selected event sequences in daily life experience before we can conclude how the schemata used in REM dream production are like or unlike those used in other contexts.

Whatever the fate of such research, however, the suggestion that a dream's content be considered as well as its form remains an apt one. For example, rather than proceeding at the highly abstract level that permits us to characterize generalities in story form or life experience, we might begin by focusing on particular scripts (Chapter 3) that are portrayed in dream imagery. What, for example, are the differences between going to a restaurant in a dream and in life? Never mind that, on leaving the dream restaurant, you're suddenly the engineer of a transcontinental train: so long as the restaurant theme is sustained, how is it like, and how is it unlike, waking evocations of relevant script knowledge? Do the deviations suggest the simultaneous activation of unrelated scripts, or are they more an indication of a greater possibility of omissions or alternative slot-fillers in the operative script?

Focus on such questions might begin with preoperational and early concrete operational children. Their waking script knowledge is still relatively limited and relatively accessible to experimental determination (and even control). Their dreaming script knowledge also seems correspondingly limited, and it may be less subject to the simultaneous or successive distractive influence of other script schemata. It would be interesting, for example, to determine the evolution of both waking and dreaming script knowledge following children's exposure to a new class of environmental events (e.g., going to school). When children reflect on their own dreams, what do they find different or unusual about the sequence of dream events as compared to the class of waking events on which the dream seems to be modeled? The very "mundaneness" of children's dreams suggests that questions such as these define feasible research objectives.

To the extent that generalized "content" schemata are employed in organizing mnemonic activation for dream representation, there may be a problem in my earlier characterization of dream processing as being syntactically rather than semantically constrained. At the broadest level of analysis, we still can say that, *whatever* the contents of dream experience, that experience generally meets minimally acceptable criteria of momentary (imaginal) and sequential (thematic) coherence. The question we have been considering more recently is to what degree the dream is scriptually coherent. We have good reason to believe that its scriptual coherence is generally less than perfect. The oddness of dreaming lies in its juxtaposition of unrelated elements in familiar contexts and in its stringing together of somewhat implausible events. In my dream, rocks rather than food can be served at the restaurant, and the waiter can put down his dishes and begin an algebra lesson. But the actual incidence of such improbability in REM dreams is, in fact, quite rare, and far less than our stereotyped notion of dreaming would suggest.[25] The mundaneness of most REM dreams suggests that, once a script or other generalized-event knowledge structure has been selected to organize dream experience, the momentary representations and the sequences of the dream conform fairly well to the pattern implicit in that structure.

This is *more* than saying that the dream has formal thematic coherence. I could, for example, define formal thematic coherence in terms of character persistence and sequential self–other behavioral interchange. For instance, I could dream that I was sitting in a restaurant, was served rocks, asked the waiter about them, whereupon he undertook to show me a mountainous area just outside the back door where he obtained them, whereupon we set to prospecting for gold-colored rocks, whereupon we inadvertently opened up a cave from which a small child emerged holding a dog in her arms, etc. In this "dream" each event flows smoothly from the preceding one, even though there is no waking script to which the unfolding of dream events seems to conform. Thematic coherence, in this sense, does not presuppose scriptual coherence, which is adherence to a pattern of temporally sequenced events with which we are familiar in our waking lives. The scriptual coherence of REM dreams remains to be determined, but there's reason to believe that it is generally (if not invariably) fairly good.

To the extent that it is good, there is indeed a generalized semantic constraint on the organization of dream experience. The constraint is semantic in the sense that it dictates that, for example, events in a dream restaurant bear some degree of correspondence to events we've learned to expect to take place in that sort of situation. However, to the degree that the constraint is also generalized, it can be viewed as an extension, rather than a refutation, of the principle that the dream is formed more to say something (anything) well rather than to convey some particular message. That is, we can use evidence of scriptual coherence better to argue that the dream is keeping events generally consistent with waking expectations about what happens in situation X than to argue that the dream reflects an intention to use dream imagery to say something very specific about that situation or anything else. "Keeping the dream well-formed" is a concept that ultimately seems to involve conformity to criteria in specific content domains, as well as to criteria that can be stated more abstractly (or "structurally"). But it is that concept, rather than any sort of intentional message propagation, which best characterizes the operative principle in dream production.

Mechanisms.   Although we don't as yet know much about the precise nature of the plans or rules that are followed in organizing dreams, we do have some interesting (and surprising) clues about how they might be implemented or enforced. The surprise is that dreaming, that most "raw sensory" form of human conscious cognition, may be organized by *verbal* production processes. The clues come from the reports of persons who are or have been severely "aphasic," i.e., with profound language impairment.[26]

Soviet researchers first described an "inhibition" of dreaming associated with language disorders. Independent of this description, and of one another, two stroke victims reported an apparent cessation of dreaming before their recovery from severe language deficits. The actress Patricia Neal sensed that, when she was most severely impaired linguistically, her sleep was "dreamless." The same impression was reported by C. Scott Moss, himself a dream researcher at the time of his stroke. He associated his loss of dreaming with a concurrent loss of "inner speech." Stimulated by these accounts, two researchers recently arranged to interview seven aphasic patients (during speech therapy sessions) about their dreams. All claimed a total loss of dreaming. The patients had not (with one exception) suffered any interference with their visual perception. They were able to communicate sufficiently well to give reliable (consistent) responses to the interviewer's questions.

Unfortunately, none of these observations comes from laboratory awakenings made during REM sleep. Thus, it isn't really clear yet how seriously they should be taken. But the initially independent convergence of accounts by observers with no particular theoretical axe to grind is impressive. Moreover, the results of the multipatient interview study suggest the aphasics' apparent dreamlessness can't be a by-product of some general cognitive impairment or an artifact of some general communication disorder. It has been suggested that some *specifically linguistic* processing system is involved, and that this system plays some central role in organizing dream consciousness.

In thinking (tentatively, of course) about how to make sense of what this role might be, it will be useful to remind ourselves of the more general role language seems to play in cognition. The form in which knowledge is represented outside of immediate memory probably cannot be linguistic. It must be more abstract than either verbal or imaginal coding permits. Speech and imagery (and feelings) are ways in which we become *consciously aware* of what we know. That is, they are representations in immediate memory. To get from what we ultimately know to what we consciously know implies, then, some active mental processing—specifically, some transformation of knowledge representations.

Psycholinguistics is concerned with characterizing such transformational processing. The kinds of evidence on which its models rest are beyond the scope of this book, but they include experimental studies of speech comprehension and (as noted earlier in this chapter) observations of speech errors.[27] Most important for our purposes here is the psycholinguistic assumption that well-defined "stages" of language processing occur *between* formulating an intention to convey a message *and* actually uttering it. These include (in order): (1) selecting a discourse plan (do you want to tell a story, make a request, state an observation, etc.?); (2) selecting particular skeletal syntactic frames to meet more immediate goals given by that larger plan (the frames are "skeletal" in that they indicate the grammatical form of a particular sentence, for instance, rather than the specific words it will contain); and (3) selecting specific words to fit those skeletal frames. These stages also are ordered, you will notice, in terms of their increasing specificity, and the decreasing size of the unit to which their planning applies.[28]

In a very rough way, we can note that intermediate stages (1) and (2) may correspond, respectively, to the higher-level narrative planning and the more momentary image planning which seem to be part of creating a dream. In dreaming, however (if my earlier argument is correct), there is no original intention, as in speech, to convey any particular message. Thus, at intermediate step (3), particular items to be expressed (in dreams, "imaged") are selected on the basis of their activation and their conformity to syntactic plans, but not on the basis of their agreement with a specific message plan. Likewise, at stage (2), syntactic plans are adopted on the basis of their conformity to the formal principles of narrative development (e.g., "this imagery must be sensibly continuous with the preceding dream imagery") and on the basis of their agreement with the more content-specific schema which has been selected to implement these principles (e.g., "this will be a dream about being in a restaurant"). And at stage (1), a content-specific schema will have been adopted because of its own activation, as well as for its suitability for incorporating other mnemonic units in a state of persistent activation. However, just as, in speech, we can change topics or digress in midcourse, so too in dreaming the operative schema can change (e.g., from restaurants to transcontinental train travel) as mnemonic activation changes. What will remain relatively more constant, however, is the formal principle that the events of the dream should unfold in a continuous sequence mimicking that of a story or life experience.

It's not clear how much credence these analogies between dream planning and mid-range speech planning should be given. But it is suggestive that there are stages of speech planning which have functional similarities to what I've taken to be necessary stages of dream planning, and that suggestiveness is only deepened by the empirical finding that disorders specific to speech organization are apparently accompanied by an absence of dreaming. Moreover, we also might ask whether humans would have two quite separate systems for planning narrative acts (speaking/writing stories versus dreaming stories), when the formal requirements of the two media seem functionally equivalent. Perhaps not.

It may seem that there is a developmental problem here. Children seem to be fluent speakers before they are fluent dreamers. But *overt* speech, at which the five-year-old is relatively fluent, may not index the child's ability to organize and experience consciousness verbally—a skill at which the waking five-year-old may not be nearly so competent. If we suppose that structures that serve specific functions in speech planning gradually come to serve a major role in the regulation of consciousness as well, then we would have a way of understanding both why children's conscious dreaming seems to lag behind their overt speech and why acquired disturbances in linguistic processing (aphasia) may be associated with deficits in dreaming. It's notable that severe aphasic deficits seem to be associated not only with disturbances in dreaming but also with a disordering of waking consciousness: this is what is meant by the patients' claims of defects in their "inner speech."[29]

Why might there be some special role for verbal processing systems in the regulation of conscious states? Why, for instance, is the quintessentially "visual" or "sensory" consciousness of dreaming seemingly more likely to be disrupted by waking speech deficits than by waking deficits in visual imaging (Chapter 1)? Why do preoperational children's skills in overt speech seem to be so much more highly developed than their skills in mental imaging (Chapter 3)?

There are several ways in which such questions (supposing their assumptions are correct) might be addressed:

1. Some current thinking in linguistics suggests a specific "instinctive" basis for linguistic competence. The evidence for this hypothesis is pretty good. With generally haphazard exposure to adult language, all humans without gross articulation or mental defects learn to speak. Even with elaborately designed training procedures, no other primate seems capable of functioning in a genuinely linguistic manner.[30] However, dreaming itself can be used to argue that there also is a species-wide (and probably species-specific) "instinctive" basis for human imaginal processing. Thus, reasoning from biological bases does not help to establish why there might be a general priority of verbal processing systems in regulating conscious states.

2. However, there is a significant difference in the degree to which social control can be exerted on verbal and imaginal processing. Speech is used for interpersonal communication, and both the specific features and the uses of language are subject to high degrees of social regulation. Imagery is inherently private, and, in the case of dreaming, it is largely outside the control of both the dreamer and the society in which he or she lives. Indeed, the autonomous process of dreaming seems to provide the only obligatory "practice" that imaginal processing systems will receive. That autonomous practice in early childhood seems much less accomplished than the social practice that children receive in listening and talking.

3. Functional considerations loom relatively larger, however, than purely ontogenetic ones in comparisons of linguistic and imaginal processing. Although the structure of language is not identical to that of thought or conceptualization, it surely is closer to it than is the structure of imaginal processing. Language is routinely suited to process the meaning of events, while imagery is routinely suited to process only their appearance properties. As we've seen, the bias of human information processing is to process events for their significance, rather than for their surface form, and in large measure symbolic memory seems to be organized conceptually rather than on the basis of appearance properties. Thus, a process such as dreaming, which is based on activation in symbolic memory, and which is thematically guided by considerations of meaning coherence rather than appearance coherence, must start from and be initially regulated by systems that are sensitive to meaning rather than appearance.

4. More formally considered, speech production systems also have functional properties required in dream production that aren't possessed by imaginal systems. Mental imagery is good at portraying particulars, but it is not good at formulating generalities. Planning and organization, however, are activities which have to be implemented at a general or abstract level, and linguistic processing systems may be better suited to such implementation than imaginal systems.

Thus, although we can consciously experience thought either in verbal or in imaginal terms, the planning which underlies consciousness may find implementation in verbal processing systems more readily than it does in specifically imaginal ones. That is, however "visual" dreaming may seem, it may be planned and regulated by the human *speech* production system. If this is the case, it may constitute the most decisive *general* test case for the regulation of consciousness, for nowhere else does our consciousness seem so vividly imaginal.

All of this is, of course, still speculative. But rich and counterintuitive speculation is the stuff on which scientific investigation thrives. An immediate task for cognitive dream psychology is to further investigate the ways in which language processing and dreaming may be related. What kinds of aphasic disorder are associated with what kinds of defects in REM dream production? Are there also reliable waking defects in *imaginal* processing in certain forms of aphasia?[31] What other sorts of brain lesions and specific cognitive defects are associated with a loss of fluency in REM dream production? Why does the development of skill in visuospatial analysis and synthesis seem to be important in the early development of dreaming (Chapter 3)? Are there communalities in the kinds of processing required for speech production and in solving block-design problems?[32] What do the REM dreams of bilinguals have to say about the role of language in dream production?[33]

3. CONSCIOUS ORGANIZATION

Nature. Dream experience is a conscious interpretation of relatively diffuse mnemonic activation. The activation of mnemonic units and networks is neither instigated nor regulated by conscious volition or intention. It is, however, subject to involuntary conscious interpretation. The implementation of the imaginal and thematic planning underlying such interpretation is achieved in, and integrated across, modular systems devoted to sensory, verbal, and affective processing.

The conditions underlying the sustainment of consciousness during sleep, sleep-induction, and other states of reduced processing of external stimulation seem to include: (a) physiological activation of the brain and the associated possibilities of mnemonic activation and symbolic activity; (b) sufficient symbolic maturation to permit the forms of symbolic processing associated with the experience of conscious states; and (c) relative preservation of the integrity of already developed systems for symbolic self-monitoring (in the face, for instance, of brain damage or degenerative disease). Whatever functions the sustainment of consciousness during sleep may serve intrasymbolically, there is some evidence suggesting that it (or the conditions permitting it) also serves some role in enhancing adaptation to the world outside the mind. For instance, extended confusional episodes sometimes are observed on arousal from profound, unconscious, early-night non-REM sleep.[34] These confusional disorders are most prevalent in preoperational children for whom, as we've seen, the maintenance of waking self-consciousness (and of dream consciousness) may be a generally difficult feat.

In consciously interpreting mnemonic activation, the dream production system serves to maintain consciousness by making sense of the only sorts of activities which typically *could* achieve awareness during states of sleep or acute inner absorption. By and large, the external world no longer exists for us when we are asleep or otherwise in the grips of the dreaming mode of mental organization. However, the interpretive nature of dreaming may most clearly be demonstrated in those relatively rare cases in which the dream seems to be almost wholly externally triggered.

During one six-year-old's REM period, for instance, an experimenter dabbed at her face with a cotton ball. When she was awakened, she reported dreaming that her brother was making some sort of designs on her head. Stimulus incorporations were rare in preoperational children's dreams, about as rare as one would expect from the children's generally low rates of reporting dreaming. They typically were accompanied by movement during stimulation, as if partial arousal were a precondition for the engagement of any effort at interpreting what was happening to the child. But the interpretive nature of the dream, here provoked by a stimulus whose nature we know, is clear. It probably is clear precisely because, at this age, REM sleep is not routinely associated with an ongoing interpretation of the more typical dream sources in symbolic memory. There was no ongoing dream experience to reject, or to obscure the role of, the external stimulus. During the concrete operational period, and later, when there is the possibility of relatively continuous interpretation of mnemonic activation (i.e., more likelihood of internally instigated dreaming), external stimuli that influence dreaming seem more likely to intrude upon, and to be used by, an already ongoing dream narrative.[35]

Modular Processing. As we've already seen (Chapter 1), a dream isn't just (or even basically) a sequence of visual images, and dreaming isn't just (or even basically) "seeing pictures." Dreaming is a multimodal simulation of waking experience. It is so lifelike that we have little difficulty understanding why we believe during a dream that what we're experiencing is "real." (We can even sympathize with those who persist in that belief after the dream is over). Dreaming recreates the spatial organization and temporal dimensions of our waking life encounters with objects and events. It has many of the sensory qualities of waking conscious perception. We are "in" our dreams, and we can "perform" a wide variety of motor acts. The verbal dimension of our communication with "others" is faithfully preserved. Even if we generally do not reflect or think *about our dreaming,* we can have an inner mental life *within the dream.* We are also capable of experiencing feelings, sometimes very intense ones.

It's interesting to contrast this portrait of "mental imaging" with traditional cognitive psychological accounts of imagery and consciousness. These accounts often seem to be influenced by the very limited contexts in which waking imagery has been studied experimentally. After so many studies of static visual images versus words as conscious mediators of verbal learning, it's as if many cognitive psychologists have come to believe that consciousness *is,* after all, either visual or verbal in just these ways. They clearly miss the sense of richness of imaginal experience that is familiar to dream psychologists and to any person who takes seriously the proposition that dreaming, too, is a symbolic activity.

We can believe that dreaming is a symbolic activity not just from theoretical considerations (what else could it be?) but also from developmental evidence. As we've seen (Chapter 3), both waking and dreaming observations suggest that the imaginal simulation of life experience is no sort of "given" in human consciousness. Instead, it is something that slowly emerges as part and parcel of the more general development of our symbolic competence.

It is, perhaps, the very fluency of our (adult) accomplishment in simulating life experience during dreaming that has led cognitive psychologists to imagine that dreaming must be something other than what they know best. But what they know best is evidently but a tiny piece of what is. Almost all waking research on mental imagery, for example, has focused on the processing of information from semantic or generic memory, rather than from our memory for events, and even Tulving's recent effort to begin redressing this imbalance "entails what we might call a 'snapshot view' of episodic memory" rather than a movielike visual (or a multimodal) view of recollective experience.[36]

How are we to understand, in a cognitive psychological sense, the fluency of the imaginal life simulation we evidence in our dreams? Since dreaming is a symbolic activity, we clearly must have some sort of information-processing framework to subsume the multimodal richness of our dream experience. What we must suppose, I think, is that there is modular memory—memory for the precise appearance, sound, affective, kinesthetic, etc. characteristics of life experiences—and that this memory, although we cannot consciously reflect on its knowledge, can be *used* in the service of symbolic processing activities. The knowledge in modular memory must be far more detailed than what we are ordinarily able to recall or to describe of the literal texture of what we've seen and heard and felt. It must be subject to a course of development that's dependent on (but may lag behind) the history of our waking perceptual experience. It must be automatic, requiring no strenuous attempts at "encoding" information.

Couldn't this memory be the source of our dreaming? Why do we have to imagine that dreaming requires conceptual processing and symbolic memory? Why couldn't any organism with a history of *perceptual* processing be able to dream? These obviously are important questions that—if the major theses of this book are to be upheld—need to be answered satisfactorily. I want, therefore, to make three main points about the hypothesis that dreaming is nothing more than a modular memory process.

First, modular memory is like what Piaget dubbed "recognition memory" (see the discussion in Chapter 3). The ordinary demonstration of recognition memory is that, when an object or event is *physically present,* we can identify or otherwise respond appropriately to it. This condition of dependence on world events for the activation of recognition memory is not met during sleep or the other states in which dreaming occurs.

Second, developmental evidence strongly suggests that the "autonomous" activation of modular memory depends on symbolic/conceptual maturation. Dream experience probably does not occur until there are independent demonstrations of symbolic competence, and, even then, children's earliest dreams seem to be far more impoverished than would have been predicted from their perceptual competence. It is striking how deficient the conscious realizations of young children's dreams seem to be. Initially, children seem not to be able to recreate a participatory self, movement of others or objects, or feelings. Then, in ways predicted by children's waking *symbolic* maturation, these components of life simulation slowly seem to fall into place.

Third, as we've also already observed, the dream creates novel experiences—outside the actual range of our perceptual experience—but they are, nonetheless, momentarily and thematically *meaningful.* It's exceedingly difficult to see how this result could occur without the mediation of symbolic (meaning) memory. Moreover, as we have also observed, the logic of the flow of dream events (my patient is sick, I'd better examine her) seems to be dictated by the meaning of those events, rather than by their appearance properties.

Thus, it seems scarcely possible that dreaming could be nothing more than a modular memory event. Both waking episodic recollection and dreaming must depend on the *symbolic* elicitation and regulation of modular processes. There's little reason to believe that these processes could, themselves, be responsible for either phenomenon (or that nonsymbolic creatures have conscious recollections or dreams).

The nearest example of what modular processing might produce by itself during sleep is what Arthur Arkin called "subideational" sleep talking. This concept refers to the (probably disinhibited) activity of speech articulation mechanisms sometimes observed during profound, early-night, non-REM sleep. Utterances are made that use meaningless sound patterns or stock phrases, such as those sometimes employed by patients with severe linguistic deficits. These utterances make little or no sense, and when awakened after making them, the erstwhile sleep-talker reports that he or she was not dreaming anything at all before being awakened.[37] One can imagine, then, that the physiological disinhibition (or activation) of modular *perceptual* processing would, in and of itself, not be associated with any conscious (dream) experience. Such experience would, among other things, require some *conceptual* regulation to produce *meaningfully organized, conscious experience.*

Although we can suspect, from our own experience, that visual dream imagery is generally well-produced (and more accomplished technically than most of our voluntary waking imagery), sophisticated descriptive studies of its (remembered) sensory qualities are just beginning to be reported. In a "psychophysical" study of the visual imagery of dreams, subjects were asked, on REM awakenings, to characterize the quality of the imagery of their last dream scene (and of their best-remembered dream scene). They responded by selecting, from 129 photographs of a standard scene that varied systematically along a number of dimensions (color saturation, illumination, figural clarity, figure-ground relationships, etc.) the one that best matched the formal quality of their dream imagery. Interestingly, subjects' ratings of various "visual" features of their dream imagery were unrelated to their ratings of the dream's emotionality or bizarreness, suggesting that visual-modular processing during dream formation is relatively uninfluenced by the plausibleness of the thematic plan being implemented therein. In a related study, the chromatic quality of subjects' REM dream imagery was assessed following 5 to 7 days in which they viewed the world through goggles which excluded all but red light. The results indicated a significant, but transitory, increase in "red" dream imagery. The effect was transitory in that it predominated only in early-night REM dreams on experimental nights and in that it disappeared when subjects no longer wore the goggles. That the effect was transitory in these ways suggests that it was due to modification of common perception/imagery *processing* systems, rather than to any fundamental reorganization in long-term depictive memory.[38]

Perhaps the most interesting studies of modular processing in REM dreams have to do with speech representations. In some imaginative studies, Frank Heynick had his subjects report, on awakening in the morning, the last line of speech they remembered from a dream. More often than not, this turned out to be speech by the self-character, it was "actually heard," and it was judged both by the dreamer and by linguists to be both meaningful and grammatically well-formed. Fully 84% of re-membered dream utterances were judged by dreamers themselves to be ones which they might either say or hear in normal waking life, and another 10% were judged to be fully acceptable speech specimens by the linguists.[39]

These findings suggest that the kind of diffuse activation which I have argued must characterize symbolic memory during dream formation does not generally exist in the modular memory systems responsible for the concrete realizations of dream expression. Either that, or what dif-fuseness there is in modular activation is overridden by the planning mechanisms overseeing modular processing. Either way, the modular sys-tems seem to be working sufficiently well, by waking standards, that we must assume that they are under effective conceptual regulation.

Freud noted what he thought were some semantic peculiarities in dream speech. He argued that the semantic oddness of dream speech occurs because, in effect, the dreamer is not actively processing speech during dreaming. Rather, the dreamer is simply stringing together, out of context, fragments of remembered speech from event memory.[40] Heynick's data indicate that both Freud's observation and his argument must be generally wrong. Dream speech can be both novel and meaningful, and its form requires us to assume the engagement of some of the same processing systems required for waking speech production.[41] Freud's argument may have been motivated by the consideration that dream speech should not be *interpreted* in the same way as waking speech, i.e., as reflecting a unitary communicative intention of the dreamer. This seems right. Neither the speech nor the other "intellectual" representations (e.g., thoughts, judgments) of dreams are intentionally formulated in the same way as their waking counterparts. They have the form, but not the sub-stance, of intentional thought products. You don't say something in a dream because you "thought" it, but because it helps to provide a consist-ent and thematically plausible interpretation of unconscious mnemonic activity. But Freud was surely wrong to insist that no conceptual compe-tence or linguistic processing is involved in the formulation of dream speech.

The apparently rare cases that caught Freud's eye, in which speech in dreams is a little odd, still bear investigation. If the general rule is that (inner) speech formulation during dreaming is conceptually regulated and effectively managed, the exceptions still might be revealing (as speech errors are more generally). Do they, for instance, seem simply to indicate a lapse in the conceptual regulation of speech processing? Or do they suggest that the conceptual structure of speech has effectively been re-

placed by the verbal-associative bias of lexical memory (e.g., "open" →
"close")? Does dream speech follow phonetic rather than conceptual lines
(e.g., "close" → "clothes")? What is the relative frequency of these "error" types, and what does this suggest about the planning of dream speech
more generally?

Another interesting question is whether the modular systems responsible for conscious dream experience can be experimentally manipulated.
Almost all attempts at "influencing" dreaming have been attempts to alter
its contents, i.e., the particular memories or knowledge processed imaginally. In another context, David Cohen proposed that dream subjects be
given verbal or nonverbal "exercises" before they go to sleep.[42] For instance, subjects might sit at a television monitor before they go to sleep
and play one of two computer games, one that forces them rapidly to
make words out of various letter combinations and one that forces them
to keep their "car" on a rapidly twisting "road." Would the game they
played on any given night increase or decrease the speech imagery in their
REM dreams?

Waking research on "priming" effects (where one experience has a
facilitating effect on a similar, later performance) has suggested that they
are not cross-modal. That is, seeing a word increases your later ability to
recognize it when it is presented visually, but not auditorially. This, in
turn, suggests that priming effects are mediated modularly rather than
conceptually. This may explain why certain brain-damaged patients can
learn perceptual-motor and cognitive *skills* without being able to demonstrate comparable gains in symbolic memory tasks. Their acquisition of
modular or procedural knowledge has not been affected, while their acquisition of conceptual knowledge is grossly impaired. They may not
"remember" if they've ever been in the laboratory before, but their performance on some procedural task may show the same kinds of im-
provement as a function of prior practice as would be seen with a
nonamnesic subject.[43]

Waking research also suggests that priming effects may be highly
specific. That is, experience in processing words may not facilitate all
later verbal processing, but only processing just like that which has been
practiced.[44] Thus, it isn't clear that effects of the hypothetical dream
experiment described above should be sought even at the level of generality of the specific modular system manipulated. They may be content-
and/or process-specific within the module. Still, the possibility of demonstrating some sort of priming effects on dream experience remains an
intriguing one. Studies in this vein would be important not only because
they use an experimental control paradigm—with which psychologists
seem most comfortable—but also because they would rely on the observation that the form of dream processing is much more readily specified in

advance than is the particular mnemonic content which is likely to be processed during the formation of any night's REM dreams.

Modular Integration. Fodor's concept of a modular system specifies that input systems for visual and linguistic analysis are automatic, modality-specific, and informationally encapsulated.[45] While it is useful to bear these properties in mind in one's first efforts to model how sensory information is processed, understood, and remembered, it's not at all clear that these properties will always survive the scrutiny of more detailed analysis. If *conscious* perception is viewed as a natural endpoint of visual information processing, for instance, Marcel's research (reviewed briefly in Chapter 3) suggests that such perception cannot be construed as being either automatic or informationally encapsulated. Fodor's focus on the informational encapsulation of modular processing and the relative shallowness of its outputs may not do full justice to later stages of information processing that we ordinarily would consider to be, for instance, specifically "visual." As has recently been noted, "True informational encapsulation . . . may be a property of only some lower level 'computational automatisms' which contribute to, but do not completely characterise, the processes that 'deliver the world to thought.' "[46]

It might well be wondered how efficient an information processing system could be that had only two levels of information access: intramodular ("encapsulated") vs. global. The more sensible way to build the system would seem to be to allow for intermediate levels of information transfer. In later stages of processing visual information, for instance, information from other modules and from symbolic memory might be accessed in a restricted (less than global) way. This still would happen before "the world was delivered to thought," i.e., to conceptual processing systems with global access to symbolic knowledge. Or, to put it another way, (the way I put it in the Introduction), we can think of an intermediate (but less than abstract) level of conceptual processing necessary to the integration (and conscious perception) of sense data. This conceptual processing would have relatively limited access to symbolic memory, as well as access to the outputs of different input modules. Thus, for example, the conscious "visual" perception of a geometric form might depend on access of lexical knowledge in the linguistic module and/or of appropriate categorical knowledge in symbolic memory.[47]

There are two reasons for introducing these complications to Fodor's view of modular systems at this point. First, the dream seems consciously to integrate information in different modalities. Second, the dream's events, although *created* via conceptual mechanisms, do not seem to receive more than a specifiably limited ("literal") interpretation. That is, the dream does not seem *itself* to stimulate global reasoning or comprehension processes. Thus, I can dream of my father, seeing and hearing him, knowing that that's my father and that it's appropriate that he's dressed as he is and that he's doing what he is doing, without remarking on how odd it is to be sharing a "life experience" with a man who has been dead for over thirty years. The conscious cross-modality integration of dreaming would seem to require some "perceptual" interaction among modules, and the comprehension we give our dream experiences would seem to require something more than modular processing, yet something much less than the sort of conceptual processing that Fodor considers symptomatic of "central" (nonmodular) processing.

Here, in fact, is another case where dream data may provide a unique view of the organizational possibilities of cognitive systems. Dreams routinely exemplify a kind of mid-range level of conceptual comprehension, a level that otherwise has to be inferred (because analysis for comprehension typically proceeds past it to "deeper" understanding), but that in dreams can be directly observed (because there generally *is* no deeper understanding in dreaming). Precisely because the unconscious mnemonic cues for "episodic recollection" in dreaming are so varied, the dream is our best demonstration of the constructive nature of conscious recollection, and our best illustration of how mnemonic information suitable to processing in different modalities simultaneously may be processed and sensibly may be integrated in conscious experience.

What do we know about the multimodal integration of knowledge in dreaming? We know, first of all, that such integration seems most poorly achieved at sleep onset. The observations we've previously noted (Chapter 2) on formal "regressivity" in conscious experience at sleep onset suggest dysfunction both at the modular level (you can be seeing two things at once, things that aren't blended into a well-formed, unified image) and at the level of intermodular integration (you can be seeing one thing, but thinking [verbally?] of another.)

But we also know that, in more typical (i.e., REM) dreaming, the integration of visual and verbal processing generally is quite effective. Heynick randomly called subjects at home during the night. He asked them for the last line of dream dialogue they could recall, and also for an account of the larger dream scenario in which that dialogue was embedded. In general, judges found the subject's dream dialogues to be appropriate to the dream narrative. Only in approximately 1 report out of every 20 was the dialogue judged to be "entirely unsuitable" to the dream narrative. In roughly 2 cases out of 3, it was judged "entirely suitable," and in most of the remainder of the cases, it was judged at least partly appropriate to the narrative. Heynick's research, as we've seen earlier in this chapter, argues for the general *grammatical* competence of dream speech (it's well-formed). The present data suggest that dream speech also generally is *pragmatically* competent. That is, however odd what is happening in the dream might be, what is said in the dream is generally appropriate to the context that otherwise has been established.[48]

Evidence on other forms of intermodular integration in dreaming still is lacking. Heynick's study provides a model that might be used in further research not only on verbal-narrative integration but on other forms of intraimaginal coherence as well. Attention clearly must be paid to the most common forms of failed integration, as well as to any general trend toward effective integration.

Anecdotal observation suggests that the domain in which coherence might least likely be observed with the dream narrative is that of affective experience. One of the peculiarities of dreaming noted by Freud (and given, by him, a characteristically deep and devious interpretation) is that the dreamer may be in a situation which in wakefulness would seem to require some conscious feeling (e.g., being stark naked in a crowd of fully-clothed people), yet feel nothing in the dream.[49] We might understand this, not as Freud did, as *inhibited* feeling, but as a failure to integrate feelings with other dream imagery. I can call into consciousness the mental image of a person's face or of some place or situation at will if I "think" about it, but if I try symbolically to generate a feeling (think about something that makes me very angry, for instance) it seems that the development of that feeling has a much slower time course. This might explain why feelings sometimes can be lacking where "required" in dreams (you haven't had enough time to work them up, given that the kind of planning which underlies dream generation may not permit much anticipation of specific situations requiring them), and why—more rarely—feelings sometimes seem to be keyed to inappropriate imagery (they were planned as accompaniments to an earlier situation).[50]

Developmental observations may be especially relevant here. As we've seen (Chapter 3), feeling competence in dream construction (i.e., having feelings accompany events that would seem to "call for" them) seems to lag behind imaginal or narrative competence in childhood. A more detailed analysis of children's waking knowledge of feelings and of their situational appropriateness might establish when the conceptual prerequisites of recreating dream feelings are first present, and such analysis could be correlated with the study of the forms in which pragmatic competence in generating dream affect is first established. Given the tendency to assimilate dreams to waking mnemonic schemata, it is essential that such research should employ the abrupt-awakening technique of dream elicitation during REM sleep episodes. Otherwise, dream experiences which had no associated affect may be reported as having had it, since it seems entirely appropriate to waking reflection that they "should have had it."[51]

We've already considered (Chapter 1) some of the reasons why the conscious experience of dreaming might be confused with the conscious experience accompanying real life events. As we've seen, the hallucinatory quality of dreaming seemingly can't be deduced simply from the fact that we're imaging, or that our imaging is wholly internally or symbolically driven, or that we're imaging so plausibly and well. Rather, it must depend on the whole quality of mental organization associated with dream production. Ultimately, it stems from the fact that the dreaming mode of mental organization does not provide the sort of judgmental framework in which the plausibility of conscious contents might be evaluated. This is, in one sense, a "descriptive" analysis rather than an "explanatory" one (the same might be said of my discussion of a related problem: why dreams seem to be so forgettable). But certain forms of description can serve explanatory purposes. They can, for example, lead us to see that, once we understand what dreaming is, it isn't really so puzzling that dream imagery is taken as real or that it can so quickly be "forgotten." Our initial puzzlement, in each case, may be a function of bringing an inappropriate frame of reference to bear on a phenomenon, one that leads us uncritically to expect that symbolically generated imaginal experiences should be recognized as being only "mental" and that momentarily impressive imaginative experiences surely should be memorable ones. Describing what dreaming seems to be can lead to changed expectations, and thus to reduced puzzlement. More importantly, it can lead us to many other important questions, and it can begin to suggest some of the ways in which they might be answered.

Whether the relatively informal model presented in this chapter is "right" or "wrong," it does open avenues to thinking about dreaming in a conceptually appropriate way. Dreaming must be a peculiar *organization* of structures and processes in the human mind. To begin to understand dreams and dreaming, we must begin to formulate hypotheses about what these structures and processes are and about their hierarchical and temporal integration. In so doing, we must begin to relate dreaming to the systematic, scientific study of mental structures, processes, and organizations more generally. That is, we must begin thinking about (and studying) dreaming in a cognitive psychological way.[52]

NOTES

[1]Jerry A. Fodor, *Psychological Explanation: An Introduction to the Philosophy of Psychology,* New York: Random House, 1968.

[2]The model discussed in this chapter is a reworking of David Foulkes, "A Cognitive-Psychological Model of REM Dream Production," *Sleep,* 1982, *5,* 169–187.

[3]On the possible adaptive role of REM sleep in mnemonic functioning in animals and humans, see Michael J. McGrath and David B. Cohen, "REM Sleep Facilitation of Adaptive

Waking Behavior: A Review of the Literature," *Psychological Bulletin*, 1978, *85*, 24–57, and William Fishbein (ed.), *Sleep, Dreams and Memory*, New York: SP Medical & Scientific Books, 1981.

[4] William B. Zimmerman, "Sleep Mentation and Auditory Awakening Thresholds," *Psychophysiology*, 1970, *6*, 540–549.

[5] Sigmund Freud, *The Interpretation of Dreams*, New York: Basic Books, 1955 (originally published, 1900).

[6] For a more detailed discussion and criticism of Freud's "deeper" dream theory, see David Foulkes, *A Grammar of Dreams*, New York: Basic Books, 1978, especially chapters 1–4.

[7] In more than twenty years of collecting laboratory reports of dreams, I can't remember *ever* having heard the identical REM dream report twice from the same person. It may be, of course, that this is because no one person has been studied often enough (although, in my research on children's dreams, longitudinal subjects were studied for as many as 40 nights each). But it also may be that spontaneously recalled "recurrent" dreams are somewhat different dream experiences which have been assimilated to a common waking mnemonic schema. The extent to which the manifest similarities in the experiences underlying these recollections are attributable to recurrent patterns of mnemonic activation per se, as compared to stereotyped nonconscious schemata which have evolved to interpret mnemonic activation, is unclear.

[8] David Foulkes and Marcella Schmidt, "Temporal Sequence and Unit Composition in Dream Reports from Different Stages of Sleep," *Sleep*, 1983, *6*, 265–280.

[9] Freud, *op. cit.*, p. 107ff. Additional associative material is from Alexander Grinstein, *On Sigmund Freud's Dreams*, Detroit: Wayne State University Press, 1968, ch. 1. The dream is quoted verbatim.

[10] Freud, *op. cit.*, p. 106.

[11] This is an unpublished observation from my own pilot research.

[12] Roger Brown and Richard J. Herrnstein, *Psychology*, Boston: Little, Brown, 1975, p. 437.

[13] Janet L. Lachman and Roy Lachman, "Theories of Memory Organization and Human Evolution," in C. Richard Puff (ed.), *Memory Organization and Structure*, New York: Academic Press, 1979, pp. 133–193.

[14] The concept of spreading activation in memory networks has been used by Allan M. Collins and Elizabeth F. Loftus, "A Spreading-Activation Theory of Semantic Processing," *Psychological Review*, 1975, *82*, 407–428.

[15] This case (originally described by Myrna F. Schwartz, Oscar S. M. Marin, and Eleanor M. Saffran, "Dissociations of Language Function in Dementia: A Case Study," *Brain and Language*, 1979, *7*, 277–306), is discussed by Loraine K. Obler, "Language and Brain Dysfunction in Dementia," in Sidney J. Segalowitz (ed.), *Language Functions and Brain Organization*, New York: Academic Press, 1983, pp. 267–282.

[16] Obler, *loc. cit.*, p. 273.

[17] *Ibid.*

[18] Donald J. Foss and David T. Hakes, *Psycholinguistics: An Introduction to the Psychology of Language*, Englewood Cliffs, N.J.: Prentice-Hall, 1978, pp. 189–197.

[19] Even Piaget, I think, in his major attempt to deal specifically with dreaming (Jean Piaget, *Play, Dreams and Imitation in Childhood*, New York: W. W. Norton, 1962 [originally published 1946]), was handicapped by the assumption that dreaming involves something more than his kind of science could comprehend. At critical points, for instance, he genuflects to such clinical concepts as repression and wish-fulfillment. For a discussion, see David Foulkes, "REM-Dream Perspectives on the Development of Affect and Cognition," *Psychiatry Journal of the University of Ottawa*, 1982, *7*, 48–55.

[20] Foss and Hakes, *op. cit.*, p. 279.

[21]See, for instance, Perry W. Thorndyke, "Cognitive Structures in Comprehension and Memory of Narrative Discourse," *Cognitive Psychology,* 1977, *9,* 77–110.

[22]For instance, subjects' chronological accounts of dreams remembered at the end of relatively brief REM episodes might be the object of study. Earlier research suggests that the end of *dream episodes* is often marked by the occurrence of gross body movements during REM sleep (e.g., Edward A. Wolpert and Harry Trosman, "Studies in Psychophysiology of Dreams. I. Experimental Evocation of Sequential Dream Episodes," *Archives of Neurology and Psychiatry,* 1958, *79,* 603–606). Thus, REM awakenings might be made during or just after such movements. The limitation that the REM episodes be relatively brief is dictated by a concern that subjects be able to recollect and be willing to describe a complete dream episode.

Kuiken and Nielsen at the University of Alberta (Edmonton) have made a promising start toward studying the "story-line" properties of dream reports. See Don L. Kuiken and Tore A. Nielsen, "Structural Analysis of Stories," unpublished manuscript, and T. Nielsen, D. Kuiken, A. Moffit, R. Hoffman, and R. Wells, "Comparisons of the Story Structure of Stage REM and Stage 2 Mentation Reports," *Sleep Research,* 1983, *12,* 181.

[23]Robert Wilensky, "Story Grammars versus Story Points," *The Behavioral and Brain Sciences,* 1983, *6,* 579–623 (see particularly the commentary by William F. Brewer, pp. 595–596); Alan Garnham, "What's Wrong with Story Grammars," *Cognition,* 1983, *15,* 145–154.

[24]Foulkes and Schmidt, *loc. cit.*

[25]Elizabeth Dorus, Walter Dorus, and Allan Rechtschaffen, "The Incidence of Novelty in Dreams," *Archives of General Psychiatry,* 1971, *25,* 364–368.

[26]The observations on dreaming and aphasia in this section come from a literature search described in David Foulkes, *A Grammar of Dreams* (New York: Basic Books, 1978), pp. 163–164, and from a study by Arthur W. Epstein and Nina N. Simmons, "Aphasia with Reported Loss of Dreaming," *American Journal of Psychiatry,* 1983, *140,* 108–109. Results of the literature search also are reported in Roger J. Broughton, "Neurology and Dreaming," *Psychiatric Journal of the University of Ottawa,* 1982, *7,* 101–110.

[27]Foss and Hakes, *op. cit.,* esp. ch. 5–6.

[28]It appears likely, both in speech planning and in dream planning, that stages such as these may not literally be sequential. Rather, they may be partly parallel in time, with some feedback from "later" to "earlier" stages. Thus, difficulties in executing a speech plan may lead to a reformulation of that plan. For didactic purposes, however, it is simplest to introduce the notion of processing stages as if they were purely sequential.

[29]The claim here is not that *overt* speech is necessary for consciousness, only that consciousness may be regulated by structures serving specific functions in speech planning. These structures can mature and become functional without overt speech, for instance, in humans with congenital articulation disorders: See Eric H. Lenneberg, "Understanding Language Without Ability to Speak: A Case Report," *Journal of Abnormal and Social Psychology,* 1962, *65,* 419–425.

[30]See H. S. Terrace, L. A. Petitto, R. J. Sanders, and T. G. Bever, "Can an Ape Create a Sentence?", *Science,* 1979, *206,* 891–902. The claims for ape language are also neatly refuted by Arden Neisser, *The Other Side of Silence: Sign Language and the Deaf Community in America,* New York: Alfred A. Knopf, 1983, pp. 202–234. Neisser points out that there is, moreover, no good evidence that linguistically trained apes ever used the "language" to *think.*

[31]An older literature (reviewed by Joyce Fitch-West, "Heightening Visual Imagery: A New Approach to Aphasia Therapy," in Ellen Perecman (ed.), *Cognitive Processing in the Right Hemisphere,* New York: Academic Press, 1983, pp. 215–228) suggests that there may be such deficits. The question obviously is important not only to dream research, but also to

attempts to remediate speech deficits by using an "alternate" imaginal processing system. (See also the following footnote.)

[32] There is some evidence that this is the case. See Patricia Marks Greenfield, "The Grammar of Action in Cognitive Development", in Donald O. Walter, Linda Rogers, and Joyce M. Finzi-Fried (eds.), *Conference on Human Brain Function*, Los Angeles: Brain Information Service, U.C.L.A., 1976, pp. 67–73, and Stuart Reifel and Patricia Marks Greenfield, "Structural Development in a Symbolic Medium: The Representational Use of Block Constructions," in George E. Forman (ed.), *Action and Thought: From Sensorimotor Schemes to Symbolic Operations*, New York: Academic Press, 1982, pp. 203–233.

One way of interpreting block-design correlations with dream production is that block-design tests measure skills of analysis and synthesis that are used in effecting flexible symbolic control over modular system processing. Thus, these skills would be used in speech regulation as well as in the symbolically motivated decomposition and recomposition of holistic visuospatial patterns. They would be (descriptively) part of a language processing system, but they would also be (conceptually) cognitive skills of wider application than to representations in or from any particular modular system. In this respect, it's interesting that C. Scott Moss reported (in personal correspondence) that, before his recovery from aphasia, he also experienced difficulty in "trying to make some sense out of" *novel* perceptual patterns. A long-time football fan, for instance, he found it so difficult to conceptually organize what was going on while watching televised games that finally, in frustration, he had to have the receiver turned off.

Another recent investigation of dream recall found that aphasic patients with left posterior (but not left anterior) hemispheric lesions were likely to be unable to remember dreams (Luigi Murri, Roberto Arena, Gabriele Siciliano, Raffaele Mazzotta, and Alberto Muratorio, "Dream Recall in Patients with Focal Cerebral Lesions," *Archives of Neurology*, 1984, *41*, 183–185). Dream recall frequency was determined by means of a questionnaire administered each morning for ten consecutive days (presumably not just as the patients awoke from sleep, although the authors do not identify the precise conditions of questionnaire administration). Six of seven (86%) patients with left posterior lesions *and* language dysfunction recalled no dreams, while only two of six (33%) patients with left posterior lesions and *no* language dysfunction were nonrecallers. The patients with language deficits *also* typically performed poorly on visuospatial analytic tasks, while those without language deficits typically did not. Right hemisphere posterior (but not anterior) lesions also were associated with visuospatial defects and with an absence of dream recall. Neither the language nor the visuospatial testing of patients was sufficiently detailed to permit one to draw conclusions about the precise manner in which defective dreaming might have been mediated. Nor, of course, was the REM awakening strategy employed, so we don't even have the best possible evidence that dreaming itself (rather than memory for dreams) was affected by the patients' visuospatial and linguistic deficits. Still, the evidence is at least consistent with the idea that mid-range processing skills that may be shared by linguistic and visuospatial systems are necessary to the production of dream experience. It isn't clear, from the author's account, that their right posterior patients were tested for language dysfunction. Thus, the dream recall of those patients is equivocal on whether specifically *linguistic* processing deficits need to be involved in defective dream production. Possibly the right posterior lesions affected only the imaginal quality and thus the later memorability of experienced dreams. Obviously, there is much further work to be done in this area, and it needs to be done with sophisticated waking cognitive testing and with REM-monitored experimental dream retrieval.

[33] There is some evidence suggesting that bilinguals may differ from unilinguals in linguistic processing strategies and that there may be interlinguistic differences in the cortical

representation of their linguistic knowledge: see Jyotsna Vaid, "Bilingualism and Brain Lateralization," in Segalowitz, *op. cit.*, pp. 315–339. If the language which achieves surface representation in dream experience can be used as a sign of the linguistic system employed in dream planning, it would be interesting to compare the formal organization of dreams "dreamed in different languages."

[34] Roger J. Broughton, "Sleep Disorders: Disorders of Arousal?" *Science*, 1968, *159*, 1070–1078.

[35] David Foulkes, *Children's Dreams: Longitudinal Studies*, New York: John Wiley and Sons, 1982. The dream is reported on p. 98; a more general discussion of results on stimulus-incorporation trials is given on pp. 256–260.

[36] Endel Tulving, *Elements of Episodic Memory*, New York: Oxford University Press, 1983. The quote is from p. 184, and the point about the neglect of imagery from episodic memory is made on p. 186. Imagery is nowhere so impressive or pervasive as in dreaming, yet most cognitive psychological discussions of waking mental imagery give no hint that the researcher has even *considered* the possible relevance of dream data. One article that does make informed use of dream observations in addressing questions about mental imagery is: Nancy H. Kerr, "The Role of Vision in 'Visual Imagery' Experiments: Evidence from the Congenitally Blind," *Journal of Experimental Psychology: General*, 1983, *112*, 265–277.

[37] Arthur M. Arkin, *Sleep Talking: Psychology and Psychophysiology*, Hillsdale, N.J.: Lawrence Erlbaum Associates, 1981. The quote is from p. 335. During lighter and later-night non-REM sleep and during REM sleep, there typically is a better correspondence between reported dream activity and sleep talking, and overt speech itself is more meaningfully organized. Sleep walking typically occurs *only* during profound, early-night non-REM sleep, and it too seems not to be accompanied by dream experience (see Allan Jacobson, Anthony Kales, Dietrich Lehmann, and J. R. Zweizig, "Somnambulism: All-Night Electroencephalographic Studies," *Science*, 1965, *148*, 975–977).

[38] The "psychophysical" study is: Allan Rechtschaffen and Cheryl Buchignani, "Visual Dimensions and Correlates of Dream Images," *Sleep Research*, 1983, *12*, 189; the goggle study is reported by Howard P. Roffwarg, John H. Herman, Constance Bowe-Anders, and Edward S. Tauber, "The Effects of Sustained Alterations of Waking Visual Input on Dream Content," in Arthur M. Arkin, John S. Antrobus, and Steven J. Ellman (eds.), *The Mind in Sleep: Psychology and Psychophysiology*, Hillsdale, N.J.: Lawrence Erlbaum Associates, 1978, 295–349.

[39] Frank Heynick, "Theoretical & Empirical Investigation into Verbal Aspects of the Freudian Model of Dream Generation," M.D. Dissertation, University of Groningen (The Netherlands), 1983.

[40] Freud, *op. cit.*, p. 418.

[41] Heynick, *op. cit.*, reports that, more often than not, his subjects did *not* identify dream speech episodes as recollections of speech they previously had said or heard. This was despite the generally commonplace nature of the dream utterances the subjects reported.

[42] David B. Cohen, *Sleep and Dreaming: Origins, Nature and Functions*, Oxford, England: Pergamon Press, 1979, p. 203. (Unlike Cohen, I'm not assuming that modular practice is necessarily the practice of one or the other cerebral hemisphere.)

Although the goggle manipulation previously mentioned (footnote 38) seemingly was conceptualized as a content manipulation (on specific waking percepts), its effects in fact best are understood as being content nonspecific. Thus, Roffwarg et al. found (*loc. cit.*, p. 324) that even events which had not been "seen" red could still be "dreamed" red.

[43] See the discussion by Tulving, *op. cit.*, pp. 100–112.

[44] *Ibid.*, p. 111.

[45] Jerry A. Fodor, *The Modularity of Mind*, Cambridge, Mass.: Bradford Books, 1983.

[46] Myrna F. Schwartz and Barry Schwartz, "In Defence of Organology," *Cognitive*

Neuropsychology, 1984, *1,* 25–42. The quote is from p. 41. The article is an extended review of Fodor's *The Modularity of Mind.*

[47] E.g., see the experimental demonstration in Rita Sloan Berndt, Alfonso Caramazza, and Edgar Zurif, "Language Functions: Syntax and Semantics," in Segalowitz, *op. cit.,* pp. 5–28.

[48] Heynick, *op. cit.,* esp. ch. 4. Heynick's judges did not even think that they were judging dreams. They were told that they would be judging how well a computer program was able to generate speech appropriate to narrative contexts. Thus, their results could not have been guided by some implicit theory about speech-narrative relationships in dreams.

[49] Freud, *op. cit.,* pp. 460–487.

[50] See the discussion in Foulkes, "REM-Dream Perspectives on the Development of Affect and Cognition," *loc. cit.* Specific questions for future research might include: How often is dream affect appropriate to the narrative? Is dream affect more often omitted or incongruous? Where it is incongruous, would the affect fit some earlier moment in the narrative? Is dream affect more appropriate to dream imagery than to free associations to that imagery (that should be the case, since thematic planning must only imperfectly reflect the potential "sources" of the dream)?

[51] E.g., see David Foulkes, "Home and Laboratory Dreams: Four Empirical Studies and a Conceptual Reevaluation," *Sleep,* 1979, *2,* 233–251.

[52] A classical objection to the possibility of an empirical dream psychology (cognitive or otherwise) is that dreaming's "causes" can neither be experimentally controlled nor empirically determined. It's true that we typically can't control or even decisively ascertain the symbolic (mnemonic) sources of the dream. Dreaming is hardly unique in this respect, however; the objection seems to rule out the systematic study of many forms of "spontaneous" cognition. The question should be, can empirical research advance our understanding of a spontaneous mental phenomenon such as dreaming? The answer clearly has to be yes. Whatever the merits of the model presented in this chapter, it summarizes and builds upon earlier research that has had precisely this effect. The model presented here suggests a further, *systematic* program of research, which should have the same knowledge-enhancing, understanding-increasing result. There may be some respects, moreover, in which dreaming is a *more* apt subject for empirical study than some of the phenomena so traditionally valued and painstakingly pursued by cognitive psychologists. To the degree that Fodor's "First Law of the Nonexistence of Cognitive Science" (*op. cit.,* p. 107) is correct, the more modular a mental process, the more possible it is to characterize or model that process. As we've just seen, modular systems play a significant role in the cognitive psychological modeling of dreaming—a more significant role, one might hazard, than they have in the modeling of human problem solving or analogical reasoning. Although we may not be able to determine or manipulate the particular mnemonic sources of dream imagery very well, this does not mean that we can't specify significant parameters of the *processing systems* that will operate on these sources, particularly when these systems themselves have a modular or quasimodular quality.

5 Meanings and Functions

The two questions people most often raise about dreams are: What do they *mean?* and *Why* do we dream? These questions often seem to be related: if you understood what any particular dream meant, then you might understand why it was dreamed. Thus, if you had some idea about the kinds of meanings dreams have, then you might also understand the general function of dreams.

But, in fact, these two questions are only closely related if you make a certain assumption about dreaming—namely that meaning is deliberately encoded during dream formation. Then, one *function* of dreaming would be that it regularly expressed certain intended meanings. Think of communicative speech. You say (generally) what you mean to say. That is, one function of speech is that it expresses intended meanings.

Another aspect of communicative speech, however, is that effects are foreseen which lie beyond the realm of speech itself. We may say that we're speaking just to "express ourselves," but typically we are likely to have certain nonlinguistic intentions as well. If a father tells his son, "Your room is messy," he's intending not just to describe a room, but also to motivate the boy to perform certain acts. Another, less immediate function of speech, then, is that a listener's behavior will be modified in specifiable ways.

For dreaming, a communication model of meaning could work in one of two ways: (1) The ultimate functions of the dream can be construed as following directly from its immediate functions. This is basically a one-person speech model. Just as you feel "better" (perhaps) for having vented your anger in some tirade, so too your behavior will predictably be modified by dreaming some particular dream. The effect follows directly from the act of expression, not from that act's mediated effect on someone or something else. Perhaps, for instance, self-confidence is directly established or reinforced by dreaming dreams in which we make ourselves behave self-confidently. (2) The ultimate effect of the dream may be less predictable than the foregoing implies. Specifically, it may depend on the use some other system makes of the dream. This is a two-person speech model, in which effects depend on how "others" construe or act upon the message we've expressed. For dream messages, the others might be other mental systems (or selves) than the system (or self) that dreamed the dream. The dream may be "saying," "See, you can do it if you try," but the waking behavioral self may not "get the message" (the dream is unnoticed or forgotten by that self) or, it may not prove capable of acting upon it.

Precisely because of the difficulties of specifying who the inner "listener" in dreaming might be, and in explaining its separation from the inner "speaker," the more popular position among dream interpreters probably has been the first. For example, Freud's theory seems to imagine that the very act of expressing some unconscious wish in a dream changes the balance of the unconscious systems that sought disguised release in dream imagery.[1] (If the release is not very well disguised, there may in fact be a "listener"—the ego—which is made anxious by the dream's expression of taboo fantasies or feelings.) However, other theorists, most notably Erich Fromm, have proposed what are essentially two-person communication models of dreaming. Fromm speaks of dreams as "important communications from ourselves to ourselves," and characterizes uninterpreted dreams as being similar to unopened letters.[2] The idea is that there is a dreaming self who see things differently, and often more wisely, than the waking self. Thus, with the aid of a therapist or of dream "groups," we may be better able to "get in touch with" who we really are and what we really want from life. But these effects don't follow routinely from simply having dreamed. Rather, they must be mediated by the hard work of self and others. We may need help both in decoding the message of the dream and in inducing our waking self to act upon it.

The model of dreaming synthesized in the last chapter suggests that there is *no* deliberate intention to express *any* particular message in dreaming. It denies the encoding either of particular wishes or fantasies which need "release," or of particular messages or gems of wisdom which, if interpreted correctly, can help us to set our lives aright. It does propose a limited hypothesis about the immediate purpose of dreaming—that it is an attempt consciously to interpret (make sense of) diffuse mnemonic activation, but it does not explain what adaptive effects it may have. Thus, it is appropriate now to consider what, if anything, the model *does* have to say about the meanings or larger functions of dreaming.

One point should be made before we embark on our course. That is that intentional meanings are not the only meanings events can have. It does not follow that, since dreams are constructed to convey no particular message, they are meaningless. There are broader senses of meaning than apply to the case of deliberate message-encoding. A speaker at a political rally may have constructed his speech to convince us that the poor are deserving, and that he is their champion. He may mean to motivate us to work on his behalf (and possibly even on behalf of the poor). But we may assign other meanings to the speech. We may see, behind a facade of concern for others, an immense self-centeredness. We may feel, behind the verbal eloquence, an attitude to the poor that is patronizing and based on no genuine experience of what it is like to be poor. These, too, are meanings, and they are precisely the sorts of meanings that psychologists long have considered their particular province. They are the unintentional behaviors by which the speaker reveals both his "real" ways of thinking and feeling about the topics he ostensibly is addressing and, in a more general way, what sort of person he is. If not messages, they are certainly *signs* of mind and of character.

Even if dreams were to contain no deliberate expressions of "deep-seated feelings" and no deliberate "messages from ourselves to ourselves," they still might be rich with meaning. Dreams come from our mind. In fact, because they are so little responsive to anything but what's in and on our mind, dreams may be one of the purest reflections we have of the structure and processes of our mind. The purpose of this chapter is to consider in what ways dreams can and can't legitimately be used to "reveal" our minds and selves to us. We'll begin by considering some limits on their revelatory possibilities. Specifically, what are the problems with the kinds of interpretations psychologists such as Fromm and Freud have proposed for our dreams?

1. THE DREAM NARRATIVE *IS* NOT
A TRANSLATED MESSAGE

Fromm seems to make relatively extreme claims for the meaningfulness of dreams. At times, at least, he seems to propose that dream content is as meaningful as is waking speech. I won't worry here about whether he consistently adheres to this position. Rather, for argument's sake, I will sketch out a position suggested by Fromm's writings and examine the implications of that position in terms of the evidence we have examined.

Fromm proposes that the dream narrative is a translation, in pictorial language (sensory/spatial mental codes), of a coherent set of underlying verbal/propositional intentions. The course of the dream, then, reflects the organization of these intentions, i.e., an underlying message sequence. Presumably, when adherents of this view ask what a particular dream means, they want to know the sequence of the underlying thoughts which are embedded in the sequence of overt dream imagery. For instance, they want to hear something like: "You find yourself tempted to move to another city, but you are made anxious by your perception of the changes this will involve. However, if you can conquer these fears, you will find the change to be a rewarding one."

Short of accepting such translations simply on an interpreter's say-so, a perennial problem with any underlying message theory has been how the messages conveyed in dream imagery shall be identified. Since Freud's time, one conventional answer has been: through free association. In free association to sequences of dream imagery, the dreamer is supposed to uncover the "latent dream thoughts" corresponding to her or his manifest dream images. As critics have often noted, free association has, in practice, rarely been standardized, and it often seems to be the interpreter's theoretical preconceptions that both guide the course of the subject's associations and select their point of termination. Even given these biases, however, a less frequently remarked result of free association methods is that *the sequence of the dreamer's associations rarely if ever coheres as well as does the sequence of the manifest dream imagery* from which the associations are elicited. That is, although individual dream events can stimulate recollections or associations which are important to the dreamer in her or his waking life, when such recollections and associations are laid out in a sequence corresponding to that of the dream events that stimulated them, the former sequence rarely (if ever) corresponds to that of an underlying story, message, or any other coherent sequence of thoughts or propositions. This certainly is true if one looks at clinicians' own examples of dream-associative data (e.g., the "Irma's Injection" dream discussed in Chapter 4). I have also observed this to be the case in application of a more standardized association methodology to subjects' laboratory collected dream reports.

This discrepancy between the undoubted sequential organization of typical manifest dream imagery and the patchy, disorganized sequence of dreamers' associations to such imagery has led me to suggest (Chapter 4) that the dramatic, coherent form of dreams does not derive from their underlying mnemonic sources at all, but that it is, instead, imposed upon such sources at a subsequent stage of dream formation.[3] The alternate view that intentions are primary, and that they then recruit mnemonic units to implement their plan, is refuted by the dreamer's general waking inability to reconstruct such an underlying plan, or even to accept the possibility of such a plan. That's why the question of dream meaning (interpretation) arises in the first place.

Thus, it seems that there is no foundation in the dreamer's own associations for the linear message view of dreaming. More generally, there are no appropriate empirical data to justify it. That is, we have no good reason to believe that messages (or coherent thought sequences) are sequentially *en*coded during dream formation. The grain of truth in the translated message view of dreaming is that the dream itself *is* a sequentially organized and coherent set of mental representations. But we have little justification for believing that the surface logic of the dream is a translation of some underlying message, and we have no reasonable way of ever determining what that message might have been.[4]

2. THE DREAM NARRATIVE DOES NOT *CONTAIN* ENCODED MEANINGS

One reading of the kind of free association evidence referred to above is that although it may refute the idea that the dream narrative *is* a translation of some underlying *message sequence,* it does not refute the idea that the dream narrative may contain deliberate (motivated) expressions of *meaning.* This, in fact, was Freud's reading of the evidence. In his view, at least some of the individual images or events in the dream express meanings (wishes) in a deliberate way. That is, some dream images are selected so as best to "represent" (carry the meaning of) underlying cognitive structures, which are not themselves imaginally coded. That the whole dream does not represent these structures is explained in terms of the simultaneous operation of "defensive" structures, which do *not* want wishes expressed. Freud thought that the linear storyline of conscious dream experience was created to obscure what was happening at strategic points within the dream itself—namely, that unconscious wishes (fantasies, etc.) were momentarily gaining an upper hand and were being expressed through dream imagery. Thus, he explicitly renounced interpreting the storyline itself:

> we should disregard the apparent coherence between a dream's constituents as an unessential illusion, and . . . we should trace back the origin of each of its elements on its own account. A dream is a conglomerate which, for purposes of investigation, must be broken up once more into fragments.[5]

Thus, the goal of Freud's interpretation was to find which elements of the dream might express hidden wishes and to determine what those wishes might be.

However, much experience with free association in dream analysis indicates that the data produced by this method are by no means easily reconciled with the hypothesis that even bits and pieces of dream imagery "encode" underlying meanings. Another typical result of free association to dream imagery is that *each dream image is capable of evoking multiple, and sometimes seemingly unrelated or even contradictory, mnemonic associates.* In contrast to speech, from which the whole concept of encoded meaning seems to be generalized to dreams, it's not typically the case that you find a compelling single underlying thought or thought complex that has been "translated" into some momentary sensory imagery in the dream. Rather, you find a number of indeterminately linked mnemonic elements that may have *contributed* to particular imagery in the dream. Thus, you can see that Irma's symptoms (Chapter 4) partake of those of her friend and of Freud's wife, but it isn't clear that these associative contributors to dream imagery can be identified with any underlying intention to express some particular, cohesive message. It certainly isn't clear what that message was, or how you'd justify any specific reading of it.

A further problem is that it isn't clear that, even if free association to some dream image led you back in a single-minded way to some particular mnemonic unit or complex, you'd want to say that the dream image "encoded" or "meant" that unit or complex. The question is *whether an associative connection between what's in memory and what's in the dream is sufficient to establish an encoding or meaning relationship* in the speech sense. It's an important question because encoding or meaning in the speech sense seems to be assumed by interpreters who, like Freud, look for "the" meaning of particular images in dreams.

Suppose, for example, that I'm singing in the shower, when suddenly, following a certain phrase in the song, I image a particular hill in a particular place. My image of "Pottersville Hill" has a childhood reference (I moved from this town when I was thirteen years old). It is connected with many feelings I experienced during childhood (for instance, I instantly recall that my favorite childhood pet is buried there). When I reflect upon this image, I can recreate a rich network of reasonably well-integrated childhood memories and feelings focused on me and that dog. I can see how the wording of the song might have led to the activation of this network. Is there, however, any sense in which the image can be construed as having deliberately encoded any of these memories or feelings? Does the question of encoding—or of meaning—ever arise in my account of what has happened? Probably not. Something has *led to* something else. But this doesn't imply that the later event meant (encoded the meaning of) the earlier one. As I think about the sequence in question, I'm not able to reconstruct any intention or deliberation about its progression. I'm more likely to think, "Isn't it funny how my mind jumped to that? I haven't thought about that place in years."

Dreams are like that. Even where a unitary connection can be demonstrated between something in dream imagery and something else you know (something "in your mind"), the connection doesn't seem to be one of translated meanings. We know that, in the most obvious of ways, dreaming is associated with a lack of intentionality and volition. And so the more appropriate model for thinking about dream imagery may be the waking situation when thoughts just pop into our (conscious) minds, rather than one in which we deliberately try to organize our thoughts to express some meaning. In both the shower example and in dreams, conscious imagery results from certain kinds of involuntary processing of memories and knowledge, kinds of processing in which the encoding of meanings seems not to be involved. Tracking down the mnemonic associates of the imagery may (or may not) reveal its sources, but it won't reveal its meanings, in the sense in which dream interpreters often seem to imagine that it will. There are no meanings in that sense.[6]

3. DOES THE DREAM HAVE A FUNCTION?

It seems that my argument is veering in the direction of asserting that dreams are without meaning, at least in the sense in which we know that speech is meaningful. While we can recognize certain respects in which the possibility of meaning has been maintained (as discussed in the introduction to this chapter), there's something unsettling about where we seem to be headed. Surely our dreams are not valueless. Surely there's some reason why nature has endowed each and every one of us with a dream-production system that is more or less continuously active during REM sleep, and is at least sporadically active in other states as well. What could that reason be? Perhaps we can restore some dignity to dreaming by establishing that it serves some valuable function.

The concept of function implies: (1) a *systematic interrelatedness* of dreaming or dream contents with something else (the dream has a *role* in some other or larger mental system[s]), and (2) *effects* of dreaming or dream contents on something else (it makes a *difference* that one has dreamed or that one has dreamed a particular sequence of dream imagery). Determining the function (or functions) of dreaming is no easy matter. Because, as we've seen (Chapter 2), dreaming is by no means limited to REM sleep, the strategy of depriving persons of their REM sleep and seeing what happens then can only be of limited value. Moreover, even if we supposed that REM sleep "indexed" dreaming, it might prove difficult to disentangle deprivation effects attributable to loss of the index (REM sleep) from those attributable to loss of the indexed (dreaming).[7] Practically speaking, the deprivation of REM sleep in humans is difficult to achieve in a methodologically clean way (leaving everything else—like non-REM sleep—the same as it was),[8] and, empirically, no clear pattern of effects has been observed for REM deprivation in humans.[9]

Contents.   Another research strategy has been to look at the inter-relatedness of particular dream contents with nondream variables. The goal is to determine what role dreaming certain kinds of dreams might play in a person's waking mental life or adjustment. To propose that the particular dreams we have are "meaningful" because they play an adaptive role and have adaptive effects is to suggest: (1) that the selection of mnemonic elements for dream processing is not random or arbitrary, and (2) that the way in which such elements are processed is not random or arbitrary. That is, what is processed and how it is processed would have to be constrained by the needs of the dream to serve some particular role(s) and to achieve some particular effect(s). One would not expect every single dream to be constrained by these needs. Yet there should be a demonstrable tendency for dream contents to have certain systematic effects and/or to be sensibly interrelated to other mental/behavioral adaptive phenomena in certain ways.

In this view, the way particular dream events unfold would be determined by priorities associated with the role served by dream processing more generally. If, to take Freud's functional hypothesis[10] as an example, repressed tension of certain sorts has been building, then the dream will attempt to discharge this tension in relatively harmless or indirect ways through a choice of images capable of mediating this responsibility. Or, to take a more recent "information processing" model[11] as an example, if, because of informational overload in the waking state, you haven't been able to fully assimilate the "lessons" of particular aspects of your waking experience, then those aspects should be reprocessed during REM sleep so as to leave their lessons more completely programmed and hence useable in subsequent waking adaptation. On either of these views, with some knowledge (and possibly control) of the current state of relevant nondream systems, there should be some predictability with respect both to the mnemonic units activated during dreaming and to the form of reprocessing such units undergo during dreaming. Conversely, where we want to establish just what the relevant nondream systems are, we should examine the co-occurrence of certain kinds of dream contents (or of their mnemonic associates) and of certain forms of dream organization with various aspects of dreamers' nondream experience/behavior.

This is, in fact, a line of research which has been fairly energetically pursued in recent years. REM dream reports have been correlated with systematic manipulations of presleep experience, with personality tests and other (e.g., age, sex) indicators of presumed variations in a person's typical daytime experience, and so forth.[12]

Research findings have generally, but not invariably, supported the hypothesis of a positive correlation between daytime experiential variables and corresponding dream experience variables. Typically, these variables have dealt with generalized dimensions of content such as "aggression," "activity-level," or "pleasantness." Thus, the questions asked have been ones such as, "Does seeing a violent movie or being insulted before you go to bed increase the aggression content in your dreams?"; "Does feeling depressed before you go to bed increase or decrease the 'depression' of your self-character in dream narratives?"; and so forth. Not surprisingly, the correlations typically observed in this sort of study between dream and waking variables have been fairly modest. That is, little dream variation seems to be explained by the manipulation or observation of waking variables.

One shortcoming of this research, which may have something to do with this unhappy situation, is that experimenters generally have looked at the correlation of dreams with waking "behaviors" in a way that neglects mental and mnemonic mediation. That is, experimenters seem to have assumed that a waking event or behavior itself will be directly reflected in dream content. But the sources of dreams are mnemonic or mental—they lie not in what we see or do or feel, but in what we know, think, and remember. It clearly is easier to describe what has been done to a person than how he or she has mentally "sized it up," but it's not adequate. Once we acknowledge that the sources of dreams are *mnemonic* rather than behavioral, however, the prediction of dream content becomes much more complex. We need to know not just what happened to people, but how they interpreted it, what other knowledge they related to it, and so on. We have to know a lot of their "minds," rather than just a piece of their behavior or presleep environment.

Correspondingly, once we acknowledge that the dream is the *end-product* of knowledge reprocessing during sleep, prediction becomes even more problematic. This is because there isn't a reliable association between mnemonic contributors to dream imagery and dream imagery itself. For instance, judging by Freud's associations to his "Irma" dream, his thoughts and feelings about Irma's friend and about his own wife were active as he dreamed it. But neither Irma's friend nor Freud's wife made it into the dream itself. Apparently it isn't enough to know what knowledge may be activated during dreaming: you also have to know how that knowledge will be processed. From the model proposed in Chapter 4, the processing of some particular complex of knowledge for "entry" into dream imagery itself would depend both on the network of knowledge simultaneously activated along with that complex, and on what dream imagery had already been dreamed. The prediction problem here would be enormous.

Consider all the knowledge a person has. From the rich variety of dream experience, consider how much of that knowledge seems at least potentially eligible to contribute to dream imagery. Yet to predict what dream you'll have during some particular REM period of some particular night, I'd have to be able to specify what particular kinds of knowledge would be active across time during that REM period, and how you'd "choose," on a moment-to-moment basis, to process it. It's little wonder, then, that we remain at quite some distance from being able to predict dream topics or the particular "resolutions" of those topics in particular dreams. It's on just this ground that Rechtschaffen has doubted the general validity of *interpretations of dream content:*

> if our postdictions (interpretations) were so right, it would imply that we had some knowledge of lawfulness between presleep events and dreams; and if we really had our finger on such lawfulness, we would be able to study a person's life circumstances and predict his dream. To the best of my knowledge, nobody has ever predicted a dream in any detail.[13]

In fact, one of the major unresolved puzzles of dream psychology is why waking experiences that seem qualitatively almost indistinguishable are sometimes followed by dreams that directly reflect them, and are sometimes followed by dreams that seem to have nothing at all to do with them.

It's possible that there's a relatively simple explanation of what individual dream images and dream sequences will be created during a given REM period. But such an explanation is not suggested by free association evidence, nor by the "unpredictable" way dreams themselves seem to intermix distantly related bits of memory and knowledge. Our general puzzlement about why we dream what we dream suggests the problem may be intractable. Most likely, there *is* relatively little rhyme or reason here. While it's difficult to imagine a definitive proof of their randomness, it begins to look as if we'll have to treat the mnemonic sources of particular dreams at particular times as being more or less unpredictable.

Granted, there are some relatively easy predictions we can make about people's dreams. If you know nothing about Anwar el-Sadat, you won't dream about him. Even *within* the boundaries of your knowledge, some almost equally confident predictions can be made. You'll probably dream more frequently of your father than of your mother, for example, if he's still around, hounding your every step (still very much "on your mind"), while she's been dead for many years. More generally, having some sense of who a person is always permits a certain range of predictiveness of her or his acts. But it's a relatively gross kind of prediction in waking life, and it's evidently at least equally gross for dreaming. What we're really talking about is consciousness prediction, and in a most difficult case, where we have no external-world cues or knowledge to help us out and where the usual guidelines seem not to be operative. This is not like predicting what you'll consciously think the first time you see Paris; this is trying to predict what you'll consciously think, period, when you're not intentionally regulating your own conscious thought.

The relative unpredictability of dream contents provides telling evidence against one version of the general functional hypothesis we've been considering. Since it seems that the activation of mnemonic elements during dreaming and their selection for dream processing *is* random and arbitrary, it's not likely that the *particular contents of our dreams*—in and of themselves—serve any adaptive functions. There is no demonstrable logic in the semantic content of particular memories that are reprocessed during dreaming. Any interpretation that proposes there is (and looks for the results thereby achieved or the functions thereby served) flies in the face of the evidence and of common sense. Common sense says it's generally unpredictable whether you will or won't dream, on a particular night at a particular time, of some event or object within your recent or distant experience. Common sense is either absolutely right, or close enough to give us our best working hypothesis about the mnemonic sources of dreams.

Processes. It's easy to overlook other respects, however, aside from their particular mnemonic sources or referents, in which dreams *are* predictable, in fact, *highly* predictable. It's an odds-on bet that, if you awaken a person (just about any person) after ten minutes of REM sleep, and ask that person to describe her or his experience prior to the awakening, she or he will:

1. describe a dramatically interrelated sequence of events that occurred within some "world analog";
2. claim that these events were known because they were, in large measure, directly sensed, i.e., seen, heard, felt, etc. rather than merely thought about in some more abstract way;
3. be able to identify *some* of these events as having rough parallels in her or his waking experience;[14]
4. be unable to identify *all* of the events as having such parallels; and

5. claim personally to have "participated" in at least some of the events in question.

In one sense, winning this bet simply establishes that REM awakenings lead to the recall of what we take to be "dreams." But this way of saying it conceals a number of important but neglected facts which may be relevant to questions of both meaning and function.

If one grants that there's something about the neurocognitive conditions of REM sleep, for instance, that permits conscious thought, it's still by no means self-evident why this conscious thought should conform to the five properties listed above. Why should we *dream* in REM sleep? Why not perform some other form of conscious ideation? Why does REM conscious ideation almost invariably have these properties, rather than others, which our conscious thought does at other times possess?

The formal regularities of dreams suggest that, however randomly particular dream contents may be initiated and sustained, dreaming itself can't be random. Judging only from the mnemonic elements represented in the dream, from their mnemonic associates, and from the apparent time sequence of both, we might guess that REM consciousness would be an undirected sequence of disconnected mental representations. But it isn't. Judging from the results of association experiments, we might guess that momentary REM imagery would be a jumble. But it isn't. Both momentarily and sequentially, the dream is coherently organized, according to certain rules or principles (some of which we just identified). Given the orderliness of dreaming, we can understand why people are reluctant to believe that dreams have no meanings and serve no functions. If so, we might expect dreaming to be a random and unpredictable process. But *dreaming* is neither random nor unpredictable.

Notice that I have emphasized the word "dreaming," because it's important to see that the focus of our discussion has changed now. We no longer are considering *what,* in terms of particular *contents,* people dream about. That, I've argued, is difficult if not impossible to predict and is hard to find rhyme or reason for. Because of this, it's difficult to believe that the particular contents of our dreams serve any adaptive function or play any adaptive role in nondreaming behaviors or mental states. But dreaming as a *process—how* consciousness is momentarily and sequentially organized—*is* orderly and predictable. In fact, we could define dreaming in terms of the formal organization to which consciousness conforms. Dreaming is the reprocessing of information which meets (among others) the five criteria listed above.

Now that, at the level of process rather than content, we have identified some regularities in dreaming, it makes sense to ask the question of function again, this time for the process of dreaming. What do the formal, organizational consistencies of dreaming suggest about possible functions that *dreaming* might serve? There is, as yet, no definitive evidence here. However, the formal characteristics of dreams do suggest some roles dreaming might play in human symbolic activity more generally.[15]

1.   The *narrative integration* of consciousness during dreaming suggests that dreaming may play a role in (have adaptive effects upon) our organization of symbolic knowledge and in the accessibility of such knowledge to conscious awareness. For example, we know that dreams do *integrate* (intermix) particularized knowledge (events we've experienced) and generalized knowledge in such a way that we can dream of events we haven't ever really experienced. Thus, knowledge can be consciously interconnected in dreams in a way waking experience typically wouldn't permit. That the form of our dream experience is *narrative* (creating chronological or causal relationships) also may indicate that narration is the basic form of human comprehension, and that dreaming affords the opportunity for this kind of comprehension to be exercised in conditions more demanding than those we typically are likely to encounter in our extrinsically-structured waking lives. Becoming human is, from this perspective, learning to understand and to be able to tell "stories". Dreaming surely might play some role in this process.

2.   The dream is experienced in visual and other forms of *sensory imagery,* and these forms of imaginal experience generally seem to be well integrated with one another. Possibly, dreaming is a major means by which conceptual control (and/or verbal control) is effected on the multimodal representation and integration of symbolic knowledge in consciousness or immediate memory.

3.   Dreams typically refer to events from our very *recent past* (day residues) and to events from our more *distant past.* Perhaps they contribute to our ability to retrieve recent experiences in evocative memory and to the integration of recent evocative memories with older evocative memories.

4.   The *lack of literal realism* in typical dreams (they may portray things that *could* have happened to us, but rarely portray things that *did* happen to us, in life) permits an enhancement of the range of "world" experiences to which our minds are exposed. On the one hand, this could help to program our minds to deal with novel situations adaptively. On the other hand, the very unreality of dreams could contribute to the development of what Freud called "reality testing."[16] By waking up from dreams, and determining that they couldn't have happened, we may first learn and later remind ourselves that just because our mind "senses" something doesn't mean it's literally so.

5.   The *consciously self-referential property* of dreaming suggests that

dream consciousness may be one way in which what we know motorically and perceptually becomes recoded and organized as (potentially) conscious self-knowledge. That is, dreaming may contribute to the development and elaboration of a distinctively human self-consciousness. What we know about dreaming in early childhood is at least consistent with this possibility.

Several points may be made about these possibilities. First (and foremost), they are just that: only possibilities, given what we now know about dreaming. Given that certain regularities characterize how we reprocess information and organize consciousness during dreaming, it makes sense to suppose that these repeated processings and organizings contribute to mental processing and organization of these sorts more generally. But we don't yet know whether these sensible suppositions are correct. *Second,* however unsure we may be about these hypothetical functions of dreaming, we do know that they are more sensible (agree better with what we know about dreams and dreaming) than hypotheses which propose that adaptive functions are served through the particular contents we happen to dream. *Third,* unlike most of these latter hypotheses, the process-level functions proposed above are functions within the same information processing systems which are engaged during dreaming itself. It seems reasonable to suppose that the most immediate effects of dreaming must be in the mind that does the dreaming, rather than on waking expressive or instrumental behaviors, which only are indirectly mediated by that mind. *Fourth,* these functions are proposed on the basis of a good understanding of what dreams are—conscious, symbolic acts—and of how they seem to develop in early life. Given these understandings, it is reasonable to suppose that dreaming contributes to our development as self-conscious, symbolic beings (and it is correspondingly unreasonable to propose that dreaming serves functions at elementary levels of behavioral adaptation and body regulation which arise for creatures such as rats and human infants).

Processes and Contents.   There's something peculiar, however, about the functional hypotheses we've just considered. They seem to be saying that the orderly recurrence of certain forms of dream processing can have adaptive effects, even when, as concluded earlier, the particular mnemonic elements being processed are haphazardly selected. How could it make so little difference *what contents* are being processed? It's possible, of course, that mental structures and processes are "exercised," no matter what the occasion for their engagement. But this doesn't seem just right. We learn to throw curve balls by throwing curve balls, not just by throwing any old ball any old way. Nevertheless, on the hypothesis that dreaming facilitates adaptive innovation by teaching us to cope with novel mnemonic configurations, it could be held that what's important about the mnemonic activation underlying dreaming is that it is unique, not *how* it's unique.

Careful attention to the other hypotheses listed above, however, reveals that they *do* specify content as well as form. It could hardly be otherwise, because rigid content–form distinctions generally don't survive scrutiny (cf. the discussion of "syntactic intentionality" in Chapter 4). When these hypotheses do specify content, however, they do so from the perspective of *mnemonic,* rather than *real-world,* status. That is, in line with the more general principle that dreaming is a symbolic activity, these hypotheses say that what's important about knowledge in dream formation is not so much what real-life event or object the knowledge is *of,* but how that knowledge is represented in memory. Is it, for example, particular (episodic) or generalized? Is it more susceptible to one form of imaginal coding in consciousness than another? Is it integrated with a whole body of accumulated knowledge or is it as yet discrete? Is it related to consciously accessible self-knowledge? If these hypotheses are at all correct, then it should be possible to demonstrate that the knowledge representations in dreams and underlying dreaming are *not* selected randomly or haphazardly. They may only look that way, because we're classifying them in the wrong way—by what they refer to rather than by their mnemonic status. The challenge here is to come up with new ways of thinking about, and classifying, the contents of dreams, and thereby to make what seems to be haphazard into something which is orderly, as orderly as the processing that occurs during dreaming. It's a considerable challenge, of course. But it illustrates once again (cf. Chapter 4) the ultimate interdependence of memory theory and dream theory, because our only hope in meeting it is to use the very best resources of waking cognitive psychology, which studies the form and structure of human knowledge representation.

4. INDICATIVE MEANINGS IN DREAMS

As suggested earlier in this chapter, although a dream does not contain a message in the sense that speech does, it still contains *signs* of the mind and thus of the character of the person who dreamed it. Likewise, dreaming, in general, contains rich clues to the nature of the human mind, in general. Thus, it is no mistake to assume that dreams are a potential source of information about the individual personality and about human nature. We do, however, need to be clear about what kind of information that is.

The kind of information we get from dreams is not the kind of information we get in verbal communication. Specifically, it is not some unitary message that the dream deliberately conveyed and that we can get some interpreter, "knowledgeable in dream language," to help us "translate." Rather, it's the kind of information that inevitably is contained in any spontaneous and organized act of the human mind. Because this act is initiated from within, it necessarily reveals some of the knowledge structures of the dreamer's mind. Because the act is organized, it necessarily reveals some of the organizational structures and processes through which the dreamer more typically assimilates information and makes conscious sense of her or his life experiences. Thus, even though the dream wasn't constructed to make any particular *statements*, it can still be read for its *indications* of the mind of the person who dreamed it. And, even though dreaming isn't any kind of communicative process, regularities of dreams can be used to index general properties of the human mind and of human character. Let's now consider some of the ways in which dreams may have diagnostic potential, both for the understanding of any particular individual, and for the more generalized analysis of the human mind.

Contents: Individual Indications.   In line with the general premises of this book, and of the evidence on which such premises are based, I am not going to stress the indicative interpretation of particular constellations of nonrecurring manifest imagery in a person's dreams. People sometimes ask me for an interpretation of what they take to be a particularly striking dream image or narrative element. Where humanly possible, I resist. That's not only because I don't see evidence for the sort of *intentional* encoding of meanings I believe these people typically imagine to be present in their dreams. It's also because, even on an *indicative* level (where one might simply wonder whether the imagery of the dream reflects some more general habits of the dreamer's thought), interpretation is fairly risky.

We've had occasion to return on a number of occasions to the general observation that dreams seem freely to intermix different bundles of the dreamer's organized knowledge. Dreams also seem to be guided, once they're under way, by narrative schemata or thematic scripts that have a logic of their own, and that use knowledge to their own ends rather than simply reflecting the inherent organization of knowledge in symbolic memory. Thus, it can't be clear that the dream-production system's particular integration of knowledge in any given dream directly reflects either how the dreamer's knowledge is organized more generally or how the dreamer typically chooses to process such information. To the extent that the processing demands of the dreaming mode of mental organization (i.e., trying to integrate disparate units in symbolic memory now in a state of effective activation) are unique, and to the extent that the pattern of units in such a state of activation is unique in any given REM period, it would be foolish to look at a particular piece of any specific dream and draw general (waking) conclusions from it.

Suppose, for example, that a woman dreams that she kills her mother. This surely is the kind of dream that will puzzle her and motivate her to seek some interpretation. Does she *really* want to kill her mother? Does she *really* hate her that much? The most reasonable answer, from the evidence of just one such dream, is: no, that's not only not what the dream means, it's not even what it indicates or suggests. The dream more likely reflects the fact that, given the dream narrative as it had developed up until the point of the murder, and given the mnemonic elements active at that point, the simplest path for the dream-production system to take at that point, given *its* requirements, was to have the dreamer kill her mother.

This conclusion may seem mind-boggling. Surely, even sleeping and dreaming, there should have been sufficient preservation of the dreamer's waking sense of self and of propriety to abort the narrative at this point. Sometimes, in fact, that seems to happen, as when we awaken in anxiety from a dream ("nightmare") that's gotten out of hand. Doesn't the fact that this dreamer could accept with apparent equanimity the evolving logic of her dream-production system suggest that she wasn't bothered by that logic because it resonated with how she really *does* feel? Not necessarily. The kind of self-monitoring that permits the development of affective responses we'd judge appropriate by waking standards may have been rendered inoperative by much more mundane systemic influences. For example, the physiology of the accompanying REM period may simply have been incompatible with that degree of waking-like self-monitoring. Awakening from anxiety dreams tends to occur more often later in the night, and toward the end of relative long REM periods, when conditions of self-monitoring may be more easily established because of the heightened "arousal" associated with those sleep contexts.[17] For example, dream lucidity (Chapter 1), the best sign we have of the potential restoration of a waking Active-I during dreaming, tends to be reported more often toward morning and in conditions of disturbed (relatively "aroused") sleep.[18] Thus, a "deep" interpretation of this woman's dream may be blaming her for something for which "she" really can't be held responsible.

But, the objection may continue, suppose we have independent waking evidence of some actual ambivalence of the dreamer toward her mother. Of course there will be such evidence. We are *all* ambivalent about our parents and about others we "love" (or "hate"). So there's a baseline problem here: we need evidence that this dreamer's ambivalance is a significant one, compared to that felt by other persons. Otherwise, we run the risk of magnifying the scanty evidence of one dream into a portrait of the dreamer which does her a grave injustice. And it does no good for the dream interpreter to reply that, in this case, a therapeutic discussion and interpretation of the dream led to much deeper evidence of the patient's ambivalence. Once again, there's a baseline problem: further therapeutic work guided by the hypothesis of mother hatred can probably produce such evidence whatever the dreamer has dreamed (including, for instance, dreams of being affectionate with her mother). The hypothesis that the dream indexes X can lead as inexorably as the hypothesis that the dream means X to its own "verification."

Freud recognized the hazards of such facile interpretations as imputing death wishes on the basis of dream deaths. One of his patients presented a dream in which her little nephew was dead, lying in a coffin. He reassured her that the dream did not mean that she wished the boy dead. His interpretation was, instead, that she dreamed her dream to fulfill another sort of wish. If her nephew were, in fact, to die, a favorite male friend would come to offer his condolences to the child's mother, and the dreamer would once again get to visit with this apple of her amorous eye.[19] Thus, although Freud was reluctant to take dream content at any kind of face value, he still held on to the idea that the dream expressed a wish. But Freud's wishful dream-instigators, as we've already noted, are at some distance from the dream itself, and it's impossible to verify their role in dream construction. Life is meaningful, and interconnected. Thus, one can start with a dream and end up with all sorts of more-or-less valid statements about the dreamer, as Freud apparently did in the case we've just considered. But it takes a considerable leap of faith—and involves a considerable degree of arbitrariness—to insist that this sort of interpretation has anything to do with the process of dreaming itself. How can we know, however true Freud's interpretation of the dreamer's feeling about her male acquaintance might be, that it was that feeling that instigated the formation of the dream's specific imagery (which, after all, did not even include the acquaintance)?

The answer seems to be that there's no way we can know that. What we *can* know is that the dream processed knowledge about the nephew by way of an episodic memory—a memory of how the nephew's *brother* looked at *his* funeral ceremony. We can know this because it's reflected in the dream imagery itself: the dreamer commented that little Karl looked just the way little Otto had, when he died.[20] Anything—literally anything—can be read into a dream's interpretation. But, when we're concerned with how the dream was put together, we must limit our attention to the particular mnemonic elements appearing in, or directly reflected in, the dream's manifest imagery. That's the only way to be on sure ground.

If we do limit ourselves to this level of analysis, are there ever any circumstances that justify our drawing any more general conclusions about the dreamer's particular habits of thought or feeling? Perhaps. Our discussion up to now has focused on the isolated, individual dream. It makes more sense, however, to think of looking for indicative meanings over a series of dreams from the same dreamer. Do there seem to be idiosyncratic patterns in the way mnemonic elements appear together in a person's dreams? Why, for example, does a given character always appear in a barren or sterile setting, and why does another always seem to be the agent of the dreamer's good fortune? Mightn't these apparently more than random conjunctions of mnemonic elements in dream imagery reflect something about the unique way in which the dreamer has organized her knowledge of her personal world? The recurrence of such patterns suggests that more than random mnemonic activation is involved here, that there is an indication of invariant mnemonic structure. Likewise, do certain narrative or thematic schemata seem, again and again, to be responsible for the organized quality of a person's dream experience, even when the specific mnemonic contents are different? If a dreamer's dreams seem recurrently to build a theme around the issue of blame for failure, mightn't this say something more general (i.e., applicable to waking life) about how she comprehends life events? One might make here the plausible (and empirically testable) assumption that that is indeed the case.

Precisely these sorts of interpretations of dream *series* have been suggested by Calvin Hall's "cognitive" theory of dreaming and dream interpretation.[21] Although adhering, in certain respects, to Freud's theory of human motivation, Hall saw that dreaming is a cognitive process and that its products therefore can be interpreted cognitively. Specifically, dreams, interpreted conservatively (i.e., through their recurrent elements and themes), can reveal the subjective reality of the dreamer's mind. They can index what the dreamer knows (the personal organization of her or his self and world knowledge) and how she or he tends conceptually to organize life experiences.

As it's applied to the unique aspects of any dreamer's dreams, this sort of content analysis must necessarily be a cautious (and tedious) business. No one dream, however striking or curious, justifies anything more than the initial and tentative formulation of a hypothesis about the dreamer's organization of knowledge, or of her or his "ways of thinking." Sequential dream analysis is required to determine that one is, in fact, seeing reflections of stable mental structures in dream imagery. Interpretations, where they are made, will necessarily be limited in scope. Specifically, they will be limited to those things that the dream, as a symbolic act, could reflect: knowledge representation and mental processing. To be truly diagnostic of the individual's mind and character—of her or his *unique* style of mental functioning—the interpretations also should be grounded, of course, in adequate baseline data about dreams and dreamers more generally.

And it may well turn out, in the end, that such interpretation won't be particularly "revealing." That is, we may not learn much (or anything) about the dreamer that we couldn't know from systematic study (or even casual observation) in wakefulness. That's why my focus here will be on the opportunities (sometimes unique opportunities) dreams provide for understanding general properties of human mental functioning. It may well be that we can learn much more about the human mind's basic structures, processes, and development from studying dreams than we can about the distinctive features of any particular human mind. Still, if in individual dream analysis we do follow the guidelines indicated above, we'll at least have the satisfaction of genuinely *knowing* what it is we think we know when we "interpret" a person's dreams.

Processes: General Indications.   Mostly by way of review, I'll now enumerate some of the ways in which recurring properties of dreams might index more general properties of human knowledge structures and of mental processing.

1.   First of all, as this book has attempted to illustrate, the study of *dreams* can be used to model the act of *dreaming*. That is, we can use dreams to suggest how our mind is organized during dreaming and how that form of organization develops.[22] Dreaming is, after all, a symbolic act in which we are engaged for a significant portion of our lives.

2.   We can also study dreams—which people generally are less self-conscious about describing—to model the development and nature of conscious waking thought that is not voluntarily regulated (mind-wandering), is not oriented to what's happening in the world around us ("spontaneous" cognition), or both. An equally significant portion of our lives must be spent using our minds in these not-quite-dreaming ways, but, until now, cognitive psychology has had very little to say about them.

3.   Although research in this vein has not yet been terribly promising, we can study the association of dream reporting with prereport brain activity, to try to determine, both developmentally and normatively, how and within what range symbolic activity is constrained by brain states. Failure to establish definite relationships up to now may merely reflect the choice of inappropriate physical variables (e.g., EEG "sleep stages"), the unavailability of suitable physical measurements (a situation likely to improve radically in the near future), or both.[23] Cognitive psychology typically has paid little attention to brain physiology, and theoretically that

inattention can be justified. Pragmatically, however, it has been useful to a purely psychological approach to dreaming to know something about sleep physiology (e.g., Chapter 2) and the same, no doubt, will someday be true for cognitive psychology more generally. And, of course, although mentalistic approaches need not be based on physical observations, the study of mind-brain relationships is itself a legitimate topic of independent interest.

4.   Dreams may, particularly in early human development, contain significant clues as to the ultimate *forms of human knowledge representation*. Specifically, as we've seen (Chapter 4), they pose an interesting (if not fatal) problem for the hypothesis of analog representations: if representation is analog, why are children's (analog) dreams so impoverished compared to what they otherwise seem to know?

5.   Dreams surely contain, as we've also seen (Chapters 1 and 4), important clues to the *organization of symbolic memory*. The way in which features of various concepts are intermixed in dream imagery, for example, must reveal our conceptual feature analysis of objects and events, as well as the "semantic distance" of such analyses to one another in a larger memory network.[24] It also seems possible that an examination of the mnemonic (rather than real-world) status of "day residues" might reveal something not only about their role in dream formation and about the information-processing function of dreaming, but also something about how, more generally, long-term memory is accessed and organized.

6.   Because of their storylike quality, dreams can also reveal the course of development and the nature of *higher-order knowledge representations* such as "scripts" (Chapter 3), narrative schemata or story grammars (Chapter 4), and (to the degree dreams are life-simulations) schemata used in naturalistic waking information processing of a highly general sort.

7.   To the degree dreams give us ideas about mental organization during the act of dreaming, they may also help us understand *amnesia* for dreams (Chapters 1 and 2). Forgetting REM dreams must be the most general and massive form of "normal" adult forgetting. Understanding this is a prerequisite for any truly general theory of human memory, and such understanding may come from detailed analysis of the kind of comprehension (encoding) we perform as we dream.

8.   A more precise description of the character of the dreamer's comprehension within the dream may be useful in other contexts than amnesia for dreams. Specifically, it may indicate a form of supra-modular conceptual processing with specifiably limited access to symbolic memory. Understanding the processes involved would help to bridge the theoretical gap between modular processing and more versatile forms of concep-

tual processing (Chapter 4). It also might help to clarify stages of conceptual comprehension more generally.

9. Because our dreams create analogs of social reality, the manner in which they portray people (their behavior, their social interactions, and their mental states) can reveal the forms through which we represent that reality. Correspondingly, developmental studies of dreams can be used to study the development of "social cognition" (Chapter 3). For example, dreams are a natural environment in which to study the growth of sex-role beliefs.

10. Dreams are involuntarily achieved, but highly organized, conscious mental acts. Thus, their study may indicate the sorts of structures that do not ever seem to have been conscious, yet which can organize "recollective" experience—i.e., memory-based rather than sensory-based consciousness. Dreams also present a nice, but heretofore unconsidered, test case for proposals about the differences between automatic and self-controlled mental processing.[25] Sleep-onset is a natural and predictable environment in which to study what it means to the organization of symbolic activity and of consciousness to lose voluntary self-regulation.

11. Dreams indicate a form of mental organization which, although involuntary, still must be described as *self-referential* and *self-regulative*. For example, the "involuntary" process of dreaming leads (at least under certain conditions) to autobiographical recollections, and this process involves sufficient monitoring of its own ongoing symbolic activity to permit the construction of sequentially coherent narratives, even in the face of momentary disruptions (Chapters 1 and 2). Evidently self-reference and self-regulation exist in degrees or levels, and the study of dreams may help us to delineate what those degrees or levels are.

12. The study of how dreams develop in early childhood may help to index the growth of these involuntary or automatic forms of consciousness regulation. Even more significantly, it may index the growth of human consciousness itself (Chapter 3). The study of dreams *is* the study of consciousness, as it exists under certain other mental conditions. Cognitive psychologists, who study symbolic activity as it can be *inferred* from people's performances, have tended not to deal directly with consciousness. The cognitive psychological study of dreams will force us to do so. Such study should help to restore an important (if not critical, as the early introspectionists thought) phenomenon in the systematic investigation of mental phenomena. It might also help to shore up distinctions that developmental psychologists sometimes seem to ignore, such as those between recognition memory and evocative memory, and between simple representation and representation with "cognizance."[26] Dreaming is a

phenomenon which requires *both* representation *and* cognizance (consciousness). It may be significant, then (no matter how many contemporary psychologists will tell you, "Piaget got it all wrong; actually, experimentation reveals that the child must know this or that much earlier than Piaget said"), that children's dreams suggest that Piaget got it pretty much right, timetable and all. The reason for the difference may be that dreams represent a kind of cognition in which Piaget was particularly interested when he first studied preoperational children—a cognition indexed not just by behavioral showing, but also by conscious knowing. The study of dreams may provide our single most reliable clue as to how that kind of cognition develops.

13.   Through coordinated study of the *form* of children's dreams (which seems to depend on certain automatic self-regulations) and of their self-referential *content* (including animal surrogates, a passively observing self, and an actively participating self), it may be possible to reconstruct the developmental growth of, and interrelationships among, self-regulation, self-knowledge, and self-awareness. As was suggested in Chapter 3, such observations may also help to clarify the origins and early nature of autobiographical (episodic, self-contextual) memory.

14.   Because dreams are conscious mental representations, their study can help to reveal the nature and development of *conscious mental codes* at early childhood ages where these otherwise are difficult to determine. Such evidence, as we've seen (Chapters 3 and 4), will be relevant to developmental theories proposing that preoperational children code their knowledge differently than adults. It will also bear on theories that explain our amnesia for our early childhood years in precisely those terms. An additional possibility (suggested by the evidence described in Chapter 4 that dream imagery depends on linguistic processing) is that the study of children's dreams in relation to their overt and inner speech may indicate interrelations of what conventionally have been taken to be separate conscious coding formats: words and visual images.

15.   Dreams surely are relevant data in attempting to determine "the qualitative nature of images."[27] As we've already noted (Chapter 4), dreams cast great doubt on some psychologists' tendencies to think of mental imagery as being merely visual, "pictorial," or "two-dimensional." Dream imagery creates world analogs, with the full array of conscious representations we experience in life. Thus, it is most likely to reveal the multifaceted ways in which we mentally simulate life. Developmental research on dreams may also indicate the stages through which we acquire such representational competence.

16.   Neuropsychology is the study of specific cognitive defects associated with circumscribed forms of brain damage. Neuropsychological

studies of dreams can reveal the waking cognitive systems which play a role in dreaming and can indicate what that role might be. Such research has already made some contribution to our understanding of dreams. Because of the apparent interdependence of waking and dreaming cognition, dreams may also be a convenient way of indexing certain forms of general cognitive impairment, such as in imaging, spatial representation, and self representation.

17.   Likewise, the study of dreams as differentially affected by waking perceptual and symbolic impairments may help to clarify the more general distinctions to be drawn between perception and symbolic cognition. As noted in Chapter 1, it seems to be possible to see without dreaming in visual imagery, and to dream in visual imagery without now being able to see. These findings need to be pursued and refined, so that we may better understand how conscious mental simulations are different from, but still related to, the perceptions they simulate.

18.   Both developmental evidence (where dreams may be "naturally" deficient in certain organizations) and neuropsychological evidence (where dreams may be "pathologically" deficient in these same organizations) can be used to study the waking consequences of individual differences in automatic strategies of self-regulation of conscious experience. What *general* difference, for example, does it make that some seven-year-olds can represent themselves consciously as active initiators of physical acts while other seven-year-olds cannot? Dreams are our best indicators of such cognitive differences, and our best "handle" for studying their implications.

19.   As we've seen (Chapter 2), there are apparent individual differences in how willingly persons relinquish voluntary self-regulation of consciousness as they fall asleep. How stable are these differences? What do they imply, more generally, about these individuals' conscious organization and regulation of their mental processing? Some people seem to relinquish voluntary control of their waking consciousness by hallucinating but not "regressing," while others "regress" without hallucination. How stable are *these* differences? What are *their* more general implications?

20.   If there is a general limitation of cognitive psychology, it lies in its neglect of feelings and of their dependence on, and their role in, symbolic behavior. Dreams should play a critical role in highlighting the interdependence of feeling and thinking. For example, does the development of feelings in dreams in early childhood index children's more general ability symbolically to recreate conscious affect? Does it have something to say about children's more general ability to "feel" feelings in the first place? We are as much in the dark now about the affective side of children's

consciousness as we were, years ago, about its more purely cognitive aspects. There's every reason to believe that dream feelings will be critical data in charting how we become "feelers" as well as "thinkers."

In summary, a number of ways have been described in which dreams might *index* general properties of mental organization and processing. Each touches on a central issue in contemporary cognitive psychology, in understanding what it means to have a mind and be a person. This is ample (although undoubtedly still partial) evidence that we can look at our dreams and learn a lot. Dreams are not meaningless. To the contrary, they are a rich source of information about our minds and ourselves. The theme of this chapter has been that intelligent use of dreams for self-knowledge depends on understanding what kinds of information they might, and might not, contain.

NOTES

[1] Sigmund Freud, *The Interpretation of Dreams,* New York: Basic Books, 1955 (originally published, 1900).

[2] Erich Fromm, *The Forgotten Language: An Introduction to the Understanding of Dreams, Fairy Tales and Myths,* New York: Grove Press, 1957 (originally published, 1951). The quotation is from p. 10.

[3] Although not similarly (or even psychologically) motivated, the "neurobiological model" of Hobson and McCarley adopts a similar position. See J. Allan Hobson and Robert W. McCarley, "The Brain as a Dream State Generator: An Activation-Synthesis Hypothesis of the Dream Process," *American Journal of Psychiatry,* 1977, *134,* 1335–1348.

[4] Kuper and Stone recently have proposed a "structuralist" alternative to "free association" which assumes linear argument within the dream itself. That is, *by assumption,* the dream demonstrates a "quasi-logical dialectic" deriving from its comparably logical sources. Kuper and Stone illustrate this method with the "Irma" dream. But they don't tell us how to abstract dialectical progressions from dreams (or even how to determine if they exist). What's notable about their approach is their frank admission that free association methods can't explain the dramatic coherence of dream imagery. Unfortunately (but not unexpectedly), their alternative to free association for determining sequential dream messages fails to meet minimal scientific standards (it doesn't follow rules). Also, as noted earlier, it seems doubtful that "Irma" (or any other single dream) is worth pursuing to the point where new methods or theories are based solely on it. See Adam Kuper and Alan A. Stone, "The Dream of Irma's Injection: A Structural Analysis," *American Journal of Psychiatry,* 1982, *139,* 1225–1234.

[5] Freud, *op. cit.,* p. 449.

[6] That Freud imagines that there are meanings in that sense depends on some additional assumptions in his theory. Those assumptions have to do with classes of psychological (mental?) phenomena whose very nature is such that they "press" for "expression" or "release." They are the "ancient mariners" of the mind, whose very reason for existence is the story they must tell. Conceptually, such elements derive from a discredited kind of 19th century neurobiology and from untrustworthy clinical formulations. Empirically, they are impossible to define or specify in any reliable way. Theoretically, they lead, as decades of

clinical practice have demonstrated, anywhere; that is to say, they lead nowhere in particular.

Another difficulty of Freud's interpretation model is not explicitly identified in the text. There are no clear rules for determining which parts of the dream have (deep) meanings and which do not.

[7] Difficult, but not perhaps wholly impossible. In agreement with findings on block-design relationships to dream reporting/experiencing reported in Chapter 3, Butler recently found that chronic adult nonreporters of dreams may, in some cases, have difficulty reporting dreams even on laboratory REM awakenings, and that this difficulty may be related to low block-design scores. Presumably, as for children, these relatively poor block-design performances indicate problems in actually generating and experiencing dreams. If so, there may be a very small number of otherwise intact adult humans whose REM sleep is *not* accompanied by dreaming. What difference does that absence make? See Stephen F. Butler, "The Relation of Block Design Scores to REM Recall in Home Dream Nonreporters", Ph.D. dissertation, Emory University, 1981.

[8] See, for instance, the discussion by David Foulkes, Terry Pivik, John B. Ahrens, and Ethel M. Swanson, "Effects of 'Dream Deprivation' on Dream Content: An Attempted Cross-Night Replication", *Journal of Abnormal Psychology,* 1968, *73,* 403–415.

[9] The definitive review is by Gerald W. Vogel, "A Review of REM Sleep Deprivation," *Archives of General Psychiatry,* 1975, *32,* 749–761.

[10] Freud, *op. cit.*

[11] E.g., Edmond M. Dewan, "The Programing (P) Hypothesis for REM Sleep," in Ernest Hartmann (ed.), *Sleep and Dreaming,* Boston: Little, Brown, 1970, pp. 295–307.

[12] See the reviews in Arthur M. Arkin, John S. Antrobus, and Stephen J. Ellman (eds.), *The Mind in Sleep: Psychology and Psychophysiology,* Hillsdale, N.J.: Lawrence Erlbaum Associates, 1978.

[13] From Allan Rechtschaffen, "The Psychophysiology of Mental Activity During Sleep," in F. J. McGuigan and R. A. Schoonover (eds.), *The Psychophysiology of Thinking: Studies of Covert Processes,* New York: Academic Press, 1973, p. 196.

[14] To the extent that this is true, dreams are "meaningful" in the sense that their mental representations *refer to* familiar persons, objects, places, or events. But this is not the same as saying that these mental representations are *conveying a message about* these referents or any others.

[15] The following arguments are, in part, adapted from David Foulkes, "Cognitive Processes During Sleep: Evolutionary Aspects," in Andrew Mayes (ed.), *Sleep Mechanisms and Functions in Humans and Animals: An Evolutionary Perspective,* Wokingham, England: Van Nostrand Reinhold, 1983, pp. 332–333.

[16] Freud, *op. cit.,* p. 566n.

[17] Ernest Hartmann, "A Note on the Nightmare," in Ernest Hartmann, *op. cit.,* pp. 192–197.

[18] Celia E. Green, *Lucid Dreams,* London: Hamish Hamilton, 1968.

[19] Freud, *op. cit.,* pp. 152–154.

[20] *Ibid.*

[21] Calvin S. Hall: "A Cognitive Theory of Dreams," *Journal of General Psychology,* 1953, *49,* 273–282; "A Cognitive Theory of Dream Symbols," *Journal of General Psychology,* 1953, *48,* 169–186; and *The Meaning of Dreams* (rev. ed.), New York: McGraw-Hill, 1966.

[22] As suggested in Chapter 2, "defective" or "ill-formed" dreams (e.g., non-REM reports) may be most revealing in both of these respects.

[23] Recent research, for instance, suggests that the quality of mentation during non-REM sleep and at sleep onset may be related to EEG spectral-power variables. See Peter Williamson, Howard Galin, and Mortimer Mamelak, "Spectral EEG Correlates of Mentation during

Sleep," *Sleep Research,* 1983, *12,* 58, and D. Lehmann, B. Meier, C. A. Meier, T. Mita, and W. Skrandies, "Sleep Onset Mentation Related to Short Epoch EEG Spectra", *Sleep Research,* 1983, *12,* 180.

[24] E.g., Roberta L. Klatzky, *Human Memory: Structures and Processes,* 2nd ed., San Francisco: W. H. Freeman, 1980, pp. 186–189.

[25] E.g., Richard M. Shiffrin and Walter Schneider, "Controlled and Automatic Human Information Processing: II. Perceptual Learning, Automatic Attending, and a General Theory," *Psychological Review,* 1977, *84,* 127–190.

[26] Jean Piaget, *The Grasp of Consciousness: Action and Concept in the Young Child,* Cambridge, Mass.: Harvard University Press, 1976 (originally published, 1974).

[27] Robert G. Crowder, *Principles of Learning and Memory,* Hillsdale, N.J.: Lawrence Erlbaum Associates, 1976, pp. 127–131.

General Index